OSF DISTRIBUTED COMPUTING ENVIRONMENT

Guide to Writing
DCE
Applications

OSF DISTRIBUTED COMPUTING ENVIRONMENT

Guide to Writing

DCE

Applications

JOHN SHIRLEY

Digital Equipment Corporation

O'Reilly & Associates, Inc.
103 Morris Street, Suite A
Sebastopol CA 95472

Guide to Writing DCE Applications
by John Shirley

Cover design by Edie Freedman
Cover illustration by Chris Reilley

Editors: Andy Oram and Steve Talbott

Printing History:

June 1992:	First Edition.
March 1993:	Minor corrections.

This book is printed on acid-free paper with 50% recycled content, 10-15% post-consumer
waste. O'Reilly & Associates is committed to using paper with the highest recycled content
available consistent with high quality.

ISBN: 1-56592-004-X

Table of Contents

Chapter 2: Using a DCE RPC Interface   25

Chapter 3: How to Write Clients   47

Figures

Examples

Tables

Preface

In this book we describe how to develop application programs that use Distributed Computing Environment Remote Procedure Call (DCE RPC) software. DCE RPC enables programs to call procedures that execute in other processes on a network. We do not describe how to migrate applications from earlier versions of RPC to this version. We developed the examples in this book on OSF/1 and MIPS ULTRIX systems.

Audience

To successfully use this book you need to know the C programming language, be experienced with common programming techniques, and understand some basic networking concepts. We designed this book for two levels of DCE application developers:

* The developer of a client for an application that has an existing interface and server.

* The developer of an interface and server.

Related Documentation

We designed this book to be used with the DCE documentation set. Especially relevant is the documentation set reference material explaining the Interface Definition Language (IDL), attribute configuration files (ACF), and DCE RPC runtime routines. The material explaining threads is also useful to the developer of multi-threaded DCE applications.

Another book in this series, *Understanding DCE*, describes how all the DCE components work together.

Utilities used in DCE application development include **uuidgen**, **idl**, and **rpccp**. Reference material on these utilities is also in the DCE documentation set.

Conventions

Throughout the book we use the following typographic conventions:

`Constant width`
indicates a code example, system output, or user input. Words in constant width also represent application-specific variables and procedures.

Bold
introduces new terms or concepts. Words in bold also represent system elements such as filenames and directory names, and literal portions of command syntax. RPC-specific routines, data types, and constants are in bold.

Italic
words or characters in command syntax or examples indicate variables for which the user supplies a value.

[]
enclose attributes in interface definitions and Attribute Configuration Files (ACFs) and are part of the syntax. Note that this is different from the common convention where brackets enclose optional items in format and syntax descriptions.

>
represents system prompts.

S>
represents a server system prompt to distinguish it from a client system prompt.

C>
represents a client system prompt to distinguish it from a server system prompt.

In order to execute commands, you must press the Return key. The Return key is assumed (not shown) in examples.

Book Organization

This book is divided into the following eight chapters and six appendices:

Chapter 1, *Overview of an RPC Application*, shows how a simple DCE application works.

Chapter 2, *Using a DCE RPC Interface*, shows how to read a DCE RPC interface definition, a file ending in **.idl**, which is a file that declares the remote procedures of an interface.

Chapter 3, *How to Write Clients*, discusses how to develop client programs for DCE RPC interfaces. Topics include binding methods, finding servers, customizing binding handles, handling errors or exceptions, and compiling clients.

Chapter 4, *Using Pointers and Arrays*, shows how pointers and arrays are defined in an interface and how to develop applications to use them.

Chapter 5, *How to Write a Server*, discusses how to develop a server program for a DCE RPC interface. Topics include initializing a server, writing remote procedures, and compiling servers.

Chapter 6, *Using a Name Service*, describes a name service database and how to use it with distributed applications.

Chapter 7, *Using Context Handles*, shows how to maintain a state (such as a file handle) on a specific server between remote procedure calls from a specific client.

Chapter 8, *Using Pipes for Large Quantities of Data*, shows how to write DCE programs that efficiently transmit data.

Appendix A, *IDL and ACF Attributes Quick Reference*, shows all the interface definition language (IDL) and attribute configuration file (ACF) attributes with brief descriptions of each.

Appendix B, *DCE RPC Runtime Routines Quick Reference*, shows all the RPC runtime routines organized into convenient categories.

Appendix C, *The Arithmetic Application*, is a small application that shows the basics of remote procedure calls.

Appendix D, *The Inventory Application*, is a somewhat richer application showing different IDL data types, how to use attribute configuration files (ACFs), and how to find servers by importing information from a name service database.

Appendix E, *The Remote_file Application*, shows how to use context handles and how to find servers using strings of network location information.

Appendix F, *The Transfer_data Application*, shows how to use advanced RPC features including pipes and customized binding handles.

How to Use This Book

We suggest you read Chapter 1 before attempting to write an application. Appropriate sections for different types of application development are listed below.

Developing a Client

If you are developing only a client for an existing DCE RPC interface and server, read the following chapters first:

- Chapter 1, *Overview of an RPC Application*
- Chapter 2, *Using a DCE RPC Interface*
- Chapter 3, *How to Write Clients*

Read other chapters as needed to learn how to develop applications that use more features of interface definitions.

Developing a Network Interface and Server

If you are developing a network interface with accompanying server, read the following:

- Chapter 1, *Overview of an RPC Application*
- Chapter 2, *Using a DCE RPC Interface*
- Chapter 3, *How to Write Clients*
- Chapter 4, *Using Pointers and Arrays*
- Chapter 5, *How to Write a Server*

Obtaining the Example Programs

The example programs in this book are available electronically in a number of ways: by ftp, ftpmail, bitftp, and uucp. The cheapest, fastest, and easiest ways are listed first. If you read from the top down, the first one that works for you is probably the best. Use *ftp* if you are directly on the Internet. Use ftpmail if you are not on the Internet but can send and receive electronic mail to internet sites (this includes CompuServe users). Use BITFTP if you send electronic mail via BITNET. Use UUCP if none of the above works.

FTP

To use FTP, you need a machine with direct access to the Internet. A sample session is shown, with what you should type in boldface.

```
% ftp ftp.uu.net
Connected to ftp.uu.net.
220 ftp.UU.NET FTP server (Version 6.34 Thu Oct 22 14:32:01 EDT 1992) ready.
Name (ftp.uu.net:andyo): anonymous
```

```
331 Guest login ok, send e-mail address as password.
Password: andyo@ora.com (use your user name and host here)
230 Guest login ok, access restrictions apply.
ftp> cd /published/oreilly/dce/applic_guide
250 CWD command successful.
ftp> binary (Very important! You must specify binary transfer for compressed files.)
200 Type set to I.
ftp> prompt (Convenient, so you are not queried for every file transferred)
Interactive mode off.
ftp> mget *
200 PORT command successful.
150 Opening BINARY mode data connection for README (1737 bytes).
226 Transfer complete.
local: README remote: README
1737 bytes received in 0.39 seconds (4.3 Kbytes/s)
200 PORT command successful.
150 Opening BINARY mode data connection for arithmetic.tar.Z (6763 bytes).
226 Transfer complete.
local: arithmetic.tar.Z remote: arithmetic.tar.Z
6763 bytes received in 1.2 seconds (5.3 Kbytes/s)
200 PORT command successful.
150 Opening BINARY mode data connection for inventory.tar.Z (26090 bytes).
226 Transfer complete.
local: inventory.tar.Z remote: inventory.tar.Z
26090 bytes received in 5.4 seconds (4.8 Kbytes/s)
200 PORT command successful.
150 Opening BINARY mode data connection for remote_file.tar.Z (9279 bytes).
226 Transfer complete.
local: remote_file.tar.Z remote: remote_file.tar.Z
9279 bytes received in 3.1 seconds (2.9 Kbytes/s)
200 PORT command successful.
150 Opening BINARY mode data connection for transfer_data.tar.Z (12169 bytes).
226 Transfer complete.
local: transfer_data.tar.Z remote: transfer_data.tar.Z
12169 bytes received in 4.5 seconds (2.6 Kbytes/s)
ftp> quit
221 Goodbye.
%
```

Each .Z archive contains all the source code and configuration information required for building one example. Extract each example through a command like:

```
% zcat arithmetic.tar.Z | tar xf -
```

System V systems require the following tar command instead:

```
% zcat arithmetic.tar.Z | tar xof -
```

If *zcat* is not available on your system, use separate uncompress and tar commands.

The *tar* command creates a subdirectory that holds all the files from its archive. The README file in this subdirectory describes the goals of the example and how to build and run it; the text is an ASCII version of the introductory material from the corresponding appendix in this book.

FTPMAIL

FTPMAIL is a mail server available to anyone who can send and receive electronic mail to and from Internet sites. This includes most workstations that have an email connection to the outside world, and CompuServe users. You do not need to be directly on the Internet. Here's how to do it.

You send mail to *ftpmail@decwrl.dec.com*. In the message body, give the name of the anonymous ftp host and the ftp commands you want to run. The server will run anonymous ftp for you and mail the files back to you. To get a complete help file, send a message with no subject and the single word "help" in the body. The following is an example mail session that should get you the examples. This command sends you a listing of the files in the selected directory, and the requested example files. The listing is useful in case there's a later version of the examples you're interested in.

```
% mail ftpmail@decwrl.dec.com
Subject:
reply andyo@ora.com                  (where you want files mailed)
connect ftp.uu.net
chdir /published/oreilly/dce/applic_guide
dir
get README
binary
uuencode                             (or btoa if you have it)
get remote_file.tar.Z
get arithmetic.tar.Z
get transfer_data.tar.Z
get inventory.tar.Z
quit
%
```

A signature at the end of the message is acceptable as long as it appears after "quit."

All retrieved files will be split into 60KB chunks and mailed to you. You then remove the mail headers and concatenate them into one file, and then *uudecode* or *btoa* it. Once you've got the desired .Z files, follow the directions under FTP to extract the files from the archive.

VMS, DOS, and Mac versions of *uudecode*, *btoa*, *uncompress*, and *tar* are available. The VMS versions are on *gatekeeper.dec.com* in */archive/pub/VMS*.

BITFTP

BITFTP is a mail server for BITNET users. You send it electronic mail messages requesting files, and it sends you back the files by electronic mail. BITFTP currently serves only users who send it mail from nodes that are directly on BITNET, EARN, or NetNorth. BITFTP is a public service of Princeton University. Here's how it works.

To use BITFTP, send mail containing your ftp commands to *BITFTP@PUCC*. For a complete help file, send HELP as the message body.

The following is the message body you should send to BITFTP:

```
FTP   ftp.uu.net   NETDATA
USER   anonymous
PASS your Internet email address (not your bitnet address)
CD   /published/oreilly/dce/applic_guide
DIR          .
GET README
BINARY
GET remote_file.tar.Z
GET arithmetic.tar.Z
GET transfer_data.tar.Z
GET inventory.tar.Z
QUIT
```

Once you've got the desired .Z files, follow the directions under FTP to extract the files from the archive. Since you are probably not on a UNIX system, you may need to get versions of *uudecode, uncompress, btoa,* and *tar* for your system. VMS, DOS, and Mac versions are available. The VMS versions are on *gatekeeper.dec.com* in */archive/pub/VMS.*

Questions about BITFTP can be directed to Melinda Varian, *MAINT@PUCC* on BITNET.

UUCP

UUCP is standard on virtually all UNIX systems, and is available for IBM-compatible PCs and Apple Macintoshes. The examples are available by UUCP via modem from UUNET; UUNET's connect-time charges apply.

You can get the examples from UUNET whether you have an account or not. If you or your company has an account with UUNET, you will have a system with a direct UUCP connection to UUNET. Find that system, and type:

uucp uunet\!~/published/oreilly/dce/applic_guide/ *yourhost*\!~/*yourname*/

The backslashes can be omitted if you use the Bourne shell (*sh*) instead of *csh*. The files should appear some time later (up to a day or more) in the directory */usr/spool/uucppublic/**yourname***. If you don't have an account but would like one so that you can get electronic mail, then contact UUNET at 703-204-8000.

If you don't have a UUNET account, you can set up a UUCP connection to UUNET using the phone number 1-900-468-7727. As of this writing, the cost is 50 cents per minute. The charges will appear on your next telephone bill. The login name is "uucp" with no password. For example, an *L.sys/Systems* entry might look like:

```
uunet Any ACU 19200 1-900-468-7727 ogin:--ogin: uucp
```

Your entry may vary depending on your UUCP configuration. If you have a PEP-capable modem, make sure `s50=255s111=30` is set before calling.

It's a good idea to get the file */published/oreilly/dce/applic_guide/ls-lR.Z* as a short test file containing the filenames and sizes of all the files in the directory.

Once you've got the desired **.Z** files, follow the directions under FTP to extract the files from the archives.

Acknowledgments

This book originated as a companion to Digital Equipment Corporation's DCE documentation set. I am in debt to Tonie Franz and Frank Willison of Digital, who contracted me to write this book. Their confidence in me gave me an opportunity that I have found exceptionally rewarding. I especially thank the architects and developers of the IDL compiler at Digital, including Jerry Harrow, Tony Hinxman, Dick Annicchiarico, and Al Simons. I found it a great pleasure to learn from them. I received numerous reviews and good advice from developers, writers, and editors at Digital, including David Magid, Margie Showman, Ken Ouellette, Mary Orcutt, and Marll McDonald.

After several drafts were complete, some people thought this book should be published on its own. This required significant additions of material to explain portions of DCE. Andrew Oram and Steve Talbott were the driving force coaxing me to find the important explanatory information to accompany the programming examples. Some of the people at O'Reilly and Associates who made great efforts toward this book include Eileen Kramer, Jeff Robbins, and Edie Freedman. Engineers at Locus Computing Corporation who reviewed portions of this book include Mark Heroux, Clem Cole, and Marty Port. We are indebted to the management at Locus for making Clem available to us in a general advisory role.

Additional help and support came from Ram Sudama, Diane Sherman, Susan Scott, David Strohmeyer, Karol McIntyre, Wei Hu, Susan Hunziker, Andy Ferris, Vicki Janicki, Beth Martin, Dan Cobb, Lois Frampton, Steve

Miller, Madeline Cormier, Jim Teague, Eric Jendrock, Gary Schmitt, Ellen Vliet, Judy Davies, Judy Egan, Ward Rosenberry, Collis Jackson, David Kenney, Suzanne Lipsky, Darrell Icenogle, Terry Tvrdik, Howard Mayberry, and of course my wife, Linda McClary.

Joint Venture

This book was produced as a cooperative effort between Digital Equipment Corporation and O'Reilly and Associates. We wish in particular to thank Tonie Franz, a Publications Supervisor at Digital, and Frank Willison, Publications Manager. Tonie's intelligent and energetic oversight of the writing process was a key to the book's successful completion, while Frank's surpassing skill and delicacy in clearing a path through corporate formalities was essential both to get the project under way and to keep it moving smoothly.

While we at O'Reilly and Associates frequently work closely with vendors of hardware and software, this book gave us an opportunity for much more extensive cooperation and mutual support than is customary. It is a model we like, and we believe the end result testifies to the value of sharing one's resources in this way.

1

Overview of an RPC Application

1.1 Introduction

A traditional (local) application is a single program where a procedure call and the procedure implementation execute in the same address space. The **client-server model** for distributed applications has a client program (client) and a server program (server), usually running on different systems of a network. The client makes a request to the server, which is usually a continuously running daemon process, and the server sends a response back to the client (see Figure 1-1).

The **remote procedure call** mechanism is the simplest way to implement client-server applications, because it keeps the details of network communications out of your application code. Figure 1-2 shows the relationship between your application code and the RPC mechanism during a remote procedure call. In client application code, a remote procedure call looks like a local procedure call, because it is actually a call to client stub code. (A **stub** is surrogate code that supports remote procedure calls. Later in this chapter we'll discuss how stubs are created and what they do.) The **client stub** communicates with the **server stub** using the RPC runtime library. (The **RPC runtime library** is a set of standard runtime routines that support all DCE RPC applications.)

The server's RPC runtime library receives the remote procedure call and communicates client information to the server stub. The server stub code invokes the **remote procedure** in the server application code, which executes in the server address space.

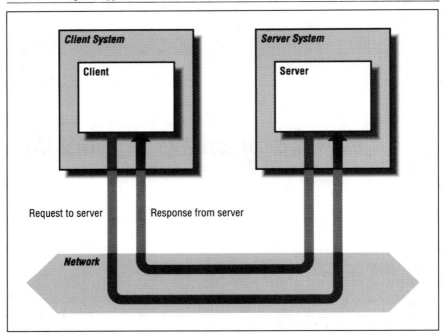

Figure 1-1: Client-server Model

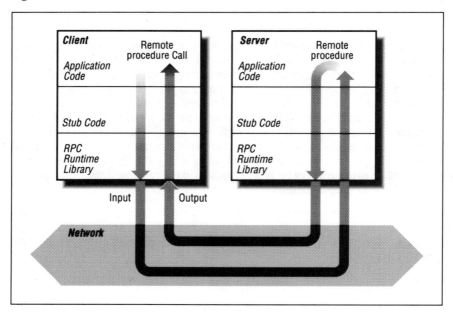

Figure 1-2: RPC Mechanism

When the server finishes executing the remote procedure, the server stub code communicates output to the client stub code using the RPC runtime library. Finally, the client stub code returns to the client application code.

Figure 1-3 shows the three phases required to develop a distributed application. An essential part of the RPC mechanism is an **interface**, which is a set of remote procedure declarations. Client and server development of an application can occur in parallel and on separate systems of the network. You may not need to develop an entire application as shown in this chapter. If the interface and server already exist, your development may require only the client.

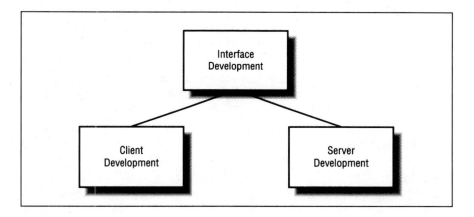

Figure 1-3: Application Development

The Arithmetic Application

The arithmetic application example in this chapter demonstrates a very simple one-client/one-server RPC application. Suppose a remote server system uses special hardware, such as an array processor. In our example, the client performs an arithmetic operation on arrays by calling a remote procedure that uses the array processor. The remote procedure executes on the server system, taking two arrays as arguments and adding together the elements of the arrays. The remote procedure returns the results to the client in a third array argument. Finally, the results of the remote procedure are displayed on the client system.

The arithmetic example is deliberately limited to demonstrate the basics of a distributed application implemented with RPC. We describe each portion of the application in this chapter, and Appendix C shows the complete application.

1.2 A Simple Interface

Every remote procedure must be declared so that the client and server programs follow the same rules when calling and implementing it. Each **procedure declaration** includes the name of the procedure, the data type of the value it returns (if any), and the order and data types of its parameters (if any). An **interface definition** contains a set of procedure declarations and data types. Just as programmers select functions from libraries, client application writers use interface definitions to determine how to call remote procedures. Server application writers use interface definitions to determine the data type of the remote procedure's return value, and the number, order, and data types of the arguments. The interface definition is like a design document that ties the client and server application code together. It is a formal definition describing the set of procedures offered by the interface.

You write the interface definition in the **Interface Definition Language** (IDL). The IDL closely resembles the declaration syntax and semantics of C, with the addition of attributes that allow procedure distribution.

You may think that we have introduced an unnecessary level of complexity here. But you will see that keeping the salient features of a distributed application in one file—the interface definition—makes it easier to scale up development to multiple servers and many clients for those servers.

Figure 1-4 shows the utilities used and the files produced when developing the arithmetic interface. The **uuidgen** utility generates a **universal unique identifier (UUID)** used in the interface definition to distinguish this interface from any other interface on the network. You use a text editor to write the rest of the interface definition, **arithmetic.idl**. When the interface definition is complete, compile it with the IDL compiler (**idl**) to generate stubs and a C header file that you use to develop the client and server programs.

1.2.1 Universal Unique Identifiers

When you write a new interface, you must first generate a universal unique identifier (UUID) with **uuidgen**. A UUID is simply a number that the **uuidgen** utility generates using time and network address information such that no matter when or where it is generated, it is guaranteed to be unique. A UUID is like a fingerprint that uniquely identifies something—such as an interface—across all network configurations.

An interface UUID enables a client to identify an interface it requires. You must use this interface UUID in all copies of the interface. The **uuidgen** utility can generate an interface definition template containing a UUID.

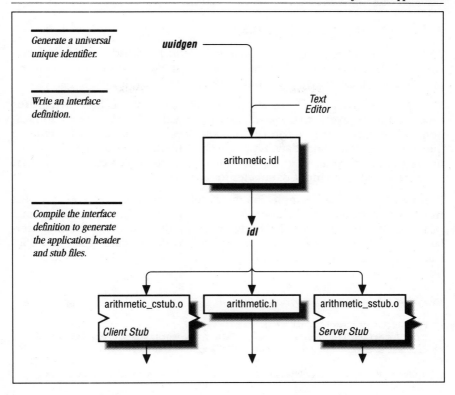

Figure 1-4: Arithmetic Application: Interface Development

Generating a UUID in an Interface Definition Template

To generate and display a UUID in a template for an interface definition, type the following command:

```
> uuidgen -i
[
uuid(A0DF7780-4C89-11C9-BD65-08002B0ECEF1),
version(1.0)
]
interface INTERFACENAME
{

}
```

In this example, the output appears at the terminal, but generally you save it in a file with the extension **.idl**. Replace the template name **INTER-FACENAME** with a name you choose for the new interface. In the next section, we use a template like this to develop the arithmetic interface definition.

1.2.2 The Interface Definition

The interface definition contains data type definitions and procedure declarations. The IDL compiler creates the header file and stubs from the interface definition, for use in your application.

The interface definition includes syntax elements called **attributes** (enclosed in brackets) that specify features needed for distributed applications. Attributes convey information about the whole interface or items in the interface, including data types, arrays, pointers, structure members, union cases, procedures, and procedure parameters. For example, the **in** attribute specifies an input parameter for a remote procedure.

Example 1-1 shows a simple interface definition. The text consists of a **header** and **body**. The header contains a **uuid** attribute and the name assigned to the interface. The body specifies all procedures for the interface; it contains the procedure declarations with the data types and constants that are used in the procedure declarations. There is only one procedure declared in our example.

Example 1-1: A Simple Interface Definition

```
/* FILE NAME: arithmetic.idl */
/* This Interface Definition Language file represents a basic arithmetic */
/* procedure that a remote procedure call application can use.           */
[
uuid(C985A380-255B-11C9-A50B-08002B0ECEF1)        /* Universal Unique ID ❶*/
]
interface arithmetic                      /* interface name is arithmetic❷*/
{
    const unsigned short ARRAY_SIZE = 10; /* unsigned integer constant  ❸*/
    typedef long long_array[ARRAY_SIZE];  /* array type of long integers❹*/

    void sum_arrays (   /* sum_arrays procedure does not return a value ❺*/
        [in] long_array a,            /* 1st parameter is passed in  */
        [in] long_array b,            /* 2nd parameter is passed in  */
        [out] long_array c            /* 3rd parameter is passed out */
    );
}
```

❶ The **uuid** attribute specifies the interface UUID. The interface definition header for any distributed application requires a **uuid** attribute.

❷ The last part of the interface definition header contains the keyword **interface** followed by the name chosen for the interface (**arithmetic**).

❸ You can define constants for type definitions and application code. In this example, we define **ARRAY_SIZE** to set the bounds of arrays.

❹ You can define data types for use in other type definitions and procedure declarations. In this example, we define a data type that is an array
of ten long integers. The indexes of arrays begin at 0, so the index values for this array range from 0 to 9.

❺ The remainder of this interface definition is a procedure declaration. A
procedure of type **void** does not return a value. The **in** and **out** parameter attributes are necessary so the IDL compiler knows which direction
the data needs to be sent over the network.

[in]: A value is passed in to the remote procedure when it is called
from the client.

[out]: A value is passed back from the server to the calling procedure
on the client when the procedure returns. A parameter with the **out**
directional attribute must be a pointer or array so that the parameter
can be passed to the client stub by reference.

1.2.3 Stub and Header Generation Using the IDL Compiler

When the interface definition is complete, you compile it with the IDL compiler, which creates the following:

- A C language header file that contains definitions needed by the stubs
and your application code. Include the header file in client and server
application code.

- A client stub file linked with the client portion of the application. During a remote procedure call, the client stub code is intermediate
between your client application code and the RPC runtime library.

- A server stub file linked with the server portion of the application. During a remote procedure call, the server stub code is intermediate
between your server application code and the RPC runtime library.

When you invoke the IDL compiler, the interface definition goes through
two phases: a preprocessing phase that generates the header file and intermediate C language stub files, and a compilation phase that generates stub
object code.

To invoke the IDL compiler and create the header and stub files for the
arithmetic interface, type the following:

```
> idl arithmetic.idl
```

In this example, we generate the header file and the object stub files of the
client and server in one compilation. The IDL compiler generates object
stub files by default, but you may retain intermediate C language stub files
by using appropriate IDL compiler options. If you develop the client and
server on different systems, copies of the interface definition and the IDL
compiler must reside on both the client and server systems. To generate

object code correctly for different kinds of systems, compile the interface definition for the client stub on the client system, and for the server stub on the server system.

1.3 A Simple Client

Developing a client requires knowledge of the interface definition. To use all the capabilities of RPC, you must also know the RPC runtime routines. The client example here, however, requires no RPC runtime routines.

Figure 1-5 shows the files and utilities needed to produce a client. You write the client application code (**client.c**) in C. Currently, DCE provides libraries only for C. Remote procedure calls in a client look like local procedure calls. (The server portion of the application implements the remote procedures themselves.) You must include the header file (**arithmetic.h**) produced by the IDL compiler, so that its type and constant definitions are available.

After compiling **client.c** with the C compiler, you can create the executable client by linking the client stub (**arithmetic_cstub.o**)—produced by the IDL compiler—with the client object file and the DCE library. Example 1-2 shows a simple client.

Example 1-2: A Simple Client

```
/* FILE NAME: client.c */
/* This is the client module of the arithmetic example. */
#include <stdio.h>
#include "arithmetic.h"    /* header file created by IDL compiler ❶*/

long_array a ={100,200,345,23,67,65,0,0,0,0};
long_array b ={4,0,2,3,1,7,5,9,6,8};

main ()
{
   long_array result;
   int       i;

   sum_arrays(a, b, result);          /* A Remote Procedure Call ❷*/
   puts("sums:");
   for(i = 0; i < ARRAY_SIZE; i++)
     printf("%ld\n", result[i]);
}
```

❶ The client code includes the header file produced by the IDL compiler.

❷ The client calls the remote procedure **sum_arrays** using the two initialized arrays as input. It then displays the elements of the resulting array.

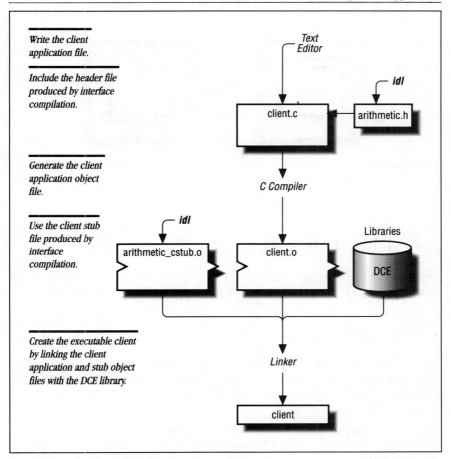

Figure 1-5: Arithmetic Application: Client Development

How a Client Finds a Server

When a client makes a remote procedure call, a **binding** relationship is established with a server (see Figure 1-6).

Binding information is network communication and location information for a particular server. We describe binding information in Section 1.4.2. Conveniently, in the arithmetic application, the client stub and the RPC runtime library automatically find the server for you during the remote procedure call.

The following section shows how to write the server for the arithmetic application.

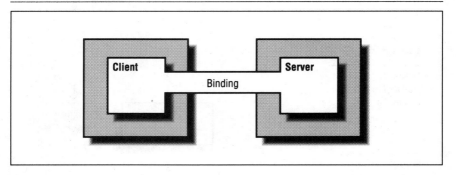

Figure 1-6: Binding

1.4 A Minimal Server

Developing a server requires knowledge of the interface definition and RPC runtime routines. You write two distinct portions of code for a server:

- code to implement the remote procedures
- code to initialize the server

You make calls to the RPC runtime routines mainly in the server initialization, which prepares the server to listen for remote procedure calls. For our arithmetic application, server initialization is the only code that requires the use of runtime routines.

Figure 1-7 shows the files and utilities needed to produce a server. You must write the remote procedures (**procedure.c**) and server initialization code (**server.c**) in C. You need the header file (**arithmetic.h**) produced by the IDL compiler because it contains definitions required by the remote procedures and runtime calls.

After compiling the server application with the C compiler, you create the executable server by linking the server stub (**arithmetic_sstub.o**)—produced by the IDL compiler—with the server application object files and the DCE library.

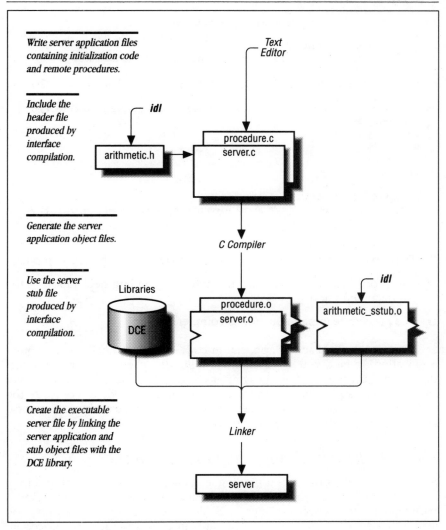

Figure 1-7: Arithmetic Application: Server Development

1.4.1 Remote Procedure Implementation

The programmer who writes a server must develop all procedures that are declared in the interface definition. Refer to the interface definition (**arithmetic.idl**) and the header file generated by the IDL compilation (**arithmetic.h**) for the procedure's parameters and data types. Example 1-3 shows the code for the remote procedure of the arithmetic application.

Example 1-3: A Remote Procedure Implementation

```
/* FILE NAME: procedure.c */
/* Implementation of procedure defined in the arithmetic interface. */
#include <stdio.h>
#include "arithmetic.h"        /* header file produced by IDL compiler ❶*/

void sum_arrays(a, b, c)       /* implementation of sum_arrays procedure ❷*/
    long_array a;
    long_array b;
    long_array c;
    {
    int i;

    for(i = 0; i < ARRAY_SIZE; i++)
       c[i] = a[i] + b[i];      /* array elements are each added together ❸*/
    }
```

❶ The server code includes the header file produced by the IDL compiler.

❷ The procedure definition matches its corresponding declaration in the interface definition.

❸ The procedure implementation is completed.

So far, the client and server application code has been much like any other application. In fact, you can compile and link the client and remote procedures, and run the resulting program as a local test. Section 1.4.3, "Server Initialization," shows how to write the final piece of code to complete the RPC application. But first, it is useful to discuss how the arithmetic application works in a distributed environment.

1.4.2 A Distributed Application Environment

Section 1.3 briefly describes a binding as a client-server relationship during a remote procedure call. Binding information tells a client how to find a particular server it needs. Figure 1-8 illustrates that binding information acts like a set of keys to a series of gates in the path a remote procedure call takes toward execution.

Binding information includes the following:

1. **Protocol Sequence**

    A protocol sequence is an RPC-specific name containing a combination of communication protocols that describe the network communication used between a client and server. For example, **ncacn_ip_tcp** represents the protocol sequence for a Network Computing Architecture connection-oriented protocol, over a network with the Internet Protocol and the Transmission Control Protocol for transport.

2. **Server Host**

The client needs to identify the server system. The server host is the name or network address of the host on which the server resides.

3. **Endpoint**

The client needs to identify a server process on the server host. An endpoint is a number representing a specific server process running on a system.

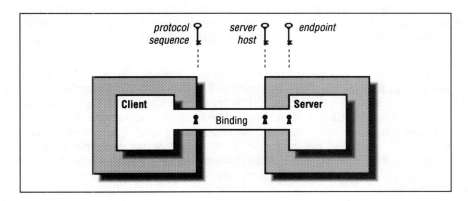

Figure 1-8: Binding Information

In order to help clients find servers in a flexible and portable manner, DCE provides a name service to store binding information. A **name service** is a distributed database service used by applications to store and retrieve information. The Cell Directory Service (CDS) is a particular name service supplied with DCE. (The terms "name service" and "directory service" are equivalent.) The RPC runtime library contains **name service routines** used to indirectly access the DCE Directory Service. These routines are independent of the particular name service on a system (name service independent) and thus can be used to access whatever name service your system uses. RPC servers store binding information in the name service database so that RPC clients can retrieve the binding information and find servers.

Distributed applications do not require the name service database, but we recommend you use it. Alternatives to using the name service are to manage binding information directly in client and server code, or to create your own application-specific method of advertising and searching for servers. These alternatives present more maintenance problems than if you use the name service routines.

Figures 1-9, 1-10, and 1-11 show how the arithmetic application uses binding information, and how the remote procedure call completes.

A server must make certain information available to clients. Figure 1-9 shows the typical steps needed each time a server starts executing. A server first registers the interface with the RPC runtime library, so that clients later know whether they are compatible with the server. The runtime library creates binding information to identify this server process. The server places the binding information in appropriate databases so that clients can find it. The server places communication and host information in the name service database. The server also places process information (endpoints) in a special database on the server system called the **local endpoint map**, which is a database used to store endpoints for servers running on a given system. In the final initialization step, a server waits while listening for remote procedure calls from clients.

When the server has completed initialization, a client can find it by obtaining its binding information, as illustrated in Figure 1-10. A remote procedure call in the client application code transfers execution to the client stub. The client stub looks up the information in the name service database to find the server system. The RPC runtime library finds the server process endpoint by looking up the information in the server system's endpoint map. The RPC runtime library uses the binding information to complete the binding of the client to the server. Chapter 3, *How to Write Clients*, discusses variations on how to obtain server binding information.

As shown in Figure 1-11, the remote procedure executes after the client finds the server. The client stub puts arguments and other calling information into an internal RPC format that the runtime library transmits over the network. The server runtime library receives the data and transfers it to the stub, which converts it back to a format the application can use. When the remote procedure completes, the conversion process is reversed. The server stub puts the return arguments into the internal RPC format, and the server runtime library transmits the data back to the client over the network. The client runtime library receives the data and gives it to the client stub, which converts the data back for use by the application.

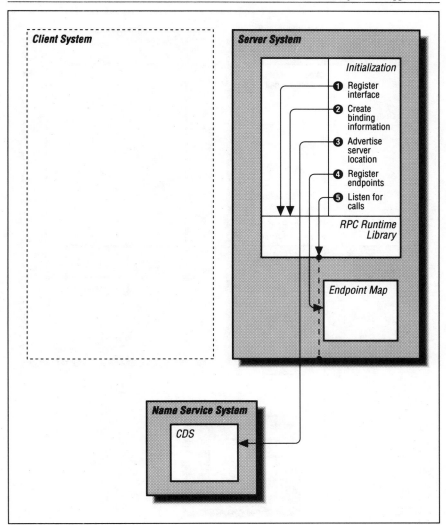

Figure 1-9: Server Initializing

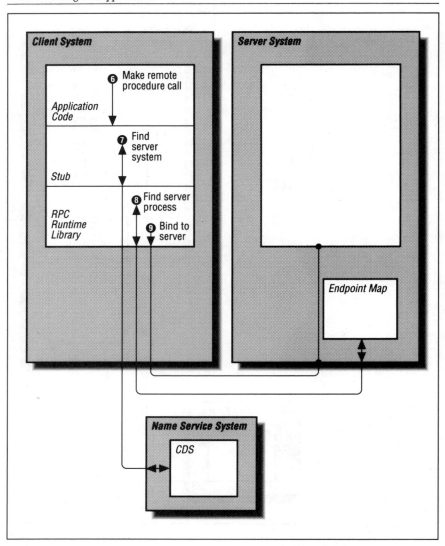

Figure 1-10: Client Finding a Server

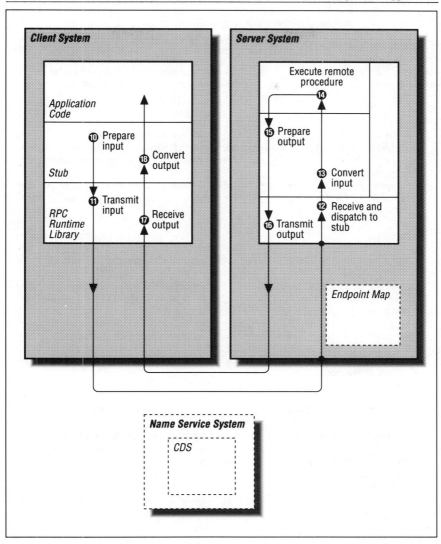

Figure 1-11: Completing a Remote Procedure Call

1.4.3 Server Initialization

As illustrated in Figure 1-9, a server must make certain information available to the RPC runtime library and clients, before it can accept remote procedure calls. Example 1-4 contains the server initialization code for the arithmetic application, illustrating the sequence of steps to initialize a typical RPC server. This code executes each time the server starts.

17

Example 1-4: A Minimal Server Initialization

```
/* FILE NAME: server.c */
#include <stdio.h>
#include "arithmetic.h"        /* header created by the idl compiler */
#include "check_status.h"      /* header with the CHECK_STATUS macro */

main ()
{
    unsigned32         status;        /* error status (nbase.h)         */
    rpc_binding_vector_t *binding_vector; /*set of binding handles(rpcbase.h)*/
    unsigned_char_t    *entry_name; /*entry name for name service (lbase.h)*/
    char *getenv();
    rpc_server_register_if(      /* register interface with the RPC runtime ❶*/
        arithmetic_v0_0_s_ifspec,  /* interface specification (arithmetic.h) */
        NULL,
        NULL,
        &status                                      /* error status */
    );
    CHECK_STATUS(status, "Can't register interface\n", ABORT);

    rpc_server_use_all_protseqs(            /* create binding information  ❷*/
        rpc_c_protseq_max_reqs_default,  /* queue size for calls   (rpcbase.h)*/
        &status
    );
    CHECK_STATUS(status, "Can't create binding information\n", ABORT);

    rpc_server_inq_bindings(   /* obtain this server's binding information ❸*/
        &binding_vector,
        &status
    );
    CHECK_STATUS(status, "Can't get binding information\n", ABORT);

    entry_name = (unsigned_char_t *)getenv("ARITHMETIC_SERVER_ENTRY");
    rpc_ns_binding_export(      /* export entry to name service database  ❹*/
        rpc_c_ns_syntax_default,    /* syntax of the entry name  (rpcbase.h) */
        entry_name,                 /* entry name for name service        */
        arithmetic_v0_0_s_ifspec,   /* interface specification (arithmetic.h)*/
        binding_vector,             /* the set of server binding handles    */
        NULL,
        &status
    );
    CHECK_STATUS(status, "Can't export to name service database\n", ABORT);

    rpc_ep_register(           /* register endpoints in local endpoint map ❺*/
        arithmetic_v0_0_s_ifspec,  /* interface specification (arithmetic.h) */
        binding_vector,            /* the set of server binding handles     */
        NULL,
        NULL,
        &status
    );
    CHECK_STATUS(status, "Can't add address to the endpoint map\n", ABORT);
```

Example 1-4: A Minimal Server Initialization (continued)

```
rpc_binding_vector_free(          /* free set of server binding handles ❻*/
    &binding_vector,
    &status
);
CHECK_STATUS(status, "Can't free binding handles and vector\n", ABORT);

puts("Listening for remote procedure calls...");
rpc_server_listen(                /* listen for remote calls          ❼*/
    rpc_c_listen_max_calls_default,/*concurrent calls serviced (rpcbase.h)*/
    &status
);
CHECK_STATUS(status, "rpc listen failed\n", ABORT);
}
```

❶ **Register the interface.** Register the interface with the RPC runtime library using the **rpc_server_register_if** routine. The **arithmetic_v0_0_s_ifspec** variable is called an **interface handle**. It is produced by the IDL compiler and refers to information that applications need, such as the UUID. We describe the NULL arguments in Chapter 5, *How to Write a Server*.

The CHECK_STATUS macro is defined in the **check_status.h** header file for the applications in this book. It is used to interpret status codes from runtime calls. (See Example 3-12.) Figure 1-9, step 1 is now complete.

❷ **Create binding information.** In order to create binding information, you must choose one or more network protocol sequences. This application, like most, calls **rpc_server_use_all_protseqs** so that clients can use all available protocols. During this call, the RPC runtime library gathers together information about available protocols, your host, and endpoints, to create binding information. The system allocates a buffer for each endpoint, to hold incoming call information. DCE sets the buffer size when you use the **rpc_c_protseq_max_calls_default** argument.

❸ **Obtain the binding information.** When creating binding information, the RPC runtime library stores binding information for each protocol sequence. A **binding handle** is a reference in application code to the information for one possible binding. A set of server binding handles is called a **binding vector**. You must obtain this information through the **rpc_server_inq_bindings** routine, in order to pass the information to other DCE services with other runtime routines. Figure 1-9, step 2 is now complete.

❹ **Advertise the server location in the name service database.** In this example, the server places all its binding information in the name service database (exports) using the **rpc_ns_ binding_export** runtime routine.

The **rpc_c_ns_syntax_default** argument tells the routine how to interpret an entry name. (The current version of DCE has only one syntax.) The `entry_name` is a string obtained in this example from an application-specific environment variable, ARITHMETIC_SERVER_ENTRY. (See Section 1.6.) The interface handle, `arithmetic_v0_0_s_ifspec`, associates interface information with the entry name in the name service database. The client later uses name service routines to obtain binding information by comparing the interface information in the name service database with information about its own interface. Figure 1-9, step 3 is now complete.

❺ **Register the endpoints in the local endpoint map.** The RPC runtime library assigns endpoints to the server as part of creating binding information. The **rpc_ep_register** runtime routine lets the endpoint map on the local host know that the process running at these endpoints is associated with this interface. Figure 1-9, step 4 is now complete.

❻ **Free the set of binding handles.** Memory for the binding handles was allocated with a call to the **rpc_server_inq_bindings** routine. When you have finished passing binding information to other parts of DCE, release the memory using the **rpc_binding_vector_free** routine.

❼ **Listen for remote calls.** Finally, the server must wait for calls to arrive. Each system has a default for the maximum number of calls that a server can accept at one time. DCE sets this maximum when you use the **rpc_c_listen_max_calls_default** argument. Figure 1-9, step 5 is now complete.

All of the server code is now complete. The compilation of the application is shown in the next section.

1.5 Producing the Application

So far we have written the interface definition, produced the stubs and header file from the interface definition with the IDL compiler, and written the client and server portions of the application. To produce the application, compile and link the client and server separately, each on the system where you want its executable to run.

1.5.1 DCE Libraries

DCE-distributed applications must be linked with the DCE libraries, which may vary depending on your system and vendor. This book uses the following options for a link on an OSF/1 system:

```
-ldce -lcma
```

The **-lcma** option (Concert Multi-threaded Architecture library) is required because DCE RPC uses threads internally. To use the makefiles shown in the appendices of this book, you may need to modify the link.

The following sections assume your client and server files are available to the respective client and server systems.

1.5.2 Compile and Link the Client Code

Recall that Figure 1-5 shows the utilities used and files produced when developing a client. The compilation and final link of the client are shown here:

1. Compile the client C language source file on the client system (represented by the shell prompt, C>) to generate the client object file.

   ```
   C> cc -c client.c
   ```

2. Link the client object file and client stub file with the DCE library to create the executable client file.

   ```
   C>  cc -o client client.o arithmetic_cstub.o -ldce -lcma
   ```

1.5.3 Compile and Link the Server Code

Recall that Figure 1-7 shows the utilities used and files produced when developing a server. The compilation and final link of the server are shown here:

1. Compile the server C language source files on the server system (represented by the shell prompt, S>), including the remote procedure implementation and the server initialization, to create the server object files.

   ```
   S> cc -c server.c procedure.c
   ```

2. Link the server object files and server stub file with the DCE library to create the executable server file.

```
S>  cc -o server server.o procedure.o arithmetic_sstub.o \
    -ldce -lcma
```

1.6 Running the Application

We designed the arithmetic application for simplicity so your client automatically finds the server by using the name service to retrieve server binding information. The client stub obtains the binding information exported by the server to the name service database, and the client RPC runtime library completes the remote procedure call. This automatic binding method requires you to set the RPC-specific environment variable, **RPC_DEFAULT_ENTRY**, on the client system, so the client stub has an entry name with which to begin looking for the binding information. More advanced applications can use binding methods not dependent on the login environment.

For this example, we use a simplistic approach by assigning to **RPC_DEFAULT_ENTRY** the same entry name used in the server initialization when exporting the binding information to the name service database. Chapter 6 describes details of naming entries and searching in a name service database.

To run the distributed arithmetic application, follow these steps:

1. This server exports binding information to a name service database. Exporting requires both read and write access permission to the name service. Use a system at your site established for testing distributed applications or see your name service administrator to establish permission.

2. Execute the server. For this example, the application-specific environment variable, ARITHMETIC_SERVER_ENTRY, is set prior to running the server. This variable represents a name for the entry that this server uses when exporting the binding information to the name service database. The usual convention for entry names is to concatenate the interface and host names. We use an environment variable here because the name can vary depending on which host you use to invoke the server. If you do not supply a valid name, the binding information will not be placed in the name service database and the program will fail. The prefix /.:/ is required to represent the global portion of a name in the

hierarchy of a name service database. For this example, assume the server resides on the system **moxie**.

```
moxie> setenv ARITHMETIC_SERVER_ENTRY /.:/arithmetic_moxie
moxie> server
```

3. For the client system (represented by the ▷ prompt), set the RPC environment variable **RPC_DEFAULT_ENTRY** to the name of the server's entry name in the name service database. The client stub can then automatically begin its search to find the server.

```
▷ setenv RPC_DEFAULT_ENTRY /.:/arithmetic_moxie
```

4. After the server is running, execute the client on the client system.

```
▷ client
sums:
104
200
347
26
68
72
5
9
6
8
```

5. The server is still running and should be terminated with a **kill** command or by typing ^C (Ctrl/C).

Figure 1-12 summarizes the development of the arithmetic application.

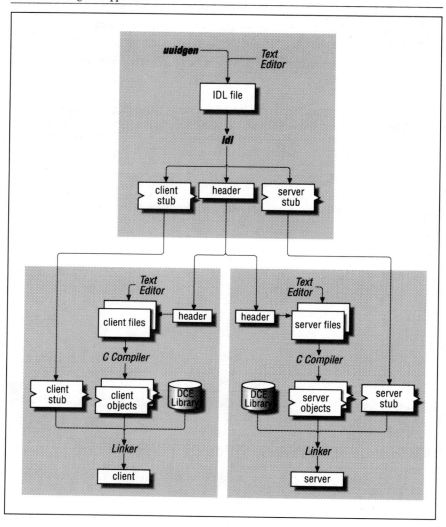

Figure 1-12: Arithmetic Application: Complete Development

2

Using a DCE RPC Interface

As we discussed in Chapter 1, the first step in creating a distributed application is to write an **interface definition**. This file contains definitions the client and server share, and a list of all the procedures offered by the server. This chapter explains what interface definitions need to contain. Server developers usually create an interface definition, which client developers need to read and interpret. All servers that support the interface must implement the remote procedures using the same format of data types and parameters. All clients must call the remote procedures consistently.

A **procedure declaration** in an interface definition specifies the procedure name, the data type of the value it returns (if any), and the number, order, and data types of its parameters (if any). Interface definition files are written in the DCE RPC Interface Definition Language (IDL) and the file names end in **.idl**.

Interface definitions are compiled with the IDL compiler (**idl**) to create the header and stub files. You use the header file with your application C code, and link the stub files with your application object code and the RPC runtime library to create a distributed application. If you make a mistake when writing an interface definition, the IDL compiler gives useful messages to help you correct what is wrong.

2.1 Interface Definition Language (IDL)

Use the Interface Definition Language (IDL) to define the necessary data types and declare the remote procedures for an interface. Declarations in IDL are similar to declarations in C,* with the addition of attributes.

---

*IDL is currently designed to work with C for programming DCE applications. However, IDL has features such as **boolean** and **byte** data types, so that it will work in future versions for languages other than C.

Attributes

Interface definition **attributes** make an application distributable using DCE RPC.

- Some attributes distinguish one interface from another on a network. They guarantee that a client finds the servers that implement the proper remote procedures. For example, the **uuid** attribute declares the UUID for the interface.

- Some attributes explicitly describe data transmitted over a network. Some aspects of data in C that you take for granted must be described explicitly for a distributed application. For example, a union is a data structure that allows different data types in the same area of memory. Your application uses another variable to keep track of which data type is valid. In a distributed program, this additional variable must be specified in IDL so it is transmitted with a union parameter.

- Some attributes make data transmission more efficient. In a local application, procedures have access to both parameters and global variables so that any amount of data can be accessed efficiently. In a distributed application, all data used by the client and the remote procedure must be passed as parameters and transmitted over the network. Since most parameters are passed in only one direction, you use attributes to specify whether each parameter is used for input, output, or both.

Tables A-1 through A-8 in Appendix A show all IDL attributes with brief descriptions of each.

Structure of an Interface Definition

An interface definition includes some or all of the following:

- The interface header
    - Interface header attributes
    - Interface name

- The interface body
    - Import statements
    - Constant definitions
    - Data type definitions
    - Procedure declarations

2.1.1 Interface Header Attributes

Interface header attributes specify RPC features that apply to an entire interface. A combination of an interface UUID (Section 1.2.1) and a version number uniquely identifies an interface. The interface UUID and version number are used to determine whether a binding can exist between a particular client and server. A complete version number consists of a major and minor version number. For example, if a version number is 2.1, the major version is 2 and the minor version is 1.

During a remote procedure call, the following rules determine whether a client can use an interface that a server supports:

- The UUID of the client and server must match.

- The major version number of the client and server must match.

- The minor version number for the client must be less than or equal to the minor version number for the server. A client minor version number that is less than the server minor version number indicates an upwardly compatible change to the interface on the server.

When you create new versions of an interface by adding new declarations and definitions, increase the minor version number. Any other changes to an interface require a major version number change, essentially creating a different interface.

The Inventory Application

The application we use in this chapter is a simple inventory: an inventory database is stored on the server system, and a client makes inquiries based on a part number. The complete application is shown in Appendix D.

Example 2-1 shows the header with associated interface header attributes in the interface definition of the inventory application.

Example 2-1: Interface Header Attributes

```
/* FILE NAME: inventory.idl */
[                                          /* brackets enclose attributes❶*/
uuid(008B3C84-93A5-11C9-85B0-08002B147A61),/* universal unique identifier❷*/
version(1.0),                              /* version of this interface❸*/
pointer_default(ptr)                       /* pointer default          ❹*/
] interface  inventory                     /* interface name           ❺*/

{
/* The body of an interface definition consists of import statements,    */
/* constant definitions, data type definitions, and procedure declarations. */
  .
  .
  .
}
```

❶ Brackets enclose attributes in interface definitions.

❷ The **uuid** is a required attribute that uniquely identifies an interface. All copies of this interface definition contain the same UUID.

❸ The **version** is an optional attribute used to identify different versions of an interface. In this example, the major version number is 1 and the minor version number is 0.

❹ The **pointer_default** is an optional attribute needed by some interface definitions so that pointer data is efficiently transmitted.

❺ The keyword **interface** and a name are required to identify the interface. The IDL compiler uses this name to construct data structure names. Client and server code use these data structures to access information about the interface.

Table A-1 lists and describes all interface header attributes.

2.1.2 Type Definitions, Data Attributes, and Constants

In C, a data type can map to different sizes on different systems. For example, a **long** data type in C may be 16, 32, or 64 bits, depending on the system. The size of an IDL data type, however, must be the same on all systems so that DCE applications can exchange data. When you compile the interface definition, the IDL compiler generates C code data types that begin with **idl_**, and places them in the header file. For example, a typedef in an interface definition uses the IDL data type **long** as follows:

```
typedef long part_num;
```

The IDL compiler generates the data type **idl_long_int**, corresponding to the **long** IDL type, and places it in the header file as follows:

```
typedef idl_long_int part_num;
```

You use the new data type, **part_num**, in your application code. Although the size of a particular IDL data type is always the same, it may map to different standard C data types on different systems. The **idl_** data types are defined in a DCE RPC-supplied header file to map to the proper sized C data types for the system on which the compile took place. For example, the **idl_long_int** data type on 32-bit systems corresponds to the **long** C type, but on a 64-bit system, its corresponding C type might be **int**. The IDL compiler takes care of the proper mapping between the generated **idl_** data types and your local system's C data types.

Table 2-1 shows the basic IDL data types, the size of each in bits, and the corresponding **idl_** data types. Use the IDL data types in interface definitions for type definitions, constant declarations, and procedure declarations. Use the **idl_** data types in your RPC application code for all return values and parameters in remote procedure calls.

Table 2-1 IDL Basic Data Types

IDL Data Type	Size	C Code Data Type
boolean	8 bits	**idl_boolean**
byte	8 bits	**idl_byte**
char	8 bits	**idl_char**
void	-	**void**
void *	opaque	application specific
handle_t	opaque	**rpc_binding_handle_t,** **handle_t**
error_status_t	32 bits	**unsigned32,** **unsigned long,** **error_status_t**
Integers		
small	8 bits	**idl_small_int**
short	16 bits	**idl_short_int**
long	32 bits	**idl_long_int**
hyper	64 bits	**idl_hyper_int**
unsigned small	8 bits	**idl_usmall_int**
unsigned short	16 bits	**idl_ushort_int**
unsigned long	32 bits	**idl_ulong_int**
unsigned hyper	64 bits	**idl_uhyper_int**
Floating Point		
float	32 bits	**idl_short_float**
double	64 bits	**idl_long_float**
International Characters		
ISO_LATIN_1	8 bits	**ISO_LATIN_1**
ISO_UCS	32 bits in a structure	**ISO_UCS**
ISO_MULTI_LINGUAL	16 bits in a structure	**ISO_MULTI_LINGUAL**

For 32-bit systems, you can use the standard C data types (**long, float**, and so on) for remote procedure return values and parameters, because most of the IDL data types map to the comparable C data type. For example, the **long** IDL type maps to **idl_long_int**, which maps to a **long** C type on a

32-bit system. However, to assure that your DCE application code will port to other systems, use the C code data types from Table 2-1 in your application code.

Table 2-2 contains notes about some of the IDL data types.

Table 2-2 Notes on IDL Data Types

IDL_Type	Notes
boolean	Data that is either **idl_true** or **idl_false**.
byte	Data is not automatically converted when transmitted over the network to a system with a different data format. Use it to transmit data that is untyped or opaque so that no conversion is performed on it.
char	An unsigned, 8-bit character. C uses the **char** data type to represent 8-bit integers as well as characters, and it interprets them as signed on some systems and unsigned on others. Use the IDL **char** data type for true character data and use **small** or **unsigned small** to represent 8-bit integers in interface definitions.
void	Indicates that a procedure does not return a value.
void *	Used with the **context_handle** attribute to define context handles. It refers to opaque data, the details of which are hidden from you. See Chapter 7, *Using Context Handles*.
handle_t	Data that denotes a binding handle. Section 3.1.3 describes how to use this data type to define binding handles in an interface definition.
error_status_t	Data that denotes an RPC communication status.
ISO_LATIN_1	The Latin character set defined by the International Standards Organization.
ISO_UCS	The universal character set defined by the International Standards Organization.
ISO_MULTI_LINGUAL	A subset of the characters of type **ISO_UCS** that can be represented in two bytes.

During a remote procedure call, the client stub prepares input parameters for transmission, and the server stub converts the data for use by the server application. When the remote procedure completes execution on the server system, the server stub prepares the output parameters for transmission and the client stub converts the data for the client application.

Marshalling is the process during a remote procedure call which prepares data for transmission across the network. Marshalling converts data into a byte-stream format and packages it for transmission using a **Network Data Representation (NDR)**. NDR allows successful data sharing between systems with different data formats. It handles differences like big-endian versus little-endian (byte order), ASCII characters versus EBCDIC characters, and other incompatibilities.

Data transmitted across the network undergoes a process called **unmarshalling**. If the data format of sender and receiver is different, the receiver's stub converts the data to the right format for that system, and passes the data to the application.

Example 2-2 shows a constant and two type definitions for the inventory interface.

Example 2-2: IDL Type Definitions

```
[
/* The header of an interface definition consists of interface header  */
/* attributes and the name of the interface.                           */
.
.
.
] interface inventory
{
    const long MAX_STRING = 30;              /* constant for string size ❶*/

    typedef long      part_num;              /* inventory part number ❷*/

    typedef [string] char part_name[MAX_STRING+1];     /* name of part ❸*/
.
.
.
/* The remainder of the interface definition consists of other data    */
/* type definitions and the procedure declarations.                    */
}
```

❶ Use the keyword **const** followed by a data type to declare a constant to use in type definitions and application code.

❷ Use the keyword **typedef** followed by a data type to define a new data type.

❸ A data type is not sufficient to completely describe some kinds of data. Attributes provide the necessary extra information. In this example, the **string** attribute enclosed in brackets applies to the character array part_name, so that it becomes a null-terminated string.

Table A-4 lists and describes all the data type attributes. So far we have seen only basic IDL data types. Now we will explain how to construct more complex data types in an interface definition.

Pointers

In a distributed application, a pointer does not provide the same convenience and efficiency that it does in a local application because there is stub overhead such as memory allocation, copying, and transmitting all the data the pointer refers to. IDL contains two kinds of pointers to balance efficiency and maximum pointer capabilities.

A **full pointer** has all of the capabilities usually associated with pointers. These capabilities require additional stub overhead during a remote procedure call to identify the data the pointer refers to, to determine whether the pointer value is NULL, and to determine whether two pointers point to the same data.

A **reference pointer** is a simpler pointer that refers to existing data. A reference pointer has a performance advantage but limited capabilities compared to a full pointer. No new memory can be allocated for the client during the remote procedure call, so memory for the data must exist in the client before the call is made.

The **ptr** attribute represents a full pointer and the **ref** attribute represents a reference pointer. Chapter 4 discusses how to use pointers.

Arrays

Array index values begin at 0 in IDL, as in C. For example, the array `arr[10]` defined in an interface definition has elements `arr[0],arr[1]` , . . . ,`arr[9]` when you use it in the client or server code. IDL provides several kinds of arrays so that array size in your interface can vary with, or conform to, the amount needed for specific client and server implementations. These kinds of arrays let the interface definition remain as flexible as possible, and help you restrict network transmission to a minimum number of elements.

fixed array　　　A fixed array has constant index values for its dimensions.

varying array　　A varrying array has a maximum size determined at compile time with subset bounds represented by variables. Only the portion of the array you need is transmitted in a remote procedure call.

conformant array   The size of a conformant array is represented by a dimension variable so that the actual size is determined when the application is running.

Chapter 4, *Using Pointers and Arrays*, discusses arrays in more detail.

Strings

In C code it is convenient to use strings to manipulate character data. C library routines, such as **strcpy**, recognize a null character as the end of a string in the character array. In IDL, all characters in an array are transmitted, including null characters. Therefore, you must explicitly define strings with the **string** attribute, so that only the characters up to a null character are transmitted. Example 2-3 shows some string definitions.

Example 2-3: Defining Strings in IDL

```
     .
     .
     .
  const long MAX_STRING = 30;              /* a constant for string size */
     .
     .
     .
  typedef [string] char part_name[MAX_STRING+1];      /* name of part ❶*/

  typedef [string, ptr] char *paragraph;      /* description of part ❷*/
     .
     .
     .
```

❶ To specify a string, apply the **string** attribute to a character or byte array. In this example, the string size is 31 but the maximum string length is 30. The data type of the array elements must be a **char** or **byte**, or defined with a type definition that resolve to a **char** or **byte**. The data type can also be a structure whose fields all resolve to a **char** or **byte**.

❷ This example specifies a **conformant string** by applying the **string** attribute to a pointer to a **char** or **byte** data type.

A conformant string has the maximum length allocated in the application code. You can also specify a conformant string using array syntax. For example, the following is another way to define the conformant string `paragraph`:

```
  typedef [string] char paragraph[];
```

When you use a conformant string as an input parameter to a remote procedure, the amount of data that is transmitted is determined from the current string length. If the string parameter is both input and output, however, apply an array attribute **size_is** or **max_is** to the string so the length can increase when the remote procedure completes. Chapter 4 discusses array attributes in greater detail.

Enumerated Types

IDL provides an enumerated type so that you can map a set of symbol names to a fixed set of integer values. An application uses the names as distinct identifiers (and the numerical values usually have no more significance than to distinguish one from another). In Example 2-4, the keyword **enum**, followed by a list of identifiers, maps the identifiers to consecutive integers starting with 0. For this example, we use enumeration to specify more than one kind of measurement unit for parts in the inventory. Some parts are counted as whole items, while other parts are measured by weight.

Example 2-4: Defining an Enumerated Type in IDL

```
    .
    .
    .
    typedef enum {
        ITEM, GRAM, KILOGRAM
    } part_units;                               /* units of measurement */
    .
    .
    .
```

Structures

You define structures in IDL the same way you do in C. In Example 2-5 the **struct** keyword is followed by a list of typed members that define a structure. For this example two structures are shown. The structure `part_price` contains a units-of-measurement member and a price-per-unit member. The `part_units` data type is an enumerated type. The structure `part_record` represents all the data for a particular part number. As in C, any user-defined types such as `part_num` must be defined before they are used.

Example 2-5: Defining Structures in IDL

```
    .
    .
    .
    typedef struct part_price {                 /* price of part */
        part_units units;
        double      per_unit;
    } part_price;
```

Example 2-5: Defining Structures in IDL (continued)

```
    .
    .
    .
    typedef struct part_record {            /* data for each part */
        part_num      number;
        part_name     name;
        paragraph     description;
        part_price    price;
        part_quantity quantity;
        part_list     subparts;
    } part_record;
    .
    .
    .
```

Discriminated Unions

In C a union is a data structure that stores different types and sizes of data in the same area of memory. For example, this union stores a long integer or a double precision floating-point number:

```
    typedef union {
        long int number;
        double   weight;
    } quantity_t;
```

To keep track of what type is stored in the union, the application must use a discriminator variable that is separate from the union data structure. If a remote procedure call includes a union parameter, the remote procedure has no way of knowing which member of the union is valid unless it receives the discriminator along with the union. In IDL, a **discriminated union** includes a discriminator as part of the data structure itself, so that the currently valid data type is transmitted with the union. When you define a discriminated union, it looks like a combination of a C union and switch statement. The switch defines the discriminator and each case of the switch defines a valid data type and member name for the union.

Example 2-6 shows how to define a discriminated union.

Example 2-6: Defining a Discriminated Union in IDL

```
    .
    .
    .
    typedef enum {
        ITEM, GRAM, KILOGRAM
    } part_units;                           /* units of measurement */
```

Example 2-6: Defining a Discriminated Union in IDL (continued)

```
        ❶              ❷                 ❸
    typedef union switch(part_units units) total {    /* quantity of part */
        case ITEM:     long int number;
        case GRAM:                        ❹
        case KILOGRAM: double   weight;
    } part_quantity;                      ❺
```

❶ You begin the definition of a discriminated union data type with the keywords **typedef union**.

❷ Use the keyword **switch** to specify the data type and name of the discriminator variable, `units`. The data type `part_units` is a previously defined enumerated type. A discriminator can be Boolean, character, integer, or an enumerated type.

❸ Define the name of the union, `total`, prior to listing the union cases.

❹ Use the keyword **case** followed by a value, to specify the data type and name of each union member. The case value is the same type as the discriminator variable. In this example, a union defines the quantity of a part in an inventory. Some parts are counted as whole items while other parts are weighed. This union offers a choice between defining the quantity as a long integer or as a double precision floating-point number. The union case GRAM has the same data type and name as the case KILOGRAM.

❺ The name of the new data type is `part_quantity`, which you use in application code to allocate a discriminated union variable.

In application code, the discriminated union is a C structure. The IDL compiler generates a C structure with the discriminator as one member and a C union as another member. Example 2-7 shows the structure in the generated header file for the corresponding discriminated union in Example 2-6.

Example 2-7: A Discriminated Union Generated by the IDL Compiler

```
    typedef struct {
      part_units units;
```

Example 2-7: A Discriminated Union Generated by the IDL Compiler (continued)

```
union {
  /* case(s): 0 */
  idl_long_int number;
  /* case(s): 1, 2 */
  idl_long_float weight;
} total;
} part_quantity;
.
.
.
```

You must manage the union discriminator in the application code to control which union case is valid at any time in the application. Example 2-8 shows how you can use the discriminated union in application code.

Example 2-8: Using a Discriminated Union in Application Code

```
part_record part;           /* structure for all data about a part */❶
.
.
.
result = order_part(part.number, &(part.quantity), account);        ❷
if(result > 0) {
    if(part.quantity.units == ITEM)                                 ❸
        printf("ordered %ld items\n", part.quantity.total.number);  ❹
    else if(part.quantity.units == GRAM)
        printf("ordered %10.2f grams\n", part.quantity.total.weight);
    else if(part.quantity.units == KILOGRAM)
        printf("ordered %10.2f kilos\n", part.quantity.total.weight);
}
```

❶ In the inventory application, the **part_quantity** discriminated union is a member of the **part_record** structure shown in Example 2-5.

❷ The **part.quantity** structure member is the discriminated union. In this example, you request a quantity of a part to order, and the remote procedure returns the actual quantity ordered.

❸ The **part.quantity.units** member is the discriminator for the union.

❹ The **part.quantity.total** member is the union, which contains number and weight cases.

If you omit the union name (**total** in Example 2-6), then the IDL compiler generates the name **tagged_union** for you. You can access the structure members in application code as follows:

```
part.quantity.units = ITEM;
part.quantity.tagged_union.number = 1;
```

Pipes

Pipes can make data transmission much more efficient in the following cases:

- Large amounts of data must be transmitted at one time.

- The total amount of data is unknown until the application is running, such as when processing files.

- The data is incrementally produced and consumed, such as with instrument data collection.

Our inventory application does not use pipes. See Chapter 8, *Using Pipes for Large Quantities of Data*, for a discussion of pipes.

2.1.3 Procedure Declarations and Parameter Attributes

The interface definition declares the procedures that a server offers. Remote procedure implementations are part of server development. All remote procedure implementations for the inventory interface are shown in Appendix D.

In C, parameters of procedure calls are passed by value, which means a copy of each parameter is supplied to the called procedure. The variable passed is an input-only parameter because any manipulation of the procedure's copy of the variable does not alter the original variable. In order for a variable to be an input and output parameter, a pointer to the variable is passed as a parameter.

With a remote procedure call, we must be concerned with whether a parameter is input, output, or both input and output, because it is more efficient to transmit data only in a relevant direction. The parameter directional attributes **in** and **out** are used in an interface definition to distinguish data transmission direction for a parameter. An output parameter must be a pointer or an array, as it must be in C. All parameters must have at least one directional attribute.

Example 2-9 shows procedure declarations and some associated parameter attributes.

Example 2-9: Procedure Declarations and Parameter Attributes

```
.
.
.
] interface inventory
{
/* The beginning of the interface definition body usually contains    */
/* constant and type definitions (and sometimes import declarations).*/
.
.
.

    /*********************** Procedure Declarations **********************/
    boolean is_part_available(        /* return true if in inventory    ❶*/
        [in] part_num number          /* input part number */
    );

    void whatis_part_name(            /* get part name from inventory   ❷*/
        [in]  part_num  number,       /* input part number */
        [out] part_name name          /* output part name   */
    );

    paragraph get_part_description(   /* return a pointer to a string   ❸*/
        [in]  part_num  number
    );

    void whatis_part_price(           /* get part price from inventory   */
        [in]  part_num   number,
        [out] part_price *price
    );

    void whatis_part_quantity(        /* get part quantity from inventory */
        [in]  part_num       number,
        [out] part_quantity *quantity
    );

    void whatare_subparts(            /* get list of subpart numbers    */
        [in]  part_num  number,
        [out] part_list **subparts    /* structure containing the array ❹*/
    );

    /* Order part from inventory with part number, quantity desired, and    */
    /* account number.  If inventory does not have enough, output lesser    */
    /* quantity ordered.  Return values: 1=ordered OK,                      */
    /* -1=invalid part, -2=invalid quantity, -3=invalid account.            */

    long order_part(  /* order part from inventory, return OK or error code */
        [in]     part_num       number,
        [in,out] part_quantity *quantity,          /* quantity ordered ❺*/
        [in]     account_num    account
    );
} /* end of interface definition */
```

❶ As in C, an IDL procedure can return a value. In this example, the `is_part_available` procedure returns a Boolean value of **idl_true** if the part number is available in the inventory.

❷ Procedures defined with the void type do not return a value. Input parameters have the **in** directional attribute and output parameters have the **out** directional attribute. As in C, arrays and strings are implicitly passed by reference, so the string name does not need a pointer operator.

❸ Some procedures return a data structure or a pointer to a data structure. In this example, the data type `paragraph` has been defined in the interface definition as `char *`. It is a full pointer to a string representing the description of the part. This remote procedure allocates new memory.

❹ Output parameters require pointers to pointers when new memory is allocated. Pointers to pointers are discussed in Section 4.1.3.

❺ Parameters that are changed by the remote procedure call use both **in** and **out**. In this example, a part is ordered with the part number, the quantity, and an account number. If the input quantity units are wrong or the quantity requested is more than the inventory can supply, the remote procedure changes the quantity on output.

Due to communication errors and disruptions that can occur, sometimes remote procedures will not complete or execute at all. If communication is disrupted, it is useful if some procedures automatically retry execution. A procedure is **idempotent** if it can execute more than once with the same arguments to produce identical results without any undesirable side-effects. If you want an idempotent procedure to automatically retry execution, use the **idempotent** attribute.

Table A-7 shows all parameter attributes and Table A-8 shows all procedure attributes.

2.2 Using the IDL Compiler

The IDL compiler generates the header and stub files needed to incorporate the interface in a client or server. The input for an IDL compilation is an interface definition file, ending in **.idl**. Figure 2-1 shows the utilities used and files produced during interface production.

An attribute configuration file (ACF) is an optional file, ending in **.acf**. It contains information that changes how the IDL compiler interprets the interface definition. (See Section 2.3).

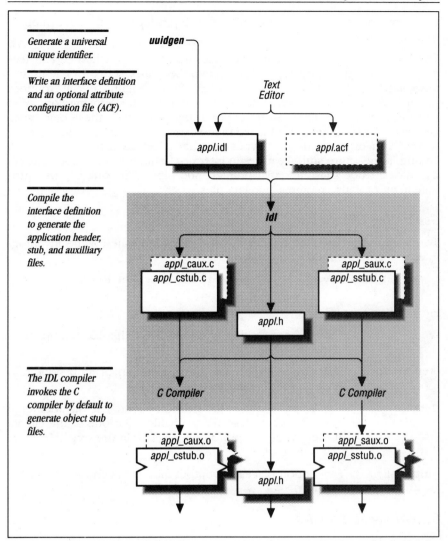

Figure 2-1: Producing an Interface

Depending on which compiler options you use, the IDL compiler produces the client stub, server stub, or both sets of stub files. The stub file names contain the **_cstub** suffix for clients and the **_sstub** suffix for servers. By default, the IDL compiler produces the header file (ending in **.h**) and object stub files (ending in **.o**) for both the client and server. The IDL compiler generates intermediate C stub code and invokes the C compiler to generate object stub files. When the IDL compiler generates object code, you can control which output and intermediate files it produces, and what options it uses.

The IDL compiler produces auxiliary files automatically when certain features are used. Auxiliary file names contain the **_caux** suffix for clients and the **_saux** suffix for servers. Auxiliary files contain special routines required for certain data types to prepare the data for transmission. You link the auxiliary object files with your application when these data types are used. These routines are placed in auxiliary files rather than in the stub, so that you can use the data types in other interface definitions without linking in the entire stub. Features in interface definitions that require auxiliary files include self-referential pointers and pipes. The **out_of_line** attribute in an ACF also requires auxiliary files.

Generating Client Files

To generate the interface header file and client stub file for the inventory interface, type the following command:

```
C> idl inventory.idl -v -server none -Iexplicit -out explicit
```

Each option is as follows:

-v   The verbose option displays what the IDL compiler is doing.

-server none This option suppresses the generation of stub none and auxiliary files for the server.

-Iexplicit The **-I** option causes the IDL compiler to use the additional directory when it searches for files. For one of the clients of the inventory application, an ACF in the **explicit** directory is needed.

-out explicit This option places the output files in the chosen directory, **explicit**.

Generating Server Files

To generate the interface header file and server stub file for the inventory interface, type the following command:

```
S> idl inventory.idl -v -client none
```

Each option is as follows:

-v   The verbose option displays what the IDL compiler is doing.

-client none This option suppresses the generation of stub and auxiliary files for the client.

2.3 Using an ACF to Customize Interface Usage

You can control some aspects of RPC on the client side without affecting the server. The opposite is also true. These aspects should not be in the interface definition because we do not want to force them on all clients and servers. A client or server developer can use an optional attribute configuration file (ACF) to modify the way the IDL compiler creates stubs, without changing the way the stubs interact across the network. This assures that all copies of an interface behave the same when clients and servers interact.

The most significant effect an ACF has on your application code can be the addition of parameters to remote procedure calls not declared in the interface definition. For example, the **explicit_handle** attribute adds a binding handle as the first parameter to some or all procedures. Also, the **comm_status** and **fault_status** attributes can add status parameters to the end of a procedure's parameter list. See Table A-9 for a complete list of ACF attributes.

If you develop both clients and servers for an interface, you can use different ACFs (or no ACF) for the client and server. Since this can cause differences between the header files generated for the client and server, it is good development practice to separate the client and server output when using ACFs.

You do not specify an ACF when you compile an interface; instead, the IDL compiler automatically uses an ACF if one is available in the search directories. The name of an ACF must match the name of the IDL file it is associated with. The file extension must be **.acf**.

An ACF is useful for a number of reasons: selecting binding methods, controlling errors, excluding procedures, and controlling marshalling.

Selecting a Binding Method

The **auto_handle** ACF attribute selects the automatic binding method, which causes the client stub to automatically select the server for your client. If server communication is disrupted, the client stub can sometimes find another server. If your client requires a statistical analysis server, for example, the first one found by the client stub may be sufficient.

The **implicit_handle** ACF attribute selects the implicit binding method, which allows you to select a specific server for your remote procedure calls to use. For example, if many inventory servers representing different warehouses are available on the network, you may want your client to select a specific one.

The **explicit_handle** ACF attribute selects the explicit binding method, which lets you select a specific server for each remote procedure call. For example, if your client needs data from many servers simultaneously, you need a way to control which remote procedure call uses which server.

Chapter 3, *How to Write Clients*, discusses binding methods in greater detail. Example 2-10 is an ACF used by the IDL compiler to produce the header and stub files for the implicit client example of the inventory application.

Example 2-10: An Attribute Configuration File (ACF)

```
/* FILE NAME: inventory.acf (implicit version)*/
/* This Attribute Configuration File is used in conjunction with the    */
/* associated IDL file (inventory.idl) when the IDL compiler is invoked. */
[
implicit_handle(handle_t global_binding_h)  /* implicit binding method ❶*/
]
interface  inventory    /* The interface name must match the idl file. ❷*/
{
}
```

❶ The **implicit_handle** attribute applies to the entire interface. A global binding handle of type **handle_t** is established in the client stub to refer to binding information a client uses to find a server.

❷ The interface name (`inventory`) must match the interface name in the corresponding IDL file.

Controlling Errors and Exceptions

An **exception** is a software state or condition resulting from an event to which the normal flow of control in the current procedure is unable to respond. Such an event may be produced by hardware (such as memory access violations) or software (such as array subscript range checking). DCE applications have communication and server errors raised as exceptions. Unless you design your program to handle the exceptions, the program will exit.

An ACF can save you the trouble of writing extra layers of exception handling code. The **comm_status** and **fault_status** attributes apply to procedure parameters or procedure return results. If these attributes are present, communication and server errors are communicated to the client as values in the named parameters rather than raised as exceptions. (Section 3.4 discusses error and exception control in greater detail.)

Excluding Unused Procedures

The **code** and **nocode** ACF attributes allow you to define which procedures the client stub supports. For example, if a client uses only four out of twenty remote procedures declared in the interface, the client stub code does not need the overhead of the other procedures. However, all the procedures of an interface definition must be implemented by the server.

Controlling Marshalling and Unmarshalling

The **out_of_line** ACF attribute causes constructed data types such as unions, pipes, or large structures to be marshalled or unmarshalled by auxiliary routines, thus reducing stub size. The **out_of_line** attribute directs the IDL compiler to place marshalling and unmarshalling code in IDL auxiliary stub files, rather than in the direct flow of stub code. If stub size is a concern, use **out_of_line** on constructed data types that are used in more than one remote procedure.

The **in_line** ACF attribute causes data types to be marshalled or unmarshalled as fast as possible. The **in_line** attribute directs the IDL compiler to place marshalling and unmarshalling code for constructed data types in the direct flow of stub code, rather than as a separate IDL compiler-generated auxiliary routine. This is the default for an interface.

The **in_line** and **out_of_line** attributes affect only the stub code. They require no change to application code.

3

How to Write Clients

In this chapter we discuss how to develop client programs for DCE RPC interfaces. It is a good idea to read Chapter 1 for a complete overview of a distributed application and Chapter 2 to familiarize yourself with features of interface definitions.

We discuss client development before server development because you may develop a client for an existing interface and server. We describe server development in Chapter 5. The code for all applications is shown in Appendices C through F.

The first question that probably comes to mind when you begin to develop a client is: How does a remote procedure call find the server it needs? Finding a server includes the following activities:

* Identify a data structure in the client program code that represents a server. Chapter 1 described a **binding** as a relationship between a client process and a server process involved in a remote procedure call. During each remote procedure call, the RPC runtime library needs information that defines the binding, so the client can find the server on the network. A binding handle is the principal data structure to manage binding in applications. A **binding handle** is a reference (pointer) to information for one possible binding.

  Binding information includes, among other things, a communication protocol sequence, a host name or address, and a server process address on the host (endpoint). If you are familiar with Internet Protocols, these are similar to a protocol family, an Internet address, and a port assignment. Applications use a binding handle for each remote procedure call to reference the binding information for that call.

* Manage binding handles and binding information (see Section 3.1). Binding information can be obtained automatically and be completely invisible to your client application code. To the other extreme, you can

obtain binding information by calling RPC runtime routines and using a binding handle as a parameter in a remote procedure call. The level of control you need depends on the needs of your client program.

- Locate binding information and create binding handles (see Section 3.2). DCE supplies the Cell Directory Service (CDS) as a convenient, distributed name service database to store names and locations of network services. Servers use RPC runtime routines to store binding information in the name service database. Clients use other RPC runtime routines to retrieve binding information from the name service database and create binding handles for remote procedure calls.

  A server's binding information can also be stored in an application-specific database or supplied to client programs by some other means, for example, as arguments when the client is invoked. If your client would not benefit from a name service (or your client system does not have a running name service), you can use RPC runtime routines in applications to convert strings of binding information to binding handles used by remote procedure calls.

3.1 Implementing a Binding Method

For each remote procedure call, the binding handle is managed in one of the following ways:

Automatic Method

The client stub automatically manages bindings after the application calls a remote procedure. The client stub obtains binding information from a name service database, and passes the binding handle to the RPC runtime library. If the connection is disrupted, new binding information can sometimes be automatically obtained and the call is tried again.

Implicit Method

A binding handle is held in a global area of the client stub. After the application calls a remote procedure, the stub passes the binding handle to the RPC runtime library. You write application code to obtain the binding information and set the global binding handle with RPC runtime routine calls.

Explicit Method

An individual remote procedure call in the application passes a binding handle explicitly as its first parameter. You write application code to obtain the binding information and set the binding handle with RPC runtime routine calls.

Figure 3-1 shows a comparison of binding methods in relation to the client code. For each method, the top portion of the box represents the client application code you write. The bottom portion of each box represents the client stub code that the IDL compiler generates. The shading represents the portion of the client where binding handles are managed.

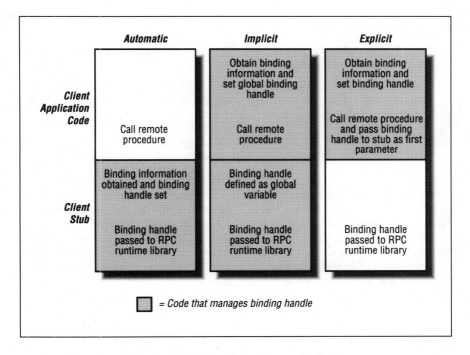

Figure 3-1: A Comparison of Binding Management Methods

For a given client instance, different methods may be employed for different remote procedure calls. For example, one remote procedure call can use the automatic method and another remote procedure call can use the explicit method.

The automatic and implicit methods apply to an entire interface. If you use either the automatic or implicit method for an interface, you can also use the explicit method for some or all remote procedure calls to that interface. The explicit method takes precedence over the automatic and implicit methods because the binding handle is visible as the first parameter in the procedure.

If a client uses more than one interface, you can use the automatic method for all remote procedure calls to one interface and the implicit method for all remote procedure calls to the other interface. However, a client cannot use the automatic and implicit methods simultaneously, for remote procedure calls to the same interface.

The implicit and explicit methods require that your application code obtain binding information and manage the binding handles. Binding handles need to be obtained and managed in the client application code under the following circumstances:

- The client uses a specific server.

- The client needs to set authentication and authorization information for specific binding handles.

- The server has more than one implementation of the same remote procedure. An application uses object UUIDs to distinguish between different remote procedure implementations.

Use an attribute configuration file (ACF) to establish a binding method with the attributes **auto_handle**, **implicit_handle**, or **explicit_handle** (see Section 2.3).

A **context handle** is a special remote procedure parameter defined in an interface definition with the **context_handle** attribute. Applications use a context handle in a sequence of remote procedure calls to refer to a context (state) on a specific server. We mention context handles briefly here with binding methods because they carry with them binding information and thus can act as a binding handle for remote procedure calls. When the context handle is active, it carries with it the binding information necessary to find the same server as it did before, and the server maintains the context for that particular client. (Chapter 7 describes context handle use.)

Deciding on Binding Methods

In some cases, you do not have to choose a binding method for procedures if you do not want to. When the interface definition is compiled, the automatic binding method is used by default except in the following cases:

- The first parameter of a procedure declaration is a binding handle.

- The procedure declaration has an input context handle.

- An ACF establishes a different binding method.

Suppose the first parameter of a procedure declaration is a binding handle. This procedure must use the explicit method. You cannot take away a parameter declared in the interface definition, so this remote procedure cannot use either the automatic or implicit methods.

The next decision you may make is whether to use the automatic or implicit method for all procedures without binding or context handle parameters. If you just want any valid server for your remote procedure calls, the automatic method should be adequate. The automatic method works fine if the network is relatively small. However, you have no control over which server you get, so applications that use servers scattered over a wide area may be inefficient. If most of your remote procedure calls need to use a specific server chosen in your application code, the implicit method is appropriate.

Suppose you have determined that individual remote procedure calls need control over which server each uses. For example, if you use a print server application, one call may request a server near you to print a file. Your next call may request a server in a different location to print another copy for your department manager. If you have determined that you need this kind of binding control for individual remote procedure calls, use the explicit method. The explicit method is necessary for clients that make multi-threaded remote procedure calls. For example, a commodity trade application may request a commodity price with remote procedure calls to many locations at the same time. This server selection control also lets you balance network load in your application. All applications in this book are single-threaded.

Depending on the method or methods you select for your application, certain requirements exist when developing the interface, the client, and the server.

3.1.1 Automatic Binding Management

The automatic binding management method is the simplest method because no binding handle manipulation is necessary in the interface definition, ACF, or your application code. The binding handle is hidden from you in the client stub. After you set an RPC-specific environment variable, the complexity of binding management is done entirely by the client stub code and the RPC runtime library. If you lose a server connection, the automatic method will try to rebind for you. With this method there is a relatively short learning curve to get a distributed application running.

Many applications do not require that you control binding so it is easier to let the underlying RPC mechanism find a server. The server is selected from a set of servers that support the interface. If the particular server makes no difference, use the automatic method. For example, for a mathematics interface, the first server that supports it is probably sufficient.

The automatic method is demonstrated in the arithmetic application and shown in detail in Chapter 1. For this chapter, however, we use one of the clients for the inventory application, so you can compare client development between different methods for the same application. The application is shown in detail in Appendix D.

Interface Development for Automatic Binding

There are no special requirements in the interface for automatic binding. If you wish, you can use the **auto_handle** attribute in an ACF for documentation.

Client Development for Automatic Binding

The client requires the following:

1. The IDL-generated header file must be included with the **#include** compiler directive in the client application code.

   ```
   /* FILE NAME: i_client.c */
   /****** Client of the inventory application ******/
   #include <stdio.h>
   #include <stdlib.h>
   #include "inventory.h" /* header file created by the IDL compiler */
   .
   .
   .
   ```

2. The client application object code must be linked with the client stub, client stub auxiliary file (if available), and the DCE libraries.

   ```
   C> cc -o i_client.exe i_client.o inventory_cstub.o -ldce -lcma
   ```

3. The RPC environment variable **RPC_DEFAULT_ENTRY** must be set to a valid name service entry so the client stub can automatically begin a name service database search.

   ```
   C> setenv RPC_DEFAULT_ENTRY /.:/inventory_group
   ```

4. The client system must have access to a name service database on the network. Your system administrator can tell you whether you have access to a name service.

The remote procedure call looks just like a local procedure call. The procedure returns a Boolean value of **idl_true** if the part number is in the inventory or **idl_false** if it is not.

```
      .
      .
      .
case 'a': if (is_part_available(part.number)) /* Remote Procedure Call */
             puts("available: Yes");
```

```
else
    puts("available: No");
break;
```

.
.
.

If your client uses the automatic method for an interface, you can override it for specific procedures using the **explicit_handle** attribute on the procedures in an ACF.

See Section 3.2.2 and Chapter 6 for more information on the name service.

Server Development for Automatic Binding

For clients to use the automatic method, a server must advertise binding information to a name service entry with the **rpc_ns_binding_export** runtime routine in the server initialization code, or with the DCE RPC control program (**rpccp**) from the shell.

3.1.2   Implicit Binding Management

The implicit binding management method gives you the control of binding management in the client application without a visible binding handle parameter in a remote procedure call. Use the implicit method for applications that need the same server for all or most remote procedure calls of an interface. An ACF defines the binding handle and the IDL compiler generates it as a client-global variable in the client stub. The client application code sets the binding handle before any remote procedure calls. During a remote procedure call, the client stub uses the global binding handle to complete the call to the RPC runtime library.

One client for the inventory application uses the implicit method because in this application you may need to choose a specific server. Once a server is found, the rest of the remote procedure calls can use the same one.

Interface Development for Implicit Binding

Use the **implicit_handle** attribute in an ACF to declare the global binding handle for the client as shown in Example 3-1. When you compile the interface definition with the ACF available, a global binding handle is defined in the client stub. The stub uses the handle every time the client calls a remote procedure for this interface.

Example 3-1: An ACF for the Implicit Binding Method

```
/* FILE NAME: inventory.acf (implicit version)*/
/* This Attribute Configuration File is used in conjunction with the   */
/* associated IDL file (inventory.idl) when the IDL compiler is invoked.*/
[
implicit_handle(handle_t global_binding_h)   /* implicit binding method */
]
interface  inventory      /* The interface name must match the idl file. */
{
}
```

The **handle_t** type is an IDL data type used to define a binding handle named `global_binding_h`.

Client Development for Implicit Binding

The client code includes the IDL-generated header file, obtains a binding handle, and assigns the binding handle to the global binding handle. (See Example 3-2.)

Example 3-2: A Client with the Implicit Binding Method

```
/* FILE NAME: implicit_client.c */
/***** Client of the inventory application with implicit method *****/
#include <stdio.h>
#include <stdlib.h>
#include "inventory.h"  /* header file created by the IDL compiler  ❶*/
 .
 .
 .

   do_import_binding("/.:/inventory_group", &global_binding_h);  /* ❷*/
 .
 .
 .

      case 'a': if (is_part_available(part.number))               /* ❸*/
         puts("available: Yes");
      else
         puts("available: No");
      break;
 .
 .
 .
```

❶ The IDL-generated header file must be included with the **#include** compiler directive.

❷ The client must obtain binding information and assign its handle to the global binding handle. The binding information can be obtained from the name service database as in this example, or it can be constructed from strings of binding information (see Section 3.2.3). Section 3.2.2

shows how to implement the application specific `do_import_binding` procedure.

❸ A remote procedure call looks just like a local procedure call.

If your client uses the implicit method for an interface, you can override it for specific procedures using the **explicit_handle** attribute on the procedures in an ACF.

Server Development for Implicit Binding

Although there are no special requirements in server development, a server must export to a name service database if the clients use a name service to find servers. As an alternative, the server binding information can be exported to the name service database with the DCE RPC control program (**rpccp**). The server for the inventory application exports binding information.

3.1.3 Explicit Binding Management

The explicit binding management method is a per-call method of managing a binding, where the first parameter of the remote procedure call is a binding handle. Use the explicit method when your application needs to make remote procedure calls to more than one server. This method is the most visible in an application because a binding handle is passed as the first parameter of the remote procedure. You completely control the binding management in the client application code.

If the procedure declaration in the interface definition has a binding handle as the first parameter, you must use the explicit method. However, if the procedure declaration does not have a binding handle parameter, you can add one by using an ACF. In this case, after you compile the interface definition, the remote procedure is defined in the header file with an additional binding handle as the first parameter.

We'll use another client from the inventory application to demonstrate the explicit method.

Interface Development for Explicit Binding

An interface definition or an ACF uses the **handle_t** data type to define binding handle parameters. Application code uses the **rpc_binding_handle_t** data type to represent and manipulate binding information.*

---

*The **handle_t** and **rpc_binding_handle_t** data types are equivalent. The **handle_t** data type exists for compatibility with earlier RPC versions. The **rpc_binding_handle_t** data type exists for consistency in data type naming for the RPC runtime routines.

Suppose we want to use the explicit method for a remote procedure that has no explicit binding handle as the first parameter. We use an ACF with the **explicit_handle** attribute, making the IDL compiler add a binding handle as the first parameter. The `is_part_available` procedure is defined in the interface as follows:

```
boolean is_part_available(    /* return true if in inventory */
    [in] part_num number       /* input part number */
);
```

An ACF that adds a binding handle parameter is shown in Example 3-3.

Example 3-3: Adding Binding Handles with an ACF

```
/* FILE NAME: inventory.acf (explicit version)*/
/* This Attribute Configuration File is used in conjunction with the   */
/* associated IDL file (inventory.idl) when the IDL compiler is invoked. */
[
explicit_handle              /* explicit binding method */
]
interface  inventory        /* The interface name must match the idl file. */
{
}
```

When the IDL compiler uses this ACF, all procedure declarations in the header file have a binding handle of type **handle_t**, named **IDL_handle**, added as the first parameter. If you use the **explicit_handle** attribute this way, none of the remote procedure calls to this interface can use the automatic or implicit method for this client instance. The header file generated by the IDL compiler contains the following:

```
    .
    .
    .
extern idl_boolean is_part_available(
#ifdef IDL_PROTOTYPES
       /* [in] */ handle_t IDL_handle,
       /* [in] */ part_num number
#endif
);
    .
    .
    .
```

You can also use the **explicit_handle** attribute on a specific procedure in the ACF to add a binding handle as the first parameter. For example, this

ACF associates a binding handle parameter only with the **is_part_available** procedure:

```
interface inventory
{
    [explicit_handle] is_part_available();
}
```

Example 3-4 defines a binding handle explicitly in the interface definition. An interface is more restrictive when a binding handle is defined this way because clients cannot use the automatic or implicit binding methods for the procedure. (The **is_part_available** procedure is not declared this way for the inventory interface.)

Example 3-4: Defining a Binding Handle in the Interface Definition

```
    .
    .
    .
boolean is_part_available(    /* return true if in inventory */
    [in] handle_t binding_h,  /* explicit, binding handle */
    [in] part_num number      /* input part number        */
);
    .
    .
    .
```

Use the remote procedure in your application code the same way whether the binding handle is declared with an ACF as in Example 3-3, or in the original interface definition as in Example 3-4. To create an application-specific, customized binding handle in the interface definition apply the **handle** attribute to a data type definition (see Section 3.3).

Client Development for Explicit Binding

Before making the remote procedure call, the client must obtain binding information and set the binding handle. The methods of obtaining binding information for the explicit method are almost the same as for the implicit method. For the explicit method you use a specific binding handle instead of assigning the binding information to the implicit global binding handle.

Example 3-5: A Client with the Explicit Binding Method

```
/* FILE NAME: explicit_client.c */
/***** Client of the inventory application with explicit method *********/
#include <stdio.h>
#include <stdlib.h>
#include "inventory.h"          /* header file created by the IDL compiler ❶*/
```

Example 3-5: A Client with the Explicit Binding Method (continued)

```
  .
  .
  .
   rpc_binding_handle_t binding_h;              /* declare a binding handle ❷*/
  .
  .
  .
   do_import_binding("/.:/inventory_group", &binding_h);   /* find server ❸*/
  .
  .
  .
    case 'a': if (is_part_available(binding_h, part.number))      /*❹*/
       puts("available: Yes");
    else
       puts("available: No");
    break;
  .
  .
  .
```

❶ The IDL-generated header file must be included with the **#include** compiler directive.

❷ Binding handles of type **rpc_binding_handle_t** must be declared in the application.

❸ The client must obtain binding information from the name service database, or it can be constructed from strings of binding information. Example 3-7 shows how the application-specific procedure do_import_binding uses the name service database.

❹ Notice that the first parameter is the binding handle. The call to is_part_available in client application code is the same whether the code in Example 3-4 or 3-3 is used to define the explicit handle.

Server Development for Explicit Binding

If the interface definition does not have a binding handle parameter for the remote procedure, and you want the remote procedure to obtain client binding information (such as authentication and authorization), you must use an ACF with the **explicit_handle** attribute to create the binding handle parameter.

If clients use a name service to find servers, the server must export to a name service database. As an alternative, the server binding information can be exported to the name service database with the DCE RPC control program (**rpccp**).

3.2 Finding Servers

Recall that Figure 1-10 shows one way to find a server. In this figure, the client stub and the RPC runtime library handle all binding management, outside of the application code. The client stub automatically finds the server system binding information in a name service database. The binding handle is set and passed to the RPC runtime library which finds the server process binding information (endpoint) in the server system's endpoint map. The RPC runtime library uses the complete binding information to bind to the server.

The key to finding a server is to obtain a protocol sequence, a server host name or address, and an endpoint. A binding handle for the remote procedure call is set to point to this binding information. Binding information may be obtained in one step, but the following discussion is a generalization of what happens during the server finding process. Included are the choices you (or the RPC runtime library) have about where to obtain the necessary binding information. Where these steps are executed (client application, client stub, or RPC runtime library) depends on the kind of binding handle and binding method used.

Finding a Protocol Sequence

A client and server can communicate over a network if they both use the same network communication protocols. A protocol sequence is found in either of two ways:

- The preferred method is to use a name service database to import or look up both a host address and protocol sequence at the same time. To set the binding handle, use the RPC runtime routines that begin with **rpc_ns_binding_import_** or **rpc_ns_binding_lookup_**. If your application uses the automatic method, the client stub does this for you.

- The other method is to use a protocol sequence string obtained from your application or from a call to the **rpc_network_inq_protseqs** routine. Use the RPC runtime routines **rpc_string_binding_compose** and **rpc_binding_from_string_binding** to set the binding handle.

A **protocol sequence** is a character string containing three items that correspond to options for network communications protocols. RPC represents each valid combination of these protocols as a protocol sequence. The protocol sequence consists of a string of the options separated by underscores. The only current, valid option combinations are shown in Table 3-1.

Table 3-1 Valid Protocol Sequences

Protocol Sequence	Common Name	Description
ncacn_ip_tcp	Connection protocol sequence	Network Computing Architecture connection over an Internet Protocol with a Transmission Control Protocol for transport.
ncadg_ip_udp	Datagram protocol sequence	Network Computing Architecture datagram over an Internet Protocol with a User Datagram Protocol for transport.
ip	Datagram protocol sequence	A short version of **ncadg_ip_udp**.

The three protocols of a protocol sequence are for RPC communication, network host addressing, and network transport.

1. The RPC protocol for communications has two options:

    — Network Computing Architecture connection-oriented protocol (**ncacn**)

    — Network Computing Architecture datagram protocol (**ncadg**)

2. The network address format used as part of the binding information is the Internet Protocol (**ip**).

3. The transport protocol for communications has two options:

    — Transmission control protocol (**tcp**)

    — User datagram protocol (**udp**)

Most servers should use all available protocol sequences so clients using the interface will have every opportunity to find and use a server.

The connection protocol sequence is good for establishing and maintaining a binding, so use it for clients that use one or a few servers. The **tcp** transport is considered reliable because the protocol guarantees message delivery.

Timeouts work differently for different protocol sequences. To find out about the availability of a specific server, **ncacn_ip_tcp** is the better protocol sequence because if the server is unavailable, you receive the error quickly. Use **ncacn_ip_tcp** for debugging your client during remote procedure calls, otherwise the process will timeout when the debugger stops it. The connection protocol sequence works better for a wide area network

(WAN) because the datagram protocol sequence will probably have timeout problems. Clients can control timeouts using the RPC runtime routines **rpc_mgmt_set_com_timeout** and **rpc_mgmt_inq_com_timeout**.

The datagram protocol sequence has low operating system overhead so use it for clients that need to bind to many servers. If a remote procedure broadcasts its call to all hosts on the local network, it must use **ncadg_ip_udp**. The **broadcast** attribute on a procedure declaration in the interface definition declares the broadcast capability.

Finding a Server Host

You can find a server host name or network address in two different ways:

- Use a name service database to import or look up a host address and at the same time get a protocol sequence. Use the RPC runtime routines that begin with **rpc_ns_binding_import_** or **rpc_ns_binding_lookup_** to set the binding handle. If your application uses the automatic method, the client stub does this for you.

- Use a host name or host network address string obtained from your application. Use the RPC runtime routines **rpc_string_binding_compose** and **rpc_binding_from_string_binding** to set the binding handle.

A **partially bound binding handle** refers to a protocol sequence and server host (but not to an endpoint). The binding to a server cannot complete until an endpoint is found. A binding handle that is partially bound corresponds to a server system but not a server process on that system. When a partially bound binding handle is passed to the RPC runtime library, an endpoint is automatically obtained for you from the interface or the endpoint map on the server's system.

Finding an Endpoint

A binding handle that has an endpoint as part of its binding information is called a **fully bound binding handle**. Endpoints can be well-known or dynamic. A **well-known endpoint** is a pre-assigned system address that a server process uses every time it runs. Usually a well-known endpoint is assigned by the authority responsible for a transport protocol. A **dynamic endpoint** is a system address of a server process that is requested and assigned by the RPC runtime library when a server is initialized. Most applications should use dynamic endpoints to avoid the network management needed for well-known endpoints.

You can use your application code to obtain an endpoint but it is best to let the RPC runtime library find an endpoint for you. An endpoint is found in one of four ways:

- If the binding information obtained during an import or lookup of the protocol sequence and host in the name service database includes an endpoint, the binding handle is fully bound in one step. The name service database can only have well-known endpoints stored in it. Dynamic endpoints are never stored in the name service database because their temporary nature requires significant management of the database, which degrades name service performance.

- A well-known endpoint is found that was established in the interface definition with the **endpoint** attribute. The RPC runtime library (or your application) finds the endpoint from an interface-specific data structure.

- An endpoint is found from the endpoint map on the server system. These endpoints can be well-known or dynamic. The RPC runtime library first looks for an endpoint from the interface specification. If one is not found, the RPC runtime library looks in the server's endpoint map. When an endpoint is found, the binding to the server process completes. To obtain an endpoint from a server's endpoint map, use the **rpc_ep_resolve_binding** routine or routines beginning with **rpc_mgmt_ep_elt_inq_** in your application.

- You can use a string from your application that represents an endpoint and then use the RPC runtime routines **rpc_string_binding_compose** and **rpc_binding_from_string_binding** to set the binding handle. These endpoints can be well-known or dynamic.

3.2.1 Interpreting Binding Information

You may interpret the binding information of a binding handle to control which server a remote procedure call will use or which binding handles a server will offer. Binding handles refer to the following binding information:

- Object UUID

- Protocol sequence

- Network address or host name

- Endpoint

- Network options

Object UUIDs are part of an advanced topic not discussed in this book. Network options are protocol-sequence specific and not relevant to the connection-oriented or datagram protocol sequences.

Example 3-6 shows how to use RPC runtime routines to interpret binding information. You use these routines in either a server or client. The `do_interpret_binding` procedure is called in the `do_import_binding` procedure (see Example 3-7).

Example 3-6: Interpreting Binding Information

```
/* FILE NAME: do_interpret_binding.c */
/* Interpret binding information and return the protocol sequence. */
#include <stdio.h>
#include <dce/rpc.h>
#include "check_status.h"

void do_interpret_binding(binding, protocol_seq)
rpc_binding_handle_t binding;  /* binding handle to interpret (rpcbase.h) */
char                 *protocol_seq;     /* protocol sequence to obtain */
{
    unsigned32      status;                           /* error status */
    unsigned_char_t *string_binding;  /* string of binding info. (lbase.h) */
    unsigned_char_t *protseq;         /* binding component of interest */

    rpc_binding_to_string_binding(      /* convert binding information */
                                        /* to string ❶*/
        binding,                        /* the binding handle to convert */
        &string_binding,                /* the string of binding data */
        &status
    );
    CHECK_STATUS(status, "Can't get string binding:", RESUME);

    rpc_string_binding_parse(       /* get components of string binding ❷*/
        string_binding,             /* the string of binding data */
        NULL,                       /* an object UUID string is not obtained */
        &protseq,                   /* a protocol sequence string IS obtained */
        NULL,                       /* a network address string is not obtained */
        NULL,                       /* an endpoint string is not obtained */
        NULL,                       /* a network options string is not obtained */
        &status
    );
    CHECK_STATUS(status, "Can't parse string binding:", RESUME);

    strcpy(protocol_seq, (char *)protseq);

                /* free all strings allocated by other runtime routines ❸*/
    rpc_string_free(&string_binding,  &status);
    rpc_string_free(&protseq,         &status);
    return;
}
```

❶ The **rpc_binding_to_string_binding** routine converts binding information to its string representation. The binding handle is passed in and the string holding the binding information is allocated.

❷ The **rpc_string_binding_parse** routine obtains the binding information items as separate allocated strings. The components include an object UUID, a protocol sequence, a network address, an endpoint, and network options. If any of the components are null on input, no data is obtained for that parameter.

❸ The **rpc_string_free** routine frees strings allocated by other RPC runtime routines.

3.2.2   Finding a Server from a Name Service Database

The usual way for a client to obtain binding information is from a name service database using the name service RPC runtime routines (routines beginning with **rpc_ns_**). This method assumes that at least one server that supports the interface has exported binding information to the name service database. Section 5.1.3 shows how servers export binding information to a name service database.

The name service database contains entries of information, each identified by a name used in programs, environment variables, and commands. A name is used to begin a search for compatible binding information in the database. Some entries contain binding information about specific servers; some contain a group of database names that represent a set of servers; and some entries contain a search list. Use RPC name service runtime routines to search entries in the name service database for binding information. The example in this section does a very simple search. See Chapter 6 for a more detailed name service description.

Importing a Binding Handle

Since the same interface can be supported on many systems of the network, a client needs a way to select one system. The runtime import routines obtain information for one binding handle at a time from the name service database, selecting from the available list of servers supporting the interface.

Example 3-7 shows how an application obtains binding information from a name service database.

Example 3-7: Importing a Binding Handle

```
/* FILE NAME: do_import_binding.c */
/* Get binding from name service database. */
#include <stdio.h>
#include "inventory.h"
#include "check_status.h"
```

Example 3-7: Importing a Binding Handle (continued)

```
void do_import_binding(entry_name, binding_h)
char                  entry_name[];        /* entry name to begin search */
rpc_binding_handle_t  *binding_h;          /* a binding handle (rpcbase.h) */
{
    unsigned32     status;                        /* error status (nbase.h) */
    rpc_ns_handle_t import_context;      /* required to import (rpcbase.h) */
    char           protseq[20];                   /* protocol sequence */

    rpc_ns_binding_import_begin(/* set context to import binding handles❶*/
        rpc_c_ns_syntax_default,                  /* use default syntax */
        (unsigned_char_t *)entry_name,     /* begin search with this name */
        inventory_v1_0_c_ifspec,  /* interface specification (inventory.h) */
        NULL,                     /* no optional object UUID required */
        &import_context,                   /* import context obtained */
        &status
    );
    CHECK_STATUS(status, "Can't begin import:", RESUME);

    while(1) {
        rpc_ns_binding_import_next(            /* import a binding handle❷*/
            import_context,      * context from rpc_ns_binding_import_begin */
            binding_h,                 /* a binding handle is obtained */
            &status
        );
        if(status != rpc_s_ok) {
            CHECK_STATUS(status, "Can't import a binding handle:", RESUME);
            break;
        }

      /* application-specific selection criteria (by protocol sequence)  ❸*/
        do_interpret_binding(*binding_h ,protseq);
        if(strcmp(protseq, "ncacn_ip_tcp") == 0)     /* select connection */
                                                     /* protocol */
            break;
        else {
            rpc_binding_free(     /* free binding information not selected❹*/
                binding_h,
                &status
            );
            CHECK_STATUS(status, "Can't free binding information:", RESUME);
        }
    } /*end while */

    rpc_ns_binding_import_done(                /* done with import context❺*/
        &import_context,      /* obtained from rpc_ns_binding_import_begin */
        &status
    );
    return;
}
```

❶ The **rpc_ns_binding_import_begin** routine establishes the beginning of a search for binding information in a name service database. An entry name syntax of **rpc_c_ns_syntax_default** uses the syntax in the RPC-specific environment variable **RPC_DEFAULT_SYNTAX**. In this example, the entry to begin the search is **/.:/inventory_group**, which is passed as a parameter. If you use a null string for the entry name, the search begins with the name in the RPC environment variable **RPC_DEFAULT_ENTRY**. In this example, an object UUID is not required so we use a null value. The interface handle **inventory_v1_0_c_ifspec** refers to the interface specification. It is generated by the IDL compiler and defined in file **inventory.h**. Finally, the import context and error status are output. You use the import context in other import routines to select binding information from the name service database or to free the context memory when you have finished with it.

❷ The **rpc_ns_binding_import_next** routine obtains binding information that supports the interface, if any exists. The routine accesses the database and does not communicate with the server. The import handle, established with the **rpc_ns_binding_import_begin** call, controls the search for compatible binding handles.

❸ Once binding information is obtained, any criteria required by the application may be used to decide whether it is appropriate. In this example, the application-specific procedure, **do_interpret_binding**, shown in Example 3-6, is used to interpret binding information by returning the protocol sequence in a parameter. The **do_import_binding** procedure then selects the binding information if it contains the connection protocol.

❹ Each call to **rpc_ns_binding_import_next** requires a corresponding call to the **rpc_binding_free** routine that frees memory containing the binding information and sets the binding handle to null. Free the binding handle after you finish making remote procedure calls.

❺ The **rpc_ns_binding_import_done** routine signifies that a client has finished looking for a compatible server in the name service database. This routine frees the memory of the import context created by a call to **rpc_ns_binding_import_begin**. Each call to **rpc_ns_binding_import_begin** must have a corresponding call to **rpc_ns_binding_import_done**.

Looking Up a Set of Binding Handles

Runtime routines whose names begin with **rpc_ns_binding_lookup_** obtain a set of binding handles from the name service database. You can then select individual binding handles from the set with the **rpc_ns_binding_select** routine or you may use your own selection criteria. Lookup routines give a client program a little more control than import routines because **rpc_ns_binding_import_next** returns a random binding handle from a list of compatible binding handles. Use the lookup routines when you want to select a server or servers by more specific binding information; for example, to select a server that is running on a system in your building or to use servers supporting a specific protocol sequence.

3.2.3 Finding a Server from Strings of Binding Data

If you bypass the name service database, you need to construct your own binding information and binding handles. Binding information may be represented with strings. You can compose a binding handle from appropriate strings of binding information or interpret information that a binding handle refers to (see Section 3.2.1).

The minimum information required in your application to obtain a binding handle includes the following:

- a protocol sequence of communication protocols

- a server network address or host name

Remember that an endpoint is required for a remote procedure call to complete, but you can let the RPC runtime library obtain one for you. To set a binding handle, obtain and present the binding information to RPC runtime routines.

Example 3-8 shows a procedure to set a binding handle from strings of binding information. The remote_file application uses this procedure. A network address or host name is input for this procedure and the protocol sequence is obtained. This procedure creates a partially bound binding handle, so the RPC runtime library obtains the endpoint when a remote procedure uses the binding handle.

Example 3-8: Setting a Binding Handle from Strings

```
/* FILE NAME: do_string_binding.c */
/* Find a server binding handle from strings of binding information */
/* including protocol sequence, host address, and server process endpoint. */
#include <stdio.h>
#include <dce/rpc.h>
#include "check_status.h"              /* contains the CHECK_STATUS macro */
```

Example 3-8: Setting a Binding Handle from Strings (continued)

```
int do_string_binding(host, binding_h)/* return=0 if binding valid, else -1 */
char            host[];      /* server host name or network address input ❶*/
rpc_binding_handle_t *binding_h;   /* binding handle is output (rpcbase.h) */
{
   rpc_protseq_vector_t *protseq_vector;          /* protocol sequence */
                                                  /* list (rpcbase.h)*/
   unsigned_char_t    *string_binding; /*string of binding info. (lbase.h)*/
   unsigned32         status;             /* error status (nbase.h) */
   int                i, result;


   rpc_network_inq_protseqs(   /* obtain list of valid protocol sequences ❷*/
      &protseq_vector,              /* list of protocol sequences obtained */
      &status
   );
   CHECK_STATUS(status, "Can't get protocol sequences:", ABORT);

   /* loop through protocol sequences until a binding handle is obtained */
   for(i=0; i < protseq_vector->count; i++) {
      rpc_string_binding_compose(  /* make string binding from components ❸*/
         NULL,                          /* no object UUIDs are required */
         protseq_vector->protseq[i],           /* protocol sequence */
         (unsigned_char_t *)host,       /* host name or network address */
         NULL,                          /* no endpoint is required */
         NULL,                     /* no network options are required */
         &string_binding,           /* the constructed string binding */
         &status
      );
      CHECK_STATUS(status, "Can't compose a string binding:", RESUME);

      rpc_binding_from_string_binding(            /* convert string to */
                                                  /* binding handle ❹*/
         string_binding,               /* input string binding */
         binding_h,                 /* binding handle is obtained here */
         &status
      );
      if(status != rpc_s_ok) {
         result = -1;
         CHECK_STATUS(status, "Can't get binding handle from string :", RESUME);
      }
      else
         result = 0;

      rpc_string_free(                /* free string binding created ❺*/
         &string_binding,
         &status
      );
      CHECK_STATUS(status, "Can't free string binding:", RESUME);
      if(result == 0)  break;                /* got a valid binding */
   }
```

Example 3-8: Setting a Binding Handle from Strings (continued)

```
rpc_protseq_vector_free(          /* free the list of protocol sequences ❻*/
    &protseq_vector,
    &status
);
CHECK_STATUS(status, "Can't free protocol sequence vector:", RESUME);
return(result);
}
```

❶ The network address or host name on which a server is available is required binding information. For this example, the information is input as a parameter.

❷ The **rpc_network_inq_protseqs** routine creates a list of valid protocol sequences. This example uses each protocol sequence from the list until a binding handle is created.

❸ The **rpc_string_binding_compose** routine creates a string of binding information in the argument `string_binding` from all the necessary binding information components. The component strings include an object UUID, a protocol sequence, a network address, an endpoint, and network options.

❹ The **rpc_binding_from_string_binding** routine obtains a binding handle from the string of binding information. The string of binding information comes from the **rpc_string_binding_compose** routine or from the **rpc_binding_to_string_binding** routine.

When you are finished with the binding handle, use the **rpc_binding_free** routine to set the binding handle to null and free memory referred to by the binding handle. In this example, another part of the application frees the binding handle.

❺ The **rpc_string_free** routine frees strings allocated by other RPC runtime routines. This example frees the string `string_binding` allocated by the **rpc_string_binding_compose** routine.

❻ The **rpc_protseq_vector_free** routine is called to free the list of protocol sequences. An earlier call to **rpc_network_inq_protseqs** requires a corresponding call to **rpc_protseq_vector_free**.

3.3 Customizing a Binding Handle

You need to manage binding handles in client application code when you use implicit or explicit binding management methods. A binding handle can be either primitive or customized.

To declare a **primitive binding handle** in an interface definition, use a parameter of type **handle_t** as the first parameter of a procedure declaration. You can also establish a primitive binding handle by using the **handle_t** type with the **explicit_handle** or **implicit_handle** attribute in an ACF. So far, we have seen applications that use only primitive binding handles.

A **customized binding handle** associates your choice of data type with a primitive binding handle. You can use a customized binding handle when application-specific data is appropriate to use for finding a server, and the information is also needed as a procedure parameter. For example, in the transfer_data application, a structure contains a host name and a remote filename. The application creates the necessary binding information from the host name and the filename is passed with the binding information so the server knows what data file to use. You can use a customized binding handle with the explicit or implicit binding methods, but the automatic method uses only primitive binding handles.

Figure 3-2 shows how a customized binding handle works during a remote procedure call.

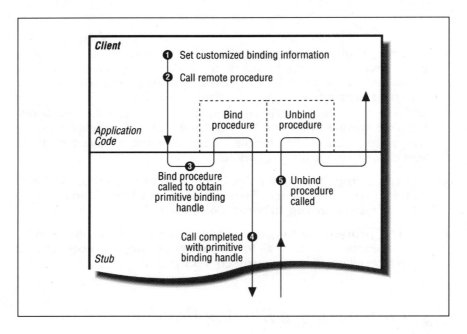

Figure 3-2: How a Customized Binding Handle Works

To define a customized binding handle apply the **handle** attribute to a type definition in an interface definition.

Use a customized binding handle in a client just like a primitive binding handle, but you must write special **bind** and **unbind** procedures. Your code does not call these procedures; the client stub calls them during each remote procedure call. For a primitive binding handle, the client stub already has the necessary code to prepare the binding information for the call. For application-specific binding information, you must supply the code. The tasks of the bind and unbind procedures are to obtain a primitive binding handle and do application cleanup when finished with the binding handle.

Manipulate the data structure in your application the same as any structure, including passing data in the remote procedure call. However, the client stub uses the special procedures to manage the binding. The customized binding handle must be the first parameter in a remote procedure (or the global handle for the implicit method) to act as the binding handle for the call. A customized handle acts as a standard parameter if it is not the first parameter.

Example 3-9 shows how to define a customized binding handle in the transfer_data interface definition (see Appendix F).

Example 3-9: Defining a Customized Binding Handle

```
/* FILE NAME: transfer_data.idl */
[
uuid(A6876974-F555-11CA-BAE1-08002B245A28),
version(1.0)
]
interface transfer_data     /* data transfer to and from a remote system */
{
    const long NAME_LENGTH = 200;

    typedef [handle] struct {            /* a customized handle type ❶*/
       char host[NAME_LENGTH+1];
       char filename[NAME_LENGTH+1];
    } file_spec;                                                     /*❷*/
 .
 .
 .
```

Example 3-9: Defining a Customized Binding Handle (continued)

```
void send_floats(        /* send pipe of floats to a file on the server ❸*/
   [in] file_spec  cust_binding_h,    /* customized binding for server */
   [in] pipe_type data                /* input pipe of float data      */
);
   .
   .
   .
```

❶ Use the **handle** attribute in the interface definition to associate a customized binding handle with a data type.

❷ The `file_spec` data type is a structure whose members are file specifications. This is application-specific information used by the bind procedure to obtain server binding information.

❸ The customized binding handle is the first parameter of a procedure declaration. This is an example of explicit binding.

You must implement bind and unbind procedures (see Example 3-10).

Example 3-10: Bind and Unbind Procedures

```
/* FILE NAME: binding.c */
#include "transfer_data.h"        /* header created by the IDL compiler */
#include "check_status.h"         /* contains the CHECK_STATUS macro     */

handle_t file_spec_bind(spec)  /* "bind" procedure for customized handle❶*/
file_spec spec;
{
   rpc_binding_handle_t binding_h;
   if(do_string_binding(spec.host, &binding_h) < 0) {
      fprintf(stderr, "Cannot get binding\n");
      exit(1);
   }
   return(binding_h);
}

void file_spec_unbind(spec, binding_h) /* "unbind" for customized handle❷*/
file_spec spec;
handle_t binding_h;
{
   unsigned32 status;  /* error status */

   rpc_binding_free(&binding_h, &status);
   CHECK_STATUS(status, "Can't free binding handle:", RESUME);
   return;
}
```

❶ The bind procedure takes an input parameter of the customized handle data type, and returns a primitive binding handle. You construct the procedure name from the data type name, **file_spec**, to which you append **_bind**. In this example **file_spec_bind** calls the application-specific `do_string_binding` procedure (defined in the remote_file application and shown in Example 3-8) to obtain a primitive binding handle.

❷ The unbind procedure takes input parameters of the customized handle data type and a primitive binding handle. You construct the procedure name from the data type name, **file_spec**, to which you append **_unbind**. In this example **file_spec_unbind** calls the RPC runtime routine, **rpc_binding_free**, to free the binding handle. This procedure can simply act as a dummy procedure, leaving all binding management to the bind procedure.

Example 3-11 shows how a transfer_data application client uses a customized binding handle.

Example 3-11: A Client with a Customized Binding Handle

```
/* FILE NAME: client_send.c */
 .
 .
 .
main(argc, argv)
int argc;
char *argv[];
{
    file_spec   cust_binding_h;          /* customized binding handle❶*/
    char        local_source[100];
 .
 .
 .
    void        send_floats();

    /* get user input */
    if(argc < 4) {
       printf("USAGE: %s  local_source  host  file\n", argv[0]);
       exit(0);
    }
    /* initialize customized binding handle structure */          /*❷*/
    strcpy(local_source, argv[1]);
    strcpy(cust_binding_h.host, argv[2]);
    strcpy(cust_binding_h.filename, argv[3]);
 .
 .
 .
    send_floats(cust_binding_h, data); /* remote procedure with input❸*/
}
```

❶ The application allocates the customized binding handle.

❷ Initialize the customized binding information in the client before calling the remote procedure. For this example, when we invoke the client, we input the server host name and remote data filename as arguments.

❸ The remote procedure is called with the customized binding handle as the first parameter.

3.4 Error Parameters or Exceptions

DCE RPC client applications require special error-handling techniques to deal with errors that may occur during a remote procedure call. The following discussion pertains to both client and server development.

Server and communication errors are raised to the client as exceptions during a remote procedure call. An **exception** is a software state or condition resulting from an event to which the current procedure's normal flow of control is unable to respond. Such an event may be produced by hardware (such as memory access violations) or software (such as array subscript range checking).

RPC exceptions are equivalent to the RPC error status codes. For example, the exception **rpc_x_comm_failure** is the same as the error code **rpc_s_comm_failure**.*

Types of exceptions include the following:

- Exceptions raised on the client system, such as when the client process is out of memory (**rpc_x_no_memory**).

- Exceptions raised to the client application by the client stub due to communication errors, such as remote system crashes (**rpc_x_comm_failure**).

- Exceptions raised by the client stub on behalf of the server. These errors can occur in the server stub (**rpc_x_fault_remote_no_memory**), in the remote procedures (**rpc_x_call_faulted**), in pipe support routines (**rpc_x_fault_pipe_order**), or in the server's RPC runtime library.

A distributed application can have errors from a number of sources, so you will need to decide whether you want to handle errors with exception

---

*The RPC runtime routines define error status codes as **unsigned32** so that data type naming is consistent. The IDL compiler-generated header file contains procedure definitions whose error parameters are defined as **error_status_t** so that data type naming in IDL is consistent. The data types **unsigned32** and **error_status_t** are equivalent. The applications in this book use the data type **unsigned32** for exceptions and error parameters.

handling code or error parameters. This may simply be a matter of personal preference or consistency.

Using Exception Handlers in Clients or Servers

You can handle exceptions by writing exception handler code in the application to recover from an error or gracefully exit the application. DCE threads supply macros as a framework to handle exceptions in your client or server code. (Example 5-6 uses exception handling macros.)

Using Remote Procedure Parameters to Handle Errors

Remote procedure call communication and server errors can be handled using an ACF to specify error parameters for the remote procedures. Errors are presented to the client application code as values of these parameters rather than raised as exceptions. You can also use a combination of exception handlers and error parameters.

The following procedure is declared in the interface definition for the inventory application. Notice that there is one input parameter.

```
boolean is_part_available(    /* Return true if part is in inventory */
    [in] part_num number      /* input part number */
);
```

To establish an error parameter for the procedure, include the following statement in an ACF:

```
is_part_available([comm_status, fault_status] status);
```

The ACF attributes, **comm_status** and **fault_status**, establish a parameter in which to report communication and server errors, if they occur during this remote procedure call. These ACF attributes can be associated with one parameter or separate parameters. In a client, the remote procedure call to this procedure now has an additional parameter written as follows:

```
unsigned32 status;
.
.
.
available = is_part_available(part.number, &status);
CHECK_STATUS(status, "", ABORT);
```

Notice the added error parameter at the end of the parameter list. In this example, if a communication or server error occurs during the remote procedure call, the error code is assigned to **status** when the call returns. You can interpret the error code with the RPC runtime routine **dce_error_inq_text**. Example 3-12 shows this routine in the application-specific **CHECK_STATUS** macro.

Example 3-12: The CHECK_STATUS Macro

```
/* FILE NAME: check_status.h */
#include <stdio.h>
#include <dce/dce_error.h>/* required to call dce_error_inq_text routine */
#include <dce/pthread.h>          /* needed if application uses threads */
#include <dce/rpcexc.h> /* needed if application uses exception handlers */

#define RESUME 0
#define ABORT  1

#define CHECK_STATUS(input_status, comment, action) \
{ \
  if(input_status != rpc_s_ok) { \
     dce_error_inq_text(input_status, error_string, &error_stat); \
     fprintf(stderr, "%s %s\n", comment, error_string); \
     if(action == ABORT) \
     exit(1); \
  } \
}

static int           error_stat;
static unsigned char error_string[dce_c_error_string_len];

void exit();
```

For most applications that use ACFs, you compile the interface separately for the client and server because their header files are different. Each show the correct number, order, and type of parameters where the client has the error parameter but the server does not. If an error occurs during a remote procedure call, the stubs deliver and assign the value to the additional error parameter in the client.

If an error parameter already exists for the procedure in the interface definition, the **comm_status** and **fault_status** ACF attributes can be applied to that parameter to override the exception mechanism. In this case, the error parameter must be a pointer to the **error_status_t** type and be an output parameter with the out directional attribute. For example, the following procedure declaration in an interface definition has an error parameter:

```
proc([out] error_status_t *status);
```

The ACF must have the following declaration to report communication errors through the parameter:

```
     .
     .
     .
proc([comm_status] *status);
     .
     .
     .
```

3.5 Compiling and Linking Clients

Figure 3-3 shows the files and libraries required to produce an executable client. If needed, the IDL compiler produces the client stub auxiliary file (*appl_caux*.o) when the interface is compiled. The following features cause the production of a client auxiliary file:

- self-referential pointers in the interface definition

- the **out_of_line** attribute in an ACF

To compile the implicit client of the inventory application, type the following from the **implicit** directory:

1. Compile all the client modules with the C compiler.

    ```
    C> cc -c implicit_client.c do_import_binding.c \
    do_interpret_binding.c
    ```

2. Link the client application, client stub, and client auxiliary object files (if available) with the DCE libraries to produce the executable client. The IDL compiler does not produce auxiliary files for the inventory interface.

    ```
    C> cc -o implicit_client.exe \
    implicit_client.o do_import_binding.o do_interpret_binding.o \
    inventory_cstub.o -ldce -lcma
    ```

Local Testing

You can compile a local version of your client to test and debug remote procedures without using remote procedure calls. To do a local test, compile the client object files and remote procedure implementations without the stub or auxiliary files. The code that finds a server is also unnecessary for a local test. Applications in this book use the compiler directive, –DLOCAL, to distinguish a test compilation used in a local environment from a compilation used in a distributed environment. Type the following from the **implicit** directory:

```
C> cc -I../ -I../../arithmetic -DLOCAL -o local_implicit_client.exe \
implicit_client.c ../i_procedures.c ../implement_inventory.c
```

Be sure to delete the object files created with the –DLOCAL compiler directive so they do not interfere with a build for the distributed version of the applications.

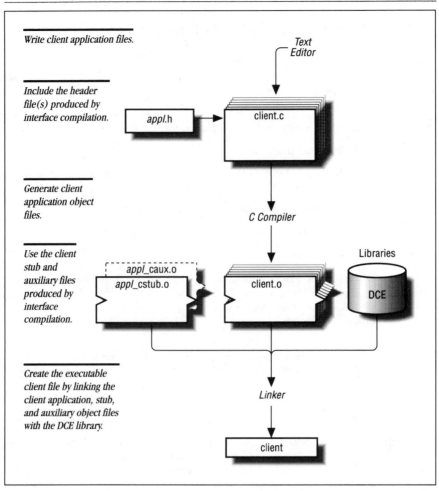

Figure 3-3: Producing a Client

4

Using Pointers and Arrays

In C, pointers and arrays have a close correlation due to the way applications access the information they contain. Pointers and arrays work essentially the same in distributed and local applications. But there are a few restrictions in distributed applications because the client and server have different address spaces. In most of this chapter we discuss pointers and arrays for clients. See also Section 5.2 for a discussion of memory allocation for pointers and arrays in remote procedures.

To make your applications more efficient, IDL offers several kinds of pointers and arrays to reduce network traffic and stub overhead. This chapter uses the inventory application to demonstrate the use of pointers and arrays in distributed applications.

4.1 Kinds of Pointers

A pointer is a variable containing the address of another data structure or variable. As in C, you declare a pointer in an interface definition by using an asterisk (*) followed by a variable. For example, the inventory application has the following procedure declaration:

```
void whatis_part_price(            /* get part price from inventory */
    [in]  part_num    number,
    [out] part_price *price
);
```

In a distributed application, the client and server do not share the same address space. This means the data a pointer refers to in the client is not available in the remote procedure of the server. The opposite is also true. Therefore, pointer data is copied between the client and server address spaces during a remote procedure call. For the **whatis_part_price** procedure, data that the pointer argument refers to on the server is copied back to the client and placed in the memory referred to by the **price** pointer. This copying of pointer data does not occur during a local procedure call. IDL has two kinds of pointers: full pointers and reference pointers.

A **full pointer** has all the capabilities usually associated with pointers. Interface definitions require full pointers for the following:

- When a remote procedure call allocates new memory for the client. The client stub actually allocates the memory.

- When the value of the pointer is **NULL**, as with an optional parameter.

- When two pointers refer to the same address, as in a double-linked list.

The **ptr** attribute specifies a full pointer in an interface definition. Full pointer capability comes at a cost of significant stub overhead, so IDL provides a second kind of pointer, a reference pointer.

A **reference pointer** is used to refer to existing data. A reference pointer has a performance advantage over a full pointer because stub overhead is reduced. For example, the **whatis_part_price** procedure uses a reference pointer. This procedure passes by reference a pointer to an allocated **part_price** data structure. The remote procedure returns output data to the same memory location with the part price. Thus for reference pointers, the data can change but not the address itself. The **ref** attribute specifies a reference pointer in an interface definition.

You can apply a pointer attribute to pointers in an interface definition, only where there is a visible asterisk.

The following sections discuss using pointers, and when you need a reference or full pointer. Table 4-1 and Example 4-5 in Section 4.1.5 summarize what you need to know to declare and use pointers.

4.1.1 Pointers as Output Parameters

Due to the overhead of transmitting data, IDL parameters can be input, output, or both. In IDL as in C, input parameters are passed in by value, which means a copy of each input parameter is available in the procedure. Passing input parameters by value makes sense for remote procedure calls since data must be copied and transmitted from the client to the server anyway. However, passing by value also means that any change to the variable in the procedure cannot reflect back to the original parameter when the call completes.

To fill in data for an output parameter (or modify an input/output parameter), both C and IDL must pass by reference a memory address using a pointer or array parameter. During a remote procedure call, the parameter refers to existing memory, which is passed by reference to the client stub.

When the remote procedure completes execution, data is sent back by the server stub to the client stub, which unmarshalls it into the memory referred to by the pointer. Therefore, the data is available to the client application when the client stub returns to the application.

Example 4-1 shows an output parameter in the **whatis_part_price** procedure declaration from the inventory interface definition. Pointer parameters (***price**) are reference pointers by default.

Example 4-1: Defining an Output Parameter

```
void whatis_part_price(            /* get part price from inventory */
    [in]  part_num   number,
    [out] part_price *price                 /* reference pointer */
);
```

The **part_price** structure must be allocated in the client prior to the remote procedure call, but values are assigned in the remote procedure and transmitted back. The **whatis_part_price** remote procedure call in the client looks like this:

```
    part_record part;          /* structure for all data about a part */
    .
    .
    .
        case 'p': whatis_part_price(part.number, &(part.price));
                  printf("price:%10.2f\n", part.price.per_unit);
                  break;
```

In the server, **whatis_part_price** reads a part record from the database for the part number input. It then assigns the values from the part record to the price structure members. Finally, the procedure returns and the price information is marshalled and transmitted by the server stub. The **whatis_part_price** remote procedure looks like this:

```
    void whatis_part_price(number, price)
    part_num   number;
    part_price *price;
    {
        part_record *part;              /* a pointer to a part record */

        read_part_record(number, &part);
        price->units = part->price.units;
        price->per_unit = part->price.per_unit;
        return;
    }
```

You can see from the preceding explanation that an output parameter must refer to existing storage on the client, and therefore that it is always a reference pointer. In fact, the IDL compiler refuses to let you declare an output only parameter with the **ptr** attribute.

Suppose we don't know how much memory should be allocated for output data, so we want a procedure to return data in a parameter as newly allocated memory. We cannot just allocate some memory and hope it's enough because if the data output is greater, data will overwrite into other memory. To solve this, we pass a pointer to a pointer. We describe how to do this in Section 4.1.3.

A parameter used as both input and output is passed by reference. Programs commonly modify data by passing a pointer to a data structure into a procedure, which passes back the same pointer but with modified data. Pointer features including optional parameters and pointer aliasing can apply to input/output parameters. These features apply to the input and are described in Section 4.1.2.

4.1.2   Pointers as Input Parameters

Suppose our inventory interface has the following procedure declaration:

```
void store_parts(
    [in] part_record *part1,
    [in] part_record *part2
);
```

Assume this procedure adds new parts to the database. The procedure takes as parameters two pointers to structures of type **part_record**, (already defined in the interface) to store all data about a part.

The remote procedure call in a client can look like the following:

```
part_record *part1, *part2;
part1 = (part_record *)malloc(sizeof(part_record));
part2 = (part_record *)malloc(sizeof(part_record));
/* part structures are filled in */
part1->number = 123;
part2->number = 124;
    .
    .
    .
store_parts(part1, part2);
```

In this simple case, the client stub marshalls and transmits the data the pointers refer to. (This procedure is not implemented in any applications in this book, so no server code is shown.)

One way reference pointers reduce the overhead involved with pointer management is that the stubs make certain assumptions. Since pointer parameters are reference pointers by default, one of these assumptions is that a pointer parameter points to valid data of the type specified.

Suppose we want optional parameters in our procedure definition. In this case, the client passes a null pointer value for the parameter, so the remote procedure knows to ignore it. In order for the stubs to know the parameter is a null value, the parameter must be a full pointer so the stubs do not attempt to copy any data for the parameter.

Example 4-2 shows how to modify our **store_parts** procedure declaration so that both parameters are full pointers:

Example 4-2: Defining Optional Procedure Parameters

```
void store_parts_1(                    /* ❶ */
    [in,ptr] part_record *part1,
    [in,ptr] part_record *part2
);
    .
    .
    .
typedef [ptr] part_record *part_record_ptr;
void store_parts_2(                    /* ❷ */
    [in] part_record_ptr part1,
    [in] part_record_ptr part2
);
```

❶ To specify an optional parameter, use the **ptr** attribute on an input (or input/output) parameter.

❷ As an alternative to method 1 for specifying an optional parameter, define a full pointer data type and use the data type for the procedure parameter.

The client can now supply a NULL pointer:

```
store_parts_1(part1, NULL);
```

If an input/output parameter is a full pointer with a null value on input, it is also null on output because the client does not have an address to store a return value.

Full pointers allow two pointers to refer to the same data. This is known as **pointer aliasing**:

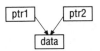

To minimize overhead, stubs cannot manage more than one reference pointer referring to the same data in a single remote procedure call. For example, suppose our **store_parts** procedure does something useful if we pass in the same pointer for both arguments. The following type of remote procedure call causes unpredictable behavior:

```
store_parts(part1, part1); /* WRONG - do not use ref pointer aliasing */
```

This call will *not* work as expected because the parameters (reference pointers) both point to the same address. Reference pointers do not allow two pointers to refer to the same data.

The following call will work correctly, however, because the pointers are specifically defined in the interface definition as full pointers with the **ptr** attribute.

```
store_parts_1(part1, part1);     /* full pointers allow aliasing */
```

4.1.3 Using Pointers to Pointers for New Output

A pointer refers to a specific amount of memory. In order for a procedure parameter to output newly allocated memory, we use a pointer to refer to another pointer that refers to data (or to another pointer and so on). This is also known as multiple levels of indirection.

If you use just one pointer for a procedure parameter, you would have to make two remote procedure calls to allocate new memory. The first remote procedure call obtains the size of the server's data structure. Then the client allocates memory for it. The second remote procedure call obtains data from the server and fills the previously allocated memory. In a distributed application, using two pointers allows the client and server stubs to allocate all the necessary memory in one remote procedure call. The client stub must generate a copy of the memory allocated on the server.

The `whatare_subparts` procedure in the inventory application contains a parameter with a pointer to a pointer:

```
[out] part_list **subparts
```

The procedure allocates memory for the left pointer, and the right pointer is a parameter passed by reference to return the address of the left pointer. To accomplish this, IDL must use both kinds of pointers:

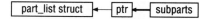

The right pointer is a reference pointer and the left pointer is a full pointer. The reference pointer by itself cannot have new memory automatically allocated because it will point to the same address throughout the remote call. However, for the full pointer, the amount of memory allocated by the server is allocated automatically by the client stub when the call returns.

When a pointer attribute is applied in an interface definition where there are pointers to pointers, it applies only to the right pointer and does not propagate to any other pointers.

Example 4-3 demonstrates how to return data in a parameter by using two pointers. The procedure needs to output a data structure (in this case a structure with a conformant array). The final size of the data structure is unknown when you call the remote procedure.

Example 4-3: Defining Pointers to Pointers for Memory Allocation

```
[
    .
    .
    .
pointer_default(ptr)          /* the pointer default is a full pointer ❶*/
] interface inventory
{
    .
    .
    .
    void whatare_subparts(     /* get list of subpart numbers for a part */
        [in]  part_num  number,
        [out] part_list **subparts          /* a pointer to a pointer ❷*/
    );
    .
    .
    .
```

❶ Parameters or type definitions with multiple pointers use a pointer default to specify the kind of pointer for all but the right one. To establish a pointer default, use the **pointer_default** attribute in the interface definition header. In this example, the **ptr** argument establishes a full pointer default.

❷ If memory is allocated during remote procedure execution, output parameters require multiple pointers. By default, the right pointer of a procedure parameter is a reference pointer. There is no default for the left pointer, which must be a full pointer. To set the left pointer, use the **pointer_default** attribute with a **ptr** argument.

The `part_list` structure is allocated during the remote procedure call. On the server, the remote procedure allocates memory and assigns data. The server stub marshalls and transmits the data back to the client. The server stub then frees the memory allocated in the remote procedure. The client stub allocates memory and unmarshalls the transmitted data into the new memory. The remote procedure call in a client for **whatare_sub-parts** looks like:

```
part_record part;          /* structure for all data about a part  */
part_list   *subparts;     /* pointer to parts list data structure */
   .
   .
   .

   case 's': whatare_subparts(part.number, &subparts);
             for(i = 0; i < subparts->size; i++)
                 printf("%ld  ", subparts->numbers[i]);
             printf("\ntotal number of subparts:%ld\n", subparts->size);
```

When you are finished with the data, free the memory allocated by full pointers:

```
free(subparts);
break;
```

See Example 5-8 for the server implementation of the remote procedure **whatare_subparts**.

4.1.4 Pointers as Procedure Return Values

As we have described previously, the client must allocate memory for reference pointer data before it is used in a remote procedure call. This simplifies the client stub by giving unmarshalling code a place to put data after the server sends it. Consider the following remote procedure call in client application code:

```
idl_long_int *a;
a = proc();
```

The address of the procedure assignment, **a**, is only available when the procedure returns and not during its execution. Therefore, we cannot use a reference pointer for the return value, then allocate memory in the client prior to the call, and expect the stub to complete the assignment for us. Procedures that return pointer results always return full pointers, so that the stub allocates any necessary memory and unmarshalls data into it for us. Example 4-4 shows an example of a procedure that returns a pointer.

Example 4-4: Defining a Procedure that Returns a Pointer

```
typedef [string, ptr] char *paragraph;        /* description of part ❶*/
.
.
.
paragraph get_part_description(         /* return a pointer to a string ❷*/
   [in]  part_num  number
);
```

❶ A pointer attribute (**ptr**) on a pointer data type (**char *paragraph**) specifies the kind of pointer for that data type wherever it is used in the interface. (If a pointer data type does not have a pointer attribute, the pointer specified with the **pointer_default** attribute applies.) To specify a pointer to a string, apply the **string** attribute as well.

❷ Procedures that return a pointer result always return a full pointer. A procedure result cannot be a reference pointer because new storage is always allocated by the client stub, which copies data into it when the call returns.

The call to **get_part_description** looks like:

```
part_record part;             /* structure for all data about a part */
.
.
.
   case 'd': part.description = get_part_description(part.number);
            printf("description:\n%s\n", part.description);
```

When you are finished with the data, free the memory allocated by full pointers:

```
      if(part.description != NULL)
         free(part.description);        /* free memory allocated */
```

On the server, the remote procedure allocates memory that the server stub copies and transmits back to the client. The server stub then frees the memory allocated. Example 5-7 shows how to allocate memory in the **get_part_description** remote procedure.

4.1.5 Pointer Summary

Reference pointers require less overhead than full pointers, but they have some restrictions. Therefore, you must differentiate between a full and reference pointer in the interface definition. Table 4-1 summarizes and compares reference pointers and full pointers. Example 4-5 shows how to recognize which kind of pointer applies in an interface definition. A visible **ref** or **ptr** pointer attribute overrides a default.

Table 4-1 A Summary of Reference and Full Pointers

	Reference Pointer	**Full Pointer**
Attribute name	**ref**	**ptr**
Characteristics	Provides indirection where the value is always the address of valid data.	Indirection and full pointer capabilities.
Stub overhead	Minimum.	Maximum.
Value of NULL	Cannot be NULL.	Can be NULL.
Address value	Never changes when a call returns.	May change when a call returns.
Storage	Storage exists prior to the call.	Storage is allocated automatically if needed.
Input and output parameter	Data is written into existing storage when the call returns.	The storage location of data on output may be different than the storage location on input. If the input value is NULL, the output value is also NULL.
Output parameter	Parameter is a reference pointer by default.	Not allowed.
Input parameter	Data is read from existing storage.	Data is read from existing storage; if the value is NULL, no data is read.
Pointer aliasing	Not allowed.	Allowed.

Example 4-5: How to Determine Kinds of Pointers

```
[
    .
    .
    .
pointer_default(ptr);                    /* ❶ */
] inventory interface
{
    .
    .
    .
typedef [string, ptr] char *paragraph;   /* ❷ */
    .
    .
    .
```

Example 4-5: How to Determine Kinds of Pointers (continued)

```
paragraph get_part_description(         /* ❸*/
   [in] part_num number,
);
   .
   .
   .

void whatis_part_price(
   [in] part_num    number,
   [out] part_price *price              /* ❹*/
);
   .
   .
   .

void whatare_subparts(
   [in] part_num   number,
   [out] part_list **subparts           /* ❺*/
);
   .
   .
   .

typedef struct {                        /* ❻*/
   [ref] part_num       *number;
   [ref] part_quantity *quantity;
   [ref] account_num    *account;
} part_order;
   .
   .
   .

void store_parts_1(                     /* ❼*/
   [in,ptr] part_record *part1,
   [in,ptr] part_record *part2
);
}
```

❶ The IDL compiler attempts to automatically assign the appropriate kind of pointer to pointers without a **ptr** or **ref** attribute. The **pointer_default** interface header attribute specifies which kind of pointer applies when one cannot be automatically determined. The **pointer_default** attribute has an argument of either **ref** or **ptr**. If a pointer attribute is not specified for the data type, the interface requires a pointer default to specify the kind of pointer for the following cases:

— Pointers in typedefs. (See callout 2.)

— Multiple pointers other than the right pointer. (See callout 5.)

— Pointers that are members of structures or cases of discriminated unions. (See callout 6.)

❷ A pointer type attribute specifies the kind of pointer used. In this example, all occurrences that use the **paragraph** data type are full pointers. If neither the **ref** nor **ptr** attribute is present in the typedef, the **pointer_default** attribute specifies the kind of pointer.

❸ A pointer return value of a procedure is always a full pointer because new memory is allocated. The **paragraph** data structure is a pointer to a string.

❹ A pointer parameter of a procedure is a reference pointer by default. Parameter reference pointers must always point to valid storage (never null). (See also callout 7.)

❺ With multiple pointers, the **pointer_default** attribute specifies all pointers except the right-most pointer. In this example, the right pointer is a reference pointer because it is a parameter pointer. The left pointer is determined by the pointer default. In this procedure, the left pointer must be a full pointer so the array of parts in the **subparts** structure is automatically allocated by the client stub when the call returns.

❻ When a structure member or discriminated union case is a pointer, you must assign it a **ptr** or **ref** attribute, either explicitly or through the **pointer_default** attribute. This interface definition specifies the structure members as reference pointers to override the full pointer default. Full pointers are unnecessary for these structure members. Therefore, it is more efficient to use reference pointers to minimize the overhead associated with full pointers.

❼ An input or input/output pointer parameter can be made an optional procedure parameter by applying the **ptr** attribute. This is required if you pass a value of NULL, or alias pointers in a call.

4.2 Kinds of Arrays

The kinds of arrays you can use in RPC applications include the following:

- **Fixed arrays** contain a specific number of elements defined in the interface definition. They are defined just like standard C declarations.

- **Varying arrays** have a fixed size but clients and servers select a portion to transmit during a remote procedure call. The interface definition specifies subset bound variables used by the clients and servers to set the bounds.

- **Conformant arrays** have their size determined in the application code. The interface definition specifies an array size variable that the clients and servers use to control the amount of memory allocated and data transmitted.

4.2.1 Selecting a Portion of a Varying Array

For some clients or servers you need to use only a portion of an array in a remote procedure call. If this is the case, it is more efficient to only transmit the needed portion of the array. Procedures or structures that use varying arrays with data limit variables allow you to select the portion of an array that is processed by a remote procedure call. A varying array has a fixed size when the application is compiled, but the portion of the array that contains the relevant, transmissible data is determined at runtime. For example, the varying array **v[100]** has index values $0 \leq L \leq U \leq 99$, where L represents the lower data limit of the array and U represents the upper data limit.

The array data limit variables are defined in the interface definition with the **first_is**, **length_is**, or **last_is** attributes. You can specify the lower limit of transmissible data (L) with the **first_is** attribute. You can specify the upper limit of transmissible data (U) with either the **length_is** or **last_is** attribute. All array attributes are shown in Table A-2.

Suppose that the following procedure appears in an interface definition:

```
const long SIZE = 100;

void proc(
    [in] long first,
    [in] long length,
    [in, first_is(first), length_is(length)] data_t arr[SIZE]
);
```

To select a portion of the array to transmit, assign values to the array data limit variables. For input parameters, the client sets them prior to the remote procedure call. Be sure the upper data limit value does not exceed the size of the array; for example:

```
long first = 23;
long length = 54;
data_t arr[SIZE];

proc(first, length, arr);
```

The transmitted array portion is represented by the indices $\boxed{23}$ . . . $\boxed{76}$ (23 + 54 - 1). The entire array is available in the client and the server, but only the portion represented by the data limit variables is transmitted and meaningful for the given remote procedure call. If the data limit parameters are also output, the remote procedure can set them to control the portion of the array transmitted back to the client.

A structure is an alternate way to define a varying array in an interface definition; for example:

```
typedef struct varray_t {
   long first;
   long length;
   [first_is(first), length_is(length)] data_t arr[SIZE];
} varray_t;

proc([in] varray_t varray);
```

4.2.2 Managing the Size of a Conformant Array

Conformant arrays are defined in an interface definition with empty brackets or an asterisk (*) in place of the first dimension value.

```
. . . c1[*] . . .
. . . c2[][10] . . .
```

The conformant array `c1[*]` has index values $\boxed{0}$ . . . $\boxed{M}$ where the dimension variable, *M*, represents the upper bound of the array. The dimension variable is specified in the interface definition and used in the application code at runtime to establish the array's actual size.

To specify an array size variable or a maximum upper bound variable, use one of the array size attributes, **size_is** or **max_is**, in an interface definition. These variables are used in the application to represent the size of the array. Example 4-6 shows how a conformant array is defined in a structure.

Example 4-6: A Conformant Array in an Interface Definition

```
      .
      .
      .
typedef struct part_list{                       /* list of part numbers */
   long                   size;       /* number of parts in array ❶*/
   [size_is(size)] part_num numbers[*]; /* conformant array of parts❷*/
} part_list;

typedef struct part_record {                         /* data for each part */
   part_num       number;
   part_name      name;
   paragraph      description;
   part_price     price;
   part_quantity quantity;
   part_list      subparts; /* Conformant array or struct must be last ❸*/
} part_record;
      .
      .
      .
```

Example 4-6: A Conformant Array in an Interface Definition (continued)

```
void whatare_subparts(            /* get list of subparts numbers for a part */
    [in] part_num number,
    [out] part_list **subparts                                    /* ❹ */
);
        .
        .
        .
```

❶ When an array member of a structure (**numbers[*]**) has an array attribute, the dimension variable (**size**) must also be a structure member. This assures that the dimension information is always available with the array when it is transmitted. The dimension variable member must be, or resolve to, an integer.

❷ The **size_is** attribute specifies a variable (size) that represents the number of elements the array dimension contains. In the application, the array indices are $\boxed{0}$ . . . $\boxed{\text{size-1}}$. For example, if **size** is equal to 8 in the application code, then the array indices are $\boxed{0}\boxed{1}\boxed{2}\boxed{3}\boxed{4}\boxed{5}\boxed{6}\boxed{7}$.

❸ If a conformant array is a member of a structure, it must be last so that your application can allocate any amount of memory needed. A conformant structure (structure containing a conformant array member) must also be the last member of a structure containing it.

❹ Use a conformant structure and multiple levels of indirection for remote procedures that allocate a conformant array. See Section 5.2.2 for the implementation of this procedure.

To specify a variable that represents the highest index value for the first dimension of the array rather than the array size, use the **max_is** attribute instead of the **size_is** attribute. For example, the conformant structure defined in Example 4-6 can also be defined as follows:

```
typedef struct part_list{
    long max;
    [max_is(max)] part_num numbers[*];
} part_list;
```

The variable **max** defines the maximum index value of the first dimension of the array. In the application the array indices are $\boxed{0}$ . . . $\boxed{\text{max}}$. For example, if max is equal to 7 in the application code, then the array indices are $\boxed{0}\boxed{1}\boxed{2}\boxed{3}\boxed{4}\boxed{5}\boxed{6}\boxed{7}$.

To avoid errors in application development code, be consistent in the interface definitions you write. Use either the **size_is** attribute or the **max_is** attribute, but not both. All array attributes are shown in Table A-2.

Conformant Arrays as Procedure Parameters

The number of elements contained by a conformant array must be available in a remote procedure call. When a client calls the **whatare_subparts** remote procedure of Example 4-3, the dimension information is available in the **part_list** structure. However, if an array is passed as a parameter, the dimension information must also be an **in** parameter of the procedure.

For example, instead of obtaining an array of all the subparts for a part (as the **whatare_subparts** procedure does) you may want only the first five subparts. This procedure is defined as follows:

```
void get_n_subparts(            /* get n subpart numbers for a part */
    [in]  part_num   number,
    [in]  long       n,
    [out,size_is(n)] part_num subparts[]
);
```

In the client, this procedure has as input the part number, a five representing the number of subparts desired, and a previously allocated array, large enough for the five subpart numbers. The output is the array with the first five subpart numbers. (The **get_n_subparts** procedure is not defined in the inventory interface definition.)

Dynamic Memory Allocation in Clients for Conformant Arrays

Suppose the following procedures appear in interface definitions:

```
proc1([in] long size, [in, size_is(size)] data_t arr[]);
proc2([in] long max,  [in, max_is(max)]   data_t arr[]);
```

Memory must then be allocated for each array needed in the application. To allocate dynamic memory for conformant arrays, use a scheme such as the following:

```
idl_long_int s,m;           /* idl data type generated in header */
data_t        *s_arr, *m_arr; /* pointers to some data structures */

    /* some application specific constants */
s = SIZE;
m = MAX;

    /* allocation of the arrays */
s_arr = (data_t *)malloc( (s)   * sizeof(data_t) );
m_arr = (data_t *)malloc( (m+1) * sizeof(data_t) );

    /* the remote procedure calls */
proc1(s, s_arr);
proc2(m, m_arr);
```

In this example, **SIZE** is defined in the client to represent an array size and MAX is defined to represent the maximum index value of an array. Notice an array that has the **max_is** attribute in its interface definition must have an extra array element allocated because arrays begin with an index value of 0.

Memory Allocation in Clients for Conformant Structures

Structures containing a conformant array require memory allocation in the client before they are input to a remote procedure call, because a statically allocated conformant structure has storage for only one array element. For example, the following is the **part_list** structure of the inventory interface:

```
typedef struct part_list{
    long                        size;
    [size_is(size)] part_num numbers[*]
} part_list;
```

The structure in the header file generated by the IDL compiler has an array size of only one, as follows:

```
typedef struct part_list {
    idl_long_int size;
    part_num numbers[1];
} part_list;
```

The application is responsible for allocating memory for as much of the array as it needs. Use a scheme such as the following to allocate more memory for a conformant structure:

```
part_list *c;       /* a pointer to the conformant structure */
long s;
s = 33;             /* the application specific array size   */

c = (part_list *)malloc(sizeof(part_list) + (sizeof(part_num)*(s-1)));
```

Notice that since the declared structure's size contains an array of one element representing the conformant array, the new memory allocated needs one array element less than the requested array size.

To allocate conformant arrays in a remote procedure of a server, see Section 5.2.2.

5

How to Write a Server

This chapter discusses how to develop a server for the inventory interface. Servers for the other applications in this book have only minor differences. Before reading this chapter, it's a good idea to read Chapter 1 for an overview of a distributed application, and Chapter 2 for features of interface definitions. You should also read Chapter 3 to understand how clients use servers.

You write the following two distinct portions of code for all servers:

- Server initialization (see Section 5.1) includes most of the RPC-specific details including RPC runtime routines. This code is executed when the server begins before it processes any remote procedure calls.

- Remote procedure implementations (see Section 5.2) include special techniques for memory management.

Chapter 1 describes how a typical distributed application works:

- Figure 1-9 shows the initialization steps to prepare a server before it processes remote procedure calls.

- Figure 1-10 shows how a client finds a server using the automatic binding method.

- Figure 1-11 shows the basic steps during a remote procedure call after the client finds the server.

To understand server initialization, it is useful at this point to explain how the RPC runtime library handles an incoming call. Figure 5-1 shows how the server system and RPC runtime library handle a client request.

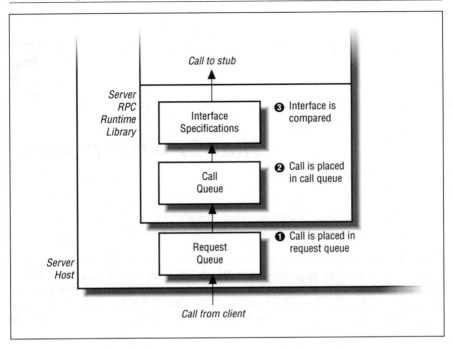

Figure 5-1: How the Server Runtime Library Handles a Call

❶ A call request for the server comes in over the network. The request is placed in a request queue for the endpoint. (The server initialization can select more than one protocol sequence on which to listen for calls, and each protocol sequence can have more than one endpoint associated with it.) Request queues temporarily store all requests; thus allowing multiple requests on an endpoint. If a request queue fills, however, the next request is rejected.

❷ The RPC runtime library dequeues requests one at a time from all request queues and places them in a single call queue. The server can process remote procedures concurrently, using threads. If a thread is available, a call is immediately assigned to it. (Server initialization can select the number of threads for processing remote procedure calls.) In this figure, only one thread is executing. If all threads are in use, the call remains in the call queue until a thread is available. If the call queue is full, the next request is rejected.

❸ After a call is assigned to a thread, the interface specification of the client call is compared with the interface specifications of the server. An **interface specification** is an opaque data structure containing information (including the UUID and version number) that identifies the interface. An **opaque data** structure simply means the details are hidden from you. If the server supports the client's interface, processing goes to the stub code. If the server does not support the client's interface, the call is rejected.

When the call finally gets to the stub, it unmarshalls the input data. Unmarshalling involves memory allocation (if needed), copying the data from the RPC runtime library, and converting data to the correct representation for the server system.

5.1 Initializing the Server

The server initialization code includes a sequence of runtime calls that prepare the server to receive remote procedure calls. The initialization code typically includes the following steps:

1. Register the interface with the RPC runtime library (see Section 5.1.1).

2. Create server binding information by selecting one or more protocol sequences for the RPC runtime library to use in your network environment (see Section 5.1.2).

3. Advertise the server location so that the clients have a way to find it. A client uses binding information to establish a relationship with a server. Advertising the server usually includes storing binding information in a name service database. Occasionally an application stores server binding information in an application-specific database or displays it or prints it (see Section 5.1.3).

4. Manage endpoints in a local endpoint map (see Section 5.1.4).

5. Listen for remote procedure calls (see Section 5.1.5).

During server execution, no remote procedure calls are processed until the initialization code completes execution. RPC runtime routines are used for server initialization. (Table B-2 lists all the RPC runtime routines for servers.)

Example 5-1 shows the necessary header files and data structures for server initialization of the inventory application.

Example 5-1: Server Header Files and Data Structures

```
/* FILE NAME: i_server.c */
#include <stdio.h>
#include <ctype.h>
```

Example 5-1: Server Header Files and Data Structures (continued)

```
#include "inventory.h"         /* header created by the IDL compiler ❶*/
#include "check_status.h"         /* contains the CHECK_STATUS macro */
#define STRINGLEN 50

main (argc, argv)
int argc;
char *argv[];
{
    unsigned32            status;            /* error status (nbase.h) ❷*/
                                                /* RPC vectors ❸*/
    rpc_binding_vector_t *binding_vector;      /* binding handle list */
    rpc_protseq_vector_t *protseq_vector;      /*protocol sequence list */
                                                /* list(rpcbase.h)*/

    char entry_name[STRINGLEN];              /* name service entry name */
    char group_name[STRINGLEN];              /* name service group name */
    char annotation[STRINGLEN];         /* annotation for endpoint map */
    char hostname[STRINGLEN];
    char *strcpy(), *strcat();
    .
    .
    .
/* For the rest of the server initialization, register interfaces,   */
/* create server binding information, advertise the server,          */
/* manage endpoints, and listen for remote procedure calls.          */
```

❶ Always include the C language header file (created by the IDL compiler) from all interfaces the server uses. This file contains the definitions of data types and structures that are needed by the RPC runtime routines.

❷ An **unsigned32** variable is needed to report errors that may occur when an RPC runtime routine is called.

❸ Some RPC runtime routines use a data structure called a vector. A **vector** in RPC applications contains a list (array) of other data structures and a count of elements in the list. Vectors keep track of lists of information for which the number of elements on the list is unknown until runtime. The **rpc_binding_vector_t** is a list of binding handles where each handle refers to some binding information. The **rpc_protseq_vector_t** is a list of protocol sequence information representing the communication protocols available to a server. RPC runtime routines create vectors, use vectors as input, and free the memory of vectors.

Many header files such as **idlbase.h** and **rpc.h** are included in the interface header **inventory.h**. The **rpc.h** file in turn has included within it header files such as **nbase.h**, **idlbase.h**, and **rpcbase.h**. Many of these header files are associated with RPC-specific interface definitions. These interface definitions contain data structure definitions you may need to refer to in order to access structure members and make runtime calls.

Object UUIDs are scattered throughout the RPC runtime routines as parameters for developing certain kinds of applications. You do not need to use object UUIDs to develop many applications so they are not covered in this book.

5.1.1 Registering Interfaces

All servers must register their interfaces so that their information is available to the RPC runtime library. This information is used when a call from a client comes in, so that the client is sure the server supports the interface and that the call can be correctly dispatched to the stub.

Binding information is used to complete a binding between a client and server, but that does not guarantee the server supports the client's interface. For example, it is possible for a complex server to temporarily suspend support for a specific interface. Therefore, when a remote procedure call arrives, a comparison is made between the client's and server's interface specifications. If the server supports the client's interface, the RPC runtime library can dispatch the call to the stub.

Use an interface handle to refer to the interface specification in application code. An **interface handle** is a pointer defined in the C language header file and generated by **idl**. For example, the server interface handle for the inventory application is **inventory_v1_0_s_ifspec**. The interface handle name contains the following:

- The interface name given in the interface definition header (**inventory**).

- The version numbers in the **version** attribute (**v1_0**). If the interface definition has no version declared, version 0.0 is assumed.

- The letter **s** or **c** depending on whether the handle is for the server or client portion of the application.

- The word **ifspec**.

Example 5-2 is a portion of C code that registers one interface.

Example 5-2: Registering an Interface with the Runtime Library

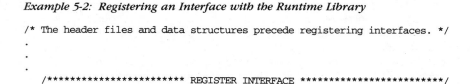

```
/* The header files and data structures precede registering interfaces. */
    .
    .
    .
/*********************** REGISTER INTERFACE ************************/
```

Example 5-2: Registering an Interface with the Runtime Library (continued)

```
rpc_server_register_if(                                    /* ❶*/
    inventory_v1_0_s_ifspec, /* interface specification (inventory.h) */
    NULL,
    NULL,
    status
);
CHECK_STATUS(status, "Can't register interface:", ABORT);   /* ❷*/
    .
    .
    .
/* For the rest of the server initialization, create server binding    */
/* information, advertise the server, manage endpoints, and listen for  */
/* remote procedure calls.                                              */
```

❶ The **rpc_server_register_if** routine is a required call to register each interface the server supports. The interface handle, **inventory_v1_0_s_ifspec**, refers to the interface specification.

❷ The **CHECK_STATUS** macro is defined in the **check_status.h** file. It is an application-specific macro used in this book to process status values returned from RPC runtime calls (see Example 3-12).

Multiple interfaces may be registered from a single server by calling the **rpc_server_register_if** routine with a different interface handle.

The second and third arguments to the **rpc_server_register_if** call are used in complex applications to register more than one implementation for the set of remote procedures. When only one implementation exists, these arguments are set to NULL. Also, in the event of a symbol name conflict between the remote procedure names of an interface and other symbols in your server (such as procedure names), you can use these arguments to assign different names to the server code's remote procedures.

5.1.2 Creating Server Binding Information

Server binding information is created when protocol sequences are selected during server initialization. RPC uses protocol sequences to identify the combinations of communications protocols that RPC supports. (See Section 3.2 for a description of protocol sequences.) Most servers offer all available protocol sequences so that you do not limit the opportunities for clients to communicate with the server. For testing purposes, however, you may want to select a specific protocol sequence. For example, to debug your server, use the connection protocol sequence **ncacn_ip_tcp** because the process will timeout when the debugger stops it if you use the datagram protocol sequence, **ncadg_ip_udp**.

Recall that besides a protocol sequence, binding information includes a host network address. A server process runs on only one host at a time, so this binding information is obtained from the system and not controlled in your server code.

When a protocol sequence is selected, an endpoint is also obtained. You have several choices when obtaining endpoints.

Using Dynamic Endpoints

Section 3.2 describes dynamic and well-known endpoints. Most servers use dynamic endpoints for their flexibility and to avoid the problem of two servers using the same endpoints. Dynamic endpoints are selected for you by the RPC runtime library and vary from one invocation of the server to the next. When the server stops running, dynamic endpoints are released and may be re-used by the server system.

Example 5-3 is a portion of the inventory server initialization showing the selection of one or all protocol sequences and dynamic endpoints. For this example, invoke the server with a protocol sequence argument to select a specific protocol sequence. If you invoke this server without an argument, the server uses all available protocols.

Example 5-3: Creating Server Binding Information

```
/* Registering interfaces precedes creating server binding information. */
   .
   .
   .

   /**************** CREATING SERVER BINDING INFORMATION ***************/
   if(argc > 1) {
       rpc_server_use_protseq(                    /* use a protocol sequence ❶*/
           (unsigned_char_t *)argv[1],       /* the input protocol sequence */
           rpc_c_protseq_max_calls_default,                  /* (rpcbase.h) */
           &status
       );
       CHECK_STATUS(status, "Can't use this protocol sequence:", ABORT);
   }
   else {
       puts("You can invoke the server with a protocol sequence argument.");
       rpc_server_use_all_protseqs(        /* use all protocol sequences ❷*/
           rpc_c_protseq_max_calls_default,                  /* (rpcbase.h) */
           &status
       );
       CHECK_STATUS(status, "Can't register protocol sequences:", ABORT);
   }

   rpc_server_inq_bindings(    /* get all binding information for server ❸*/
       &binding_vector,
       &status
   );
   CHECK_STATUS(status, "Can't get binding information:", ABORT);
```

Example 5-3: Creating Server Binding Information (continued)

.
.
.

```
/* For the rest of the server initialization, advertise the server,   */
/* manage endpoints, and listen for remote procedure calls.           */
```

❶ The **rpc_server_use_protseq** routine is called with the chosen protocol sequence string. This call selects one protocol sequence on which the server listens for remote procedure calls. For this example, when the server is invoked, **argc** is the number of arguments on the command line and **argv[1]** is the protocol sequence string argument. The constant **rpc_c_protseq_max_calls_default** sets the request queue size for the number of calls an endpoint can receive at any given moment. At this time, DCE RPC uses a system-dependent default so you cannot control request queue size (see Figure 5-1).

❷ The **rpc_server_use_all_protseqs** routine is called to select all available protocol sequences on which the RPC runtime library listens for remote procedure calls.

❸ The **rpc_server_inq_bindings** routine is a required call to obtain the set of binding handles referring to all of this server's binding information.

Dynamic endpoints must be registered with the server system's local endpoint map using the **rpc_ep_register** routine, so that clients can look them up when they try to find a server (see Section 5.1.4).

Using Well-known Endpoints

An endpoint is well-known if it is specifically selected and assigned to a single server every time it runs. Well-known endpoints are more restrictive than dynamic endpoints because, in order to prevent your servers from using the same endpoints as someone else, you need to register well-known endpoints with the authority responsible for a given transport protocol. For example, the ARPANET Network Information Center controls the use of well-known endpoint values for the Internet Protocols.

Well-known endpoints are often employed for widely-used applications such as core DCE servers. An example of a server that needs well-known endpoints is the RPC daemon, **rpcd**. This daemon runs on each system hosting DCE RPC servers, in order to maintain the database that maps servers to endpoints. When a client has a partially bound handle, and it needs to obtain an endpoint for its application's server, the client RPC runtime library contacts the server system's **rpcd** process. In short, **rpcd** is required for finding dynamic endpoints. In order for clients to contact it, **rpcd** itself must have a well-known endpoint.

Although you do not need to register well-known endpoints in the server system's endpoint map, you are encouraged to so that clients are unrestricted in finding your servers. Use the **rpc_ep_register** routine to register endpoints in the endpoint map.

Table 5-1 shows the RPC runtime routines to create server binding information with well-known endpoints.

Table 5-1 Creating Binding Information with Well-known Endpoints

RPC Runtime Routine	Description
rpc_server_use_ protseq_ep	Uses a specified protocol sequence and well-known endpoint, supplied in application code, to establish server binding information. Even though the endpoint is not dynamically generated, clients do not have an obvious way to get it, so register the endpoint in the server system's endpoint map.
rpc_server_use_ protseq_if	Uses a specified protocol sequence, but well-known endpoints are specified in the interface definition with the **endpoint** attribute. Both clients and servers know the endpoints through the interface definition.
rpc_server_use_all_protseqs_if	Uses all supported protocol sequences, but well-known endpoints are specified in the interface definition with the **endpoint** attribute. Both clients and servers know the endpoints through the interface definition.

5.1.3 Advertising the Server

Advertising the server means that you make the binding information available for clients to find this server. You can advertise the server by one of the following methods:

- Export to a name service database.

- Store binding information in an application-specific database.

- Print or display binding information for clients.

The method you use depends on the application, but the most common way is through a name service database. Binding information and the interface specification are first exported to a server entry in the database. The information is associated with a recognizable name appropriate for the application. This information can now be retrieved by a client using this name. When the client imports binding information, a comparison is made between interface specifications of the client and the name service entries, to be sure the client and server are compatible.

The convention for naming RPC server entries includes the interface name and the host name. However, this requires that your client know the specific server entry name (including the host on which a server is running) in order to find a server. A name service group associates a general group name with a set of server entries, so your client does not need to know the server entry name. The convention for naming RPC group entries includes the interface name. The server entry name is added as a member of the group. When the client imports binding information using the group name, the group members are searched until a compatible server entry is found.

Using a group name to begin a name service search eliminates the need for clients to know the specific server entry name, but now clients must know the group name. Chapter 6 describes how to set up a slightly more sophisticated naming scheme in the name service.

Example 5-4 is a portion of the inventory initialization code that uses the name service database to advertise the server.

Example 5-4: Advertising the Server to Clients

```
/* Registering interfaces and creating server binding information    */
/* precede advertising the server.                                   */
.
.
.
/*********************** ADVERTISE SERVER ***********************/
strcpy(entry_name, "/.:/inventory_");
gethostname(hostname, STRINGLEN);
strcat(entry_name, hostname);
rpc_ns_binding_export(          /* export to a name service database ❶*/
    rpc_c_ns_syntax_default,      /* syntax of entry name (rpcbase.h) */
    (unsigned_char_t *)entry_name, /* name of entry in name service */
    inventory_v1_0_s_ifspec,/* interface specification (inventory.h) */
    binding_vector,                        /* binding information */
    NULL,                          /* no object UUIDs exported */
    &status
);
CHECK_STATUS(status, "Can't export to name service database:", RESUME);

strcpy(group_name, "/.:/inventory_group");
rpc_ns_group_mbr_add(         /* add as member of name service group ❷*/
    rpc_c_ns_syntax_default,      /* syntax of group name (rpcbase.h) */
    (unsigned_char_t *)group_name, /* name of group in name service */
    rpc_c_ns_syntax_default,     /* syntax of member name (rpcbase.h) */
    (unsigned_char_t *)entry_name, /* name of member in name service */
    &status
);
```

Example 5-4: Advertising the Server to Clients (continued)

```
CHECK_STATUS(status, "Can't add member to name service group:", RESUME);

.
.
.

/* For the rest of the server initialization, manage endpoints and     */
/* listen for remote procedure calls.                                   */
```

❶ The **rpc_ns_binding_export** routine exports the server binding infor-mation to a name service database. The constant, **rpc_c_ns_syn-tax_default**, establishes the syntax the RPC runtime library uses to interpret an entry name. (DCE currently has only one syntax.) The entry name is the recognizable name used in the database for this binding information.

The interface handle (**inventory_v1_0_s_ifspec**) is needed so inter-face information is associated with the binding information in the name service database. The binding vector is the list of binding handles that represents the binding information exported. (The NULL value repre-sents an object UUID vector. For this application, no object UUIDs are used.)

❷ The **rpc_ns_group_mbr_add** routine adds the server entry exported with the **rpc_ns_binding_export** call as a member of a name service group, **/.:/inventory_group**. The binding information of an inventory server can be accessed in the name service database through the general group name, **/.:/inventory_group**, rather than a spe-cific server entry name **/.:/inventory_*serverhost***.

If all inventory servers use this combination of RPC runtime routines, clients will be able to find one of the servers.

There are three ways to manipulate the name service database:

- Use the **rpc_ns_binding_export** and other RPC runtime routines in the server initialization code (see Example 5-4).

- Use the RPC control program (**rpccp**) to export binding information (**rpccp** is discussed in Chapter 6).

- Use the **rpc_ns_mgmt_entry_create** and other RPC runtime routines in a separate management application. Management application devel-opment is an advanced subject not discussed in this book.

Exporting to the name service database requires both read and write access permission. If your access to the name service database is restricted, your name service administrator can use **rpccp** to export the binding information for you.

The **rpc_ns_binding_export** routine exports well-known endpoints to the name service database along with other binding information, but, because of their temporary nature, dynamic endpoints are not exported. Performance of the name service will degrade if it becomes filled with obsolete endpoints generated when servers restart. Also, clients will fail more often trying to bind to servers of nonexistent endpoints. Since dynamic endpoints are not in a name service database, clients need to find them from another source. The next section discusses how to manage endpoints.

5.1.4 Managing Server Endpoints

When the server uses dynamic endpoints, clients need a way to find them, because neither the name service database nor the interface specification store dynamic endpoints. The **endpoint map** is a database on each RPC server system that associates endpoints with other server binding information. As a general rule, have your server store all endpoints (dynamic and well-known) in the endpoint map. If all endpoints are placed in the endpoint map, system administrators have an easier time monitoring and managing all RPC servers on a host system.

The RPC daemon (**rpcd**) process maintains the endpoint map for the particular host system. Access the endpoint map through the RPC daemon with calls to RPC runtime routines or with the RPC control program (**rpccp**).

When a client uses a partially bound binding handle for a remote procedure call, the RPC runtime library obtains an endpoint from the server system's endpoint map. (However, if a well-known endpoint is available in the interface specification, the server's endpoint map is not used.) To find a valid endpoint, the client's interface specification and binding information (protocol sequence, host, and object UUID) are compared to the information in the endpoint map. When an endpoint of an appropriate server is finally obtained, the resulting fully bound binding handle is used to complete the connection at that endpoint. Example 5-5 shows how a server registers its endpoints in the endpoint map.

Example 5-5: Managing Endpoints in an Endpoint Map

```
/* Registering interfaces, creating server binding information, and     */
/* advertising the server precede managing endpoints.                   */
 .
 .
 .
    /*********************** MANAGE ENDPOINTS ************************/
    strcpy(annotation, "Inventory interface");
```

Example 5-5: Managing Endpoints in an Endpoint Map (continued)

```
rpc_ep_register(                 /* add endpoints to local endpoint map ❶*/
    inventory_v1_0_s_ifspec, /* interface specification (inventory.h) */
    binding_vector,              /* vector of server binding handles */
    NULL,                            /* no object UUIDs to register */
    (unsigned_char_t *)annotation,            /* annotation supplied */
                                              /* (not required) */
    &status
);
CHECK_STATUS(status, "Can't add endpoints to endpoint map:", RESUME);

rpc_binding_vector_free(                 /* free server binding handles ❷*/
    &binding_vector,
    &status
);
CHECK_STATUS(status, "Can't free server binding handles:", RESUME);

open_inventory();                    /* application-specific procedure */
```

.
.
.

```
/* For the rest of the server initialization, listen for remote     */
/* procedure calls.                                                  */
```

❶ The **rpc_ep_register** routine registers the server endpoints in the local endpoint map. Use the same interface handle, binding vector, and object UUID vector as you used in the **rpc_ns_binding_export** routine (see Example 5-4). An annotation argument is recommended so the information in the endpoint map can be read more easily when using **rpccp**.

❷ The **rpc_binding_vector_free** routine is a required call that frees the memory of the binding vector and all binding handles in it. Each call to **rpc_server_inq_bindings** (see Example 5-3) requires a corresponding call to **rpc_binding_vector_free**. Make this call prior to listening for remote procedure calls, so the memory is available when remote procedure calls are processed.

The **rpc_ep_register** call is required if dynamic endpoints are established with the **rpc_server_use_protseq** or **rpc_server_use_all_protseqs** runtime routines, because each time the server is started, new endpoints are created (see Example 5-3). If well-known endpoints are established with the **rpc_server_use_protseq_ep** runtime routine, you should use the **rpc_ep_register** routine because even though the endpoint may always be the same, a client needs to find the value. If well-known endpoints are established with the **rpc_server_use_protseq_if** call or if they are established with the **rpc_server_use_all_protseqs_if** call, they need not be registered because the client has access to the endpoint values through the interface specification.

When a server stops running, endpoints registered in the endpoint map become outdated. The RPC daemon maintains the endpoint map by removing outdated endpoints. However, an unpredictable amount of time exists in which a client can obtain an outdated endpoint. If a remote procedure call uses an outdated endpoint, it will not find the server and the call will fail. To prevent clients from receiving outdated endpoints, use the **rpc_ep_unregister** routine before a server stops executing (see Section 5.1.5).

There are several ways to manage endpoints in the endpoint map:

- Use the **rpc_ep_register** and other RPC runtime routines in the server initialization code (see Example 5-5).

- Use the RPC control program (**rpccp**) to show or remove mapping information.

- Use the **rpc_mgmt_ep_elt_inq_begin** and other RPC runtime routines in a separate management application to manage a local or remote endpoint map. Managing an endpoint map with a management application is not discussed in this book.

5.1.5 Listening for Remote Procedure Calls

The final requirement for server initialization code is to listen for remote procedure calls.

Many of the RPC runtime routines used in this book have an error status variable used to determine whether the routine executed successfully. However, when the server is ready to process remote procedure calls, the **rpc_server_listen** runtime routine is called. The **rpc_server_listen** runtime routine does not return unless the server is requested to stop listening by another process, or by one of its own remote procedures using the **rpc_mgmt_stop_server_listening** routine.

Any errors occurring during stub code or remote procedure execution are reported as exceptions, and, unless your code is written to handle exceptions, it will abruptly exit. You can use a set of macros from DCE threads to help process exceptions. The macros **TRY**, **FINALLY**, and **ENDTRY** delineate code sections where exceptions are controlled. If an exception occurs in the **TRY** section, code in the **FINALLY** section is executed to handle any necessary error recovery or cleanup.

The **FINALLY** section contains clean-up code that does such things as remove outdated endpoints from the endpoint map. The **TRY** and **FINALLY** sections end with the **ENDTRY** macro.

Example 5-6 is a portion of C code that shows how the inventory server listens for remote procedure calls and handles exceptions.

Example 5-6: Listening for Remote Procedure Calls

```
/* Registering interfaces, creating server binding information,      */
/* managing endpoints, and advertising the server precede listening  */
/* for remote procedure calls.                                       */
  .
  .
  .

  /***************** LISTEN FOR REMOTE PROCEDURE CALLS *****************/
  TRY                            /* thread exception handling macro ❶*/
  rpc_server_listen(                                        /* ❷*/
     1,                 /* process one remote procedure call at a time */
     &status
  );
  CHECK_STATUS(status, "rpc listen failed:", RESUME);

  FINALLY                              /* error recovery and cleanup */
  close_inventory();                   /* application specific procedure */
  rpc_server_inq_bindings(               /* get binding information ❸*/
     &binding_vector,
     &status
  );
  CHECK_STATUS(status, "Can't get binding information:", RESUME);

  rpc_ep_unregister(       /* remove endpoints from local endpoint map ❹*/
     inventory_v1_0_s_ifspec, /* interface specification (inventory.h) */
     binding_vector,           /* vector of server binding handles */
     NULL,                              /* no object UUIDs */
     &status
  );
  CHECK_STATUS(status,"Can't remove endpoints from endpoint map:",RESUME);

  rpc_binding_vector_free(             /* free server binding handles ❺*/
     &binding_vector,
     &status
  );
  CHECK_STATUS(status, "Can't free server binding handles:", RESUME);

  puts("\nServer quit!");
  ENDTRY
} /* END SERVER INITIALIZATION */
```

❶ The **TRY** macro begins a section of code where you expect exceptions to occur. For this example, the **TRY** section contains only the **rpc_server_listen** routine. If an exception occurs during the remote procedure execution, the code section beginning with the **FINALLY** macro is executed to handle application-specific cleanup.

❷ The **rpc_server_listen** routine is a required call that causes the runtime to listen for remote procedure calls. The first argument sets the number of threads the RPC runtime library uses to process remote procedure calls. In this example, the RPC runtime library can process one remote procedure call at a time. If your remote procedures are not thread safe, set this value to 1.

❸ The **rpc_server_inq_bindings** routine obtains a set of binding handles referring to all of the server's binding information.

❹ The **rpc_ep_unregister** routine removes the server endpoints from the local endpoint map. If the server registered endpoints with a call to **rpc_ep_register**, this call is recommended before the process is removed (see Example 5-5).

❺ The **rpc_binding_vector_free** routine is called to free the memory of a binding vector and all binding handles in it. Each call to **rpc_server_inq_bindings** requires a corresponding call to **rpc_binding_vector_free**.

The server initialization code for the inventory application is now complete. All of the server initialization code is shown in Example D-6, and Table B-2 lists all the runtime routines that servers can use.

5.2 Writing Remote Procedures

Some issues to consider when writing your remote procedures include memory management, threads, and client binding handles.

Remote procedures require special memory management techniques. Suppose a procedure allocates memory for data that it returns to the calling procedure. In a local application, the calling procedure can free allocated memory because the procedure and calling procedure are in the same address space. However, remember that the client (calling procedure) is not in the same address space as the server (remote procedure), so the client cannot free memory on the server. Repeated calls to a remote procedure that allocates memory without some way to free the memory, will obviously waste the server's resources.

You must manage memory for remote procedures using special **stub support routines** in remote procedures. Stub support routines enable the server stub to free memory allocated in remote procedures, after the remote procedure completes execution. Basic memory management is described in Section 5.2.1 and memory allocation for conformant arrays is described in Section 5.2.2.

Recall that the **rpc_server_listen** routine in server initialization determines the number of threads a server uses to process remote procedure calls. If the server listens on more than one thread, the remote procedures need to be thread safe. For example, the remote procedures should not use server global data unless locks are used to control thread access. In the inventory application, when reading from or writing to the inventory application database, a lock may be needed so that data is not changed by one thread while another thread is reading it. The inventory application is single-threaded. Details of multi-threaded application development are beyond the scope of this book.

So far in this book, we have used server binding handles and server binding information to allow clients to find servers. When a server receives a call from a client, the client RPC runtime library supplies information about the client side of the binding to the server RPC runtime library. **Client binding information** is used in server code to inquire about the client. This client binding information includes the following:

- The RPC protocol sequence used by the client for the call.

- The network address of the client.

- The object UUID requested by the client. This can be simply a nil UUID.

- The client authentication and authorization information (optional).

To access client binding information in remote procedures use a **client binding handle**. If the client binding handle is available, it is the first parameter of the remote procedure. If you require client binding information and the procedure declarations in the interface definition do not have a binding handle as the first parameter, you must generate the server stub and header file using an ACF with the **explicit_handle** attribute (see Section 2.3). No further details of client binding information are described in this book.

5.2.1 Managing Memory in Remote Procedures

In typical applications, you use the C library routines, **malloc** and **free**, or your own allocation scheme, to allocate and free memory that pointers must refer to. In RPC servers, when implementing a remote procedure that returns a pointer to newly allocated memory to the client, use stub support routines to manage memory in the remote procedures. Use the stub support routine **rpc_ss_allocate** instead of the C library routine **malloc**, so bookkeeping is maintained for memory management. This also ensures that memory on the server is automatically freed by the server stub after the remote procedure has completed execution. Memory allocation will not then accumulate on the server without a release mechanism.

For reference pointers, memory on the client side must already exist, so no memory management is required for remote procedures whose output parameters are reference pointers. After you make the remote procedure call, first the server stub automatically allocates necessary memory and copies the data for the reference pointer into the new memory. Then it calls the implementation of the remote procedure. Finally, the remote procedure completes, output data is transmitted back to the client stub and the server stub frees the memory it allocated.

On both the client and server more complex memory management occurs for full pointers than for reference pointers. If a remote procedure allocates memory for an output parameter, the server stub copies and marshalls the data, then the stub frees the memory that was allocated in the remote procedure. When the client receives the data, the client stub allocates memory and copies the data into the new memory. It is the client application's responsibility to free the memory allocated by the client stub.

Example 5-7 shows how to use the **rpc_ss_allocate** routine to allocate memory for full pointers. The procedure `get_part_description` of the inventory application returns a string of characters representing the description of a part in the inventory. The call in the client is as follows:

```
part_record part; /* structure for all data about a part  */
    .
    .
    .
part.description = get_part_description(part.number);
```

Example 5-7: Memory Management in Remote Procedures

```
paragraph get_part_description(number)
part_num  number;
{
    part_record *part;                   /* a pointer to a part record */
    paragraph description;
    int size;
    char *strcpy();

    if( read_part_record(number, &part) ) {
        /* Allocated data that is returned to the client must be allocated */
        /* with the rpc_ss_allocate stub support routine.                  */
        size = strlen((char *)part->description) + 1;          /* ❶*/
        description = (paragraph)rpc_ss_allocate((unsigned)size);    /* ❷*/
        strcpy((char *)description, (char *)part->description);
    }
    else
        description = NULL;
    return(description);
}
```

❶ An additional character is allocated for the null terminator of a string.

❷ The remote procedure calls the **rpc_ss_allocate** stub support routine to allocate memory in the remote procedure.

When the procedure completes, the server stub automatically frees the memory allocated by **rpc_ss_allocate** calls. When the remote procedure call returns, the client stub automatically allocates memory for the returned string. When the client application code is finished with the data, it frees the memory allocated by the client stub as follows:

```
if(part.description != NULL)
    free(part.description);
```

For more complex memory management there is a stub support counterpart to the C library routine **free** called **rpc_ss_free**.

The only exception to using the **rpc_ss_allocate** and **rpc_ss_free** routines for memory management is when you use context handles. Memory allocated for context on the server must not use these routines because subsequent calls by the client must have access to the same context as previous calls. See Chapter 7 for more information on context handles.

5.2.2 Allocating Memory for Conformant Arrays

The `whatare_subparts` procedure of the inventory application allocates memory for a conformant array in a structure, and returns a copy of the conformant structure to the client. The `whatare_subparts` procedure is declared in the interface definition as follows:

```
typedef struct part_list{              /* list of part numbers    */
    long                    size;      /* number of parts in array */
    [size_is(size)] part_num numbers[*]; /* conformant array of parts */
} part_list;
    .
    .
    .
void whatare_subparts(     /* get list of subpart numbers for a part */
    [in]  part_num  number,
    [out] part_list **subparts  /* the structure containing the array */
);
```

Output pointer parameters are reference pointers, that must have memory allocated in the client prior to the call. Therefore, you need a full pointer in order for new memory to be automatically allocated by the client stub for the `**subparts` structure when the `whatare_subparts` procedure returns. A pointer to a pointer is required so that the reference pointer points to a full pointer, which in turn points to the structure.

Example 5-8 shows how to allocate memory in the remote procedure for a conformant structure. The call in the client is as follows:

```
part_record part;           /* structure for all data about a part  */
part_list   *subparts;      /* pointer to parts list data structure */
    .
    .
    .
    whatare_subparts(part.number, &subparts);
```

Example 5-8: Conformant Array Allocation in a Remote Procedure

```
void whatare_subparts(number, subpart_ptr)
part_num   number;
part_list **subpart_ptr;
{
    part_record *part;                      /* pointer to a part record */
    int i;
    int size;

    read_part_record(number, &part);

    /* Allocated data that is output to the client must be allocated with */
    /* the rpc_ss_allocate stub support routine.  Allocate for a part_list */
    /* struct plus the array of subpart numbers.  Remember the part_list  */
    /* struct already has an array with one element, hence the -1.        */
    size = sizeof(part_list)
            + (sizeof(part_num) * (part->subparts.size-1));       /*❶*/
    *subpart_ptr = (part_list *)rpc_ss_allocate((unsigned)size);  /*❷*/

    /* fill in the values */
    (*subpart_ptr)->size = part->subparts.size;
    for(i = 0; i < (*subpart_ptr)->size; i++)
        (*subpart_ptr)->numbers[i] = part->subparts.numbers[i];
    return;
}
```

❶ The allocated memory includes the size of the conformant structure plus enough memory for all the elements of the conformant array. The conformant structure generated by the IDL compiler already has an array of one element, so the new memory allocated for the array elements is one less than the number in the array.

❷ Use the RPC stub support routine **rpc_ss_allocate** to allocate memory so bookkeeping is maintained for memory management, and the server stub automatically frees memory on the server after the remote procedure completes execution.

When the data for the conformant structure is returned to the client, the client stub allocates memory and copies the data into the new memory. The client application code uses the data and frees the memory allocated, as follows:

```
for(i = 0; i < subparts->size; i++)
    printf("%ld ", subparts->numbers[i]);
printf("\nTotal number of subparts:%ld\n", subparts->size);
free(subparts); /* free memory allocated for conformant structure */
```

5.3 Compiling and Linking Servers

Figure 5-2 shows the files and libraries required to produce an executable server. If needed, the IDL compiler produces the server stub auxiliary file (*appl_*saux.o) when the interface is compiled. The following features cause the production of a server auxiliary file:

- self-referential pointers in the interface definition

- the **pipe** data type in the interface definition

- the **out_of_line** attribute in an ACF

No stub auxiliary files are produced for the inventory application.

To compile and link the server for the inventory application, perform the following steps:

1. Compile all the server application modules with the C compiler including the server initialization code and the remote procedures. The **arithmetic** directory is included with the compiler directive -I because this is where the **check_status.h** header file resides.

    ```
    S> cc -I../arithmetic -c i_server.c i_procedures.c \
    implement_inventory.c
    ```

2. Link the server application and server stub object files with the DCE libraries to produce the executable server.

    ```
    S> cc -o i_server.exe i_server.o i_procedures.o \
    implement_inventory.o inventory_sstub.o -ldce -lcma
    ```

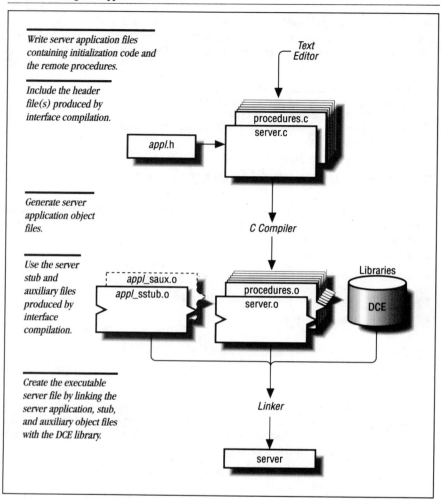

Figure 5-2: Producing a Server

6

Using a Name Service

We have seen in earlier chapters that clients query a name service to find a host where a server is running. We set up our environment in a simplistic if not inconvenient manner, so that we could avoid discussing details about the name service. For instance, in Chapter 1, we made the **RPC_DEFAULT_ENTRY** environment variable point to a specific server entry for the arithmetic application, before we ran the client.

We already discussed programming access to the name service in Chapter 3 (which shows how a client imports binding information from it) and Chapter 5 (which shows how servers export binding information to it). In this chapter we discuss administration rather than programming, and show how to make the search in the name service more flexible. After a brief introduction to the name service and its naming conventions, we discuss administration for individual servers, groups of servers, and profiles that tailor a search to your needs.

Naming

A name service accesses and maintains a distributed database of server location information (binding information). An entry name is associated with each entry in the database, that you use in programs, commands, and environment variables, to access and search the database.

DCE supplies the Cell Directory Service (CDS) as the name service used by RPC applications to locate servers. CDS tracks many kinds of resources in DCE, but its most important purpose is to provide clients with binding information so they can connect to servers.

The name service database can be quite complex and extensive. The portion that deals with your applications is only one small part of the entire distributed database. If you are working under DCE, you already know that it divides a network into cells. CDS maintains information on the servers and other resources in a cell, where they are organized into a hierarchy in the same way that files are organized into directories. Cells have unique names themselves and are represented in a larger hierarchy, but we do not discuss this level of organization in this chapter.

The following is an example of an entry name in DCE syntax:

```
/.:/product_development/test_servers/arithmetic_YAK
```

The forward slash divides the different portions of an entry name and is part of the CDS name syntax. Represent your local cell name with **/.:** as a prefix to all name service entries. Each cell also has a global name that begins with the **/...** prefix. If the cell name for this example is **/.../amoeba**, the global name for the same entry looks like this:

```
/.../amoeba/product_development/test_servers/arithmetic_YAK
```

Entry names have a hierarchy similar to a file system hierarchy. The directory pathname for this entry is **product_development/test_servers**. A leaf name identifies a specific entry for a directory pathname in the name service database. In our example, the leaf name is **arithmetic_YAK**, where **arithmetic** represents the interface the server supports and **YAK** represents the server host name.

Name service entries are generally created as management activities and may require special user permission. For example, assume only our cell administrator has permission to create or delete directories immediately under **/.:/**. And perhaps the system administrators for product development have permission to create or delete directories under **product_development**, and set appropriate user permissions for its subdirectories. Finally, the **test_servers** directory may be available for some developers to read and write entries.

You manage leaf naming by accessing CDS indirectly with the RPC control program, **rpccp**, or with RPC runtime routines that begin with **rpc_ns_** in client, server, or management programs. Use the Cell Directory Service control program (**cdscp**) to control global cell naming and to create or remove directory pathnames. We do not describe the use of **cdscp** in this book.

If an entry does not exist when information is stored in the database, it is created automatically. When new information is added to the same entry, the information in the database is updated and no entries are created or removed. For example, servers that frequently stop executing and then restart (such as during testing) have their binding information updated for the same entry. The name service operates more efficiently if you update an entry rather than remove an old entry and create a new one each time a server starts.

Environment Variables

Recall that with the automatic binding method (see Section 3.1.1), finding a server is done for you by the client stub. If your client uses this method of binding management, you must set the RPC-specific environment variable, **RPC_DEFAULT_ENTRY**, to a valid entry name, so the client stub can begin to search the name service database.

DCE uses CDS as its name service. If, however, your system uses a name service other than CDS, you must set the RPC-specific environment variable, **RPC_DEFAULT_ENTRY_SYNTAX**, to the value designated for that name service.

6.1   Server Entries

A name service **server entry** stores binding information for an RPC server. Figure 6-1 depicts server entries in the name service database.

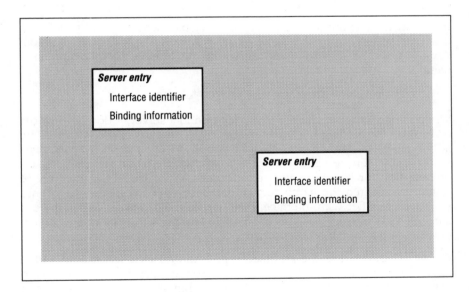

Figure 6-1: Server Entries in the Name Service Database

A server entry contains the following information:

- An **interface identifier** consists of an interface UUID and a version number. During the search for binding information, RPC name service routines use this identifier to determine if a compatible interface is found.

- **Binding information** includes one or more sets of protocol sequence and host address combinations. Well-known endpoints can also be part of the binding information, but dynamic endpoints cannot. This is the information a client needs in order to find a server.

- Some applications use optional **object UUIDs** to identify application-specific objects or resources.

A reasonable naming scheme for server entries combines the host system name and a meaningful definition of what the server offers. For example, the arithmetic interface on a host system named **YAK** can have the following name service entry:

```
/.:/arithmetic_YAK
```

Most host systems only need one server for an interface; however, if your system has multiple servers offering the same interface, you need to distinguish each server with separate name service entries and unique entry names. For example, one server might be **/.:/arithmetic1_YAK**, and another **/.:/arithmetic2_YAK**.

If you organized your name service directory pathname to point to a particular host system, using the name of the system in the leaf name is redundant. In this case, the arithmetic application might have the following entry name:

```
/.:/product_development/test_servers/host_YAK/arithmetic
```

When your client uses the name service to find a server, it does an **import** or **lookup** for binding information, starting at an entry name known to be in the database. Entry names must be supplied to you in one of two ways: by the name service administrator who knows the name service database organization, or by the server administrator. You use RPC name service routines to search the name service database which compare the client's interface identifier with interface identifiers in the database. When there is a match and the entry contains compatible binding information, the compatible binding information is returned.

Figure 6-2 shows how the arithmetic application uses a server entry in the name service database. The arithmetic server uses the **rpc_ns_binding_export** runtime routine to export binding information to the **/.:/arithmetic_YAK** server entry. The arithmetic server's use of **rpc_ns_binding_export** is shown in Example 1-4. The arithmetic client uses the automatic binding method, so the client stub finds the server. The RPC-specific environment variable, **RPC_DEFAULT_ENTRY**, is set to **/.:/arithmetic_YAK** on the client system **DUB**, so the client stub has a name with which to start a name service search. In this example, the name service simply begins and ends the search with the server entry name **/.:/arithmetic_YAK**. The server entry's binding information is returned and the remote procedure call is completed.

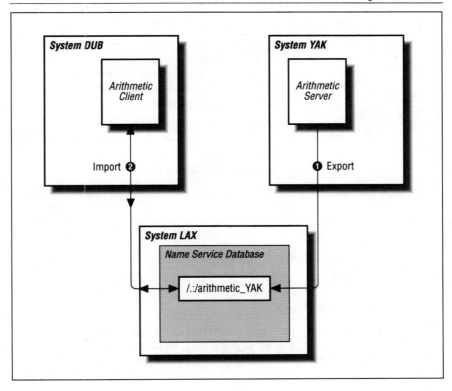

Figure 6-2: A Simple Use of a Name Service Database

Creating a Server Entry and Exporting Binding Information

Suppose the server code for the arithmetic application does not export binding information to the name service. To create a server entry, export binding information, and display the information exported, type the following sequence of **rpccp** commands:

1. Use **rpccp** to export binding information to the name service database for an entry named **/.:/arithmetic_YAK**. If the entry does not exist, the control program creates it automatically.

   ```
   > rpccp export /.:/arithmetic_YAK \
     -i C985A380-255B-11C9-A50B-08002B0ECEF1,0.0 \
     -b ncacn_ip_tcp:YAK -b ncadg_ip_udp:YAK

   >>> binding information exported
   ```

`/.:/arithmetic_YAK`   The name of the server entry.

`-i C985A380-255B-11C9-A50B-08002B0ECEF1,0.0`

The interface identifier contains the UUID and version number for the arithmetic interface. The **uuid** and **version** attributes in the interface definition contain the values.

`-b ncacn_ip_tcp:YAK -b ncadg_ip_udp:YAK`

The binding information including a protocol sequence and server host name (or network address) is added to the entry.

2. Display the binding information for the server entry created. The name service stores the host address rather than the host name. (Objects can also be exported to a server entry. If no objects are stored, a message is displayed.)

```
> rpccp show server /.:/arithmetic_YAK

>>> no matching objects found

binding information:

    <interface id>   C985A380-255B-11C9-A50B-08002B0ECEF1,0.0
    <string binding> ncadg_ip_udp:16.20.16.83[]
    <string binding> ncacn_ip_tcp:16.20.16.83[]
```

If you expect the server to be removed from service for a long period of time or permanently, you should remove the server binding information from the name service using the **rpc_ns_binding_unexport** runtime routine or the **rpccp unexport** command.

To simplify the typing of **rpccp** commands that require an interface identifier, you can set an application-specific environment variable to represent the identifier, and then use the environment variable in the **rpccp** commands. To set an environment variable representing the arithmetic interface identifier, type the following:

```
> setenv ARITHMETIC_ID C985A380-255B-11C9-A50B-08002B0ECEF1,0.0
```

6.2   Group Entries

A **group entry** is a name service entry that corresponds to a set of servers, usually offering the same interface. The members of a group can include server entries and other groups. The name service runtime routines search the members of a group to find a server. A group offers the advantage of storing server entries from many systems, under a single name. Figure 6-3 depicts a group and its members in the name service database.

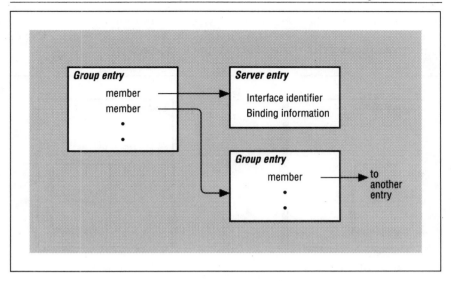

Figure 6-3: Group Entries in a Name Service Database

A group contains one or more **group members**, which are simply names referring to other entries (server entries or groups) in the name service database. Use a group name that is appropriate for all the members of a group. For example, the inventory application uses the group name `/.:/inventory_group`, to refer to all servers that offer the inventory interface.

Figure 6-4 shows how the inventory application uses a group and a server entry in the name service database. The inventory server uses the runtime routine **rpc_ns_binding_export** to export binding information to the `/.:/inventory_YAK` server entry. The inventory server then uses the runtime routine **rpc_ns_group_mbr_add** to add the server entry name as a group member to the `/.:/inventory_group`. The inventory server's use of these routines is shown in Example 5-4.

To find the inventory server, clients begin a search with the group entry named `/.:/inventory_group`. The client that uses the automatic binding method needs the RPC-specific environment variable, **RPC_DEFAULT_ENTRY**, set to `/.:/inventory_group`, so the client stub can find a server. The clients that use the implicit and explicit binding methods use the RPC name service import routines (RPC runtime routines that begin with **rpc_ns_binding_import_**) to find a server. Example 3-7 shows how to use these routines.

The search goes from the group entry to the group members and returns the binding information found in a valid server entry. The search is recursive, so if a group member is itself another group, its members are searched in the same way. The RPC name service import routines automatically select one valid server entry at a time during a search. For this example, `/.:/inventory_YAK` is the only member for the search to find.

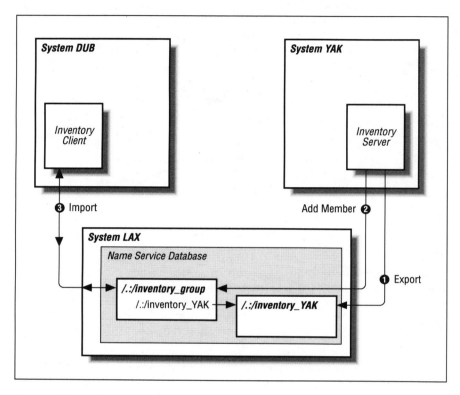

Figure 6-4: A Simple Search in a Name Service Database

Creating a Group Entry and Adding a Member

Suppose the server code for the inventory application does not add the server entry name to the group entry in the name service. To create a group entry, add a member to it, and display the information in the entry, type the following **rpccp** commands:

1. Assume `/.:/inventory_YAK` is a server entry in the name service database. Use **rpccp** to add the `/.:/inventory_YAK` server entry as a member to the group `/.:/inventory_group`.

    ```
    > rpccp add member /.:/inventory_group -m /.:/inventory_YAK

    >>> group member added
    ```

```
> rpccp add member /.:/inventory_group -m /.:/inventory_YAK

>>> group member added
```

/.:/inventory_group   The name of the group entry.

-m /.:/inventory_YAK   The name of the new member is the server entry name.

2. Display the members of the group. The name **/ . . . /amoeba** represents the cell's global name.*

```
> rpccp show group /.:/inventory_group

group members:

   /.../amoeba/inventory_YAK
```

3. Display all information for an entry, which in this example is a group entry. (Every entry has the capability to be a server, group, or profile. Since a group entry has no objects or binding information, only messages for these data are displayed.)

```
> rpccp show entry /.:/inventory_group

>>> no matching objects found

>>> no matching binding information found

group members:

   /.../amoeba/inventory_YAK
```

6.3 *Profile Entries*

A client must always start its name service search with a known entry, but you can make that entry very specific or very inclusive, depending on the variety of servers you use. The client that uses an arithmetic server in Figure 6-2 starts its search with a specific server entry. The client that uses an inventory server in Figure 6-4 conducts a broader and probably more realistic search: it starts with a group entry representing a set of servers. Thus, it can choose a server at random (in the case of automatic binding) or select

---

*When CDS encounters an entry with the /.: prefix, it expands it to a global name that includes the full name of the local cell.

the exact server that it wants from the group (in the case of implicit and explicit binding).

Profiles represent yet another layer of flexibility in searching. A **profile entry** is a name service entry that defines a search list for finding servers in the name service database. You use profiles to gather all your services together. Profiles let you tailor the database search so that all your clients begin a search from a single, general entry name. With profiles, clients do not need to know specific entry names. You usually set the RPC-specific environment variable, **RPC_DEFAULT_ENTRY**, to a profile entry name.

Like group members discussed in the previous section, profiles contain **elements**, each possessing an interface identifier and information about another entry in the database. The elements of a profile can refer to server entries, groups, and other profiles. Figure 6-5 depicts a profile and its elements in the name service database.

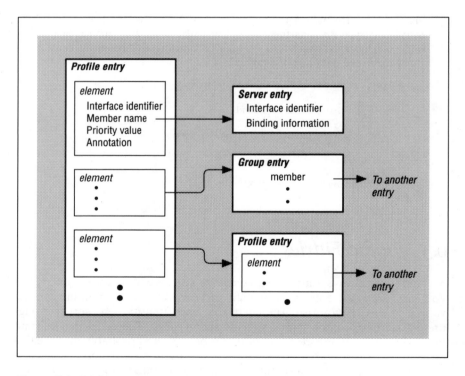

Figure 6-5: Profile Entries in a Name Service Database

Each profile element corresponds to a specific interface and contains the following information:

- The **interface identifier** consists of an interface's UUID and version number.

- A **member name** refers to another entry (server entry, group, or other profile) in the database. The RPC name service routines use this name during a search, to go to that entry for server information.

- A **priority value** (from a high of 0 to a low of 7) controls the search order of profile elements. If a profile contains more than one element for the same interface, the search uses the higher priority elements first. A priority is very useful to give you more specific control during a database search. For example, you may prefer to specify a higher priority for servers running on nearby systems, and a lower relative priority for servers running on a system much further away. In this way, the nearby servers are tried first.

- An **annotation** is optional documentation to help users and administrators understand the entry. It has no effect on the name service search.

Names can be descriptive. For example, `/.:/johns_profile` is the name of a profile the author created, to organize searches for applications that were coded and tested for the book.

Figure 6-6 shows a name service database with a new profile entry and associations we can create, so that the clients for both the arithmetic and inventory applications need only one general name service entry, `/.:/johns_profile`, to find any server. When a search begins at a profile, it looks for a matching interface identifier. If only one is found, it uses that to go to the next entry for information. If more than one element has the desired interface identifier, the search uses the one with the highest priority. In the case of equal priority, one is randomly chosen.

When an arithmetic application client begins a search in this database with the profile `/.:/johns_profile`, the search goes to a profile element whose interface identifier matches the arithmetic application's interface identifier. The search uses the element's member name as the next entry. In this case, the search goes to the server entry `/.:/arithmetic_YAK`. This server entry is the end of the search and the binding information is returned.

When an inventory application client begins a search in this database with the profile `/.:/johns_profile`, the search goes to a profile element whose interface identifier matches the inventory interface's interface identifier. The search uses the member name of the element as the next entry. In this case, the group entry `/.:/inventory_group` is the next entry in the search. The group members are searched in no particular order and binding information is returned from one of the members. If a member is itself another group, its members are also searched.

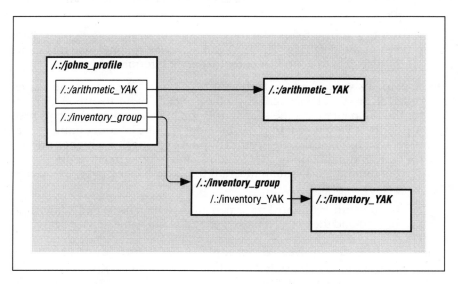

Figure 6-6: Organizing Entries in a Name Service Database

Creating a Profile and Adding Elements

Profiles tend to be created manually, through **rpccp** commands, by users customizing their environments. Programs can also create or manage profiles, using RPC routines that begin with **rpc_ns_profile_**. The following sequence of commands show how to create and add elements to the profile shown in Figure 6-6.

1. Use **rpccp** to add an element to the profile /.:/johns_profile. The member name for the element is the arithmetic server entry /.:/arithmetic_YAK. If the profile does not exist, the control program creates it automatically.

    ```
    > rpccp add element /.:/johns_profile \
        -i C985A380-255B-11C9-A50B-08002B0ECEF1,0.0 \
        -m /.:/arithmetic_YAK \
        -a "Arithmetic IF"

    >>> profile element added
    ```

`/.:/johns_profile`   The name of the profile to which the element is added.

`-i C985A380-255B-11C9-A50B-08002B0ECEF1,0.0`
The interface identifier contains the UUID and version number for the server interface.

`-m /.:/arithmetic_YAK`
The member name of the element added to the profile is /.:/arithmetic_YAK.

`-a "Arithmetic IF"`   An annotation in the profile is Arithmetic IF.

2. Add another element to the profile `/.:/johns_profile`. The member name for this element is the entry `/.:/inventory_group`.

```
> rpccp add element /.:/johns_profile \
  -i 008B3C84-93A5-11C9-85B0-08002B147A61,1.0 \
  -m /.:/inventory_group \
  -a "Inventory IF"

>>> profile element added
```

`/.:/johns_profile`   The name of the profile to which the element is added.

`-i 008B3C84-93A5-11C9-85B0-08002B147A61,1.0`
The interface identifier contains the UUID and version number for the server interface.

`-m /.:/inventory_group`
The member name of the element added to the profile is /.:/inventory_group.

`-a "Inventory IF"`   An annotation in the profile is Inventory IF.

3. Display the elements of the profile.

```
> rpccp show profile /.:/johns_profile

profile elements:

    <interface id>    C985A380-255B-11C9-A50B-08002B0ECEF1,0.0
    <member_name>     /.../amoeba/arithmetic_YAK
    <priority>        0
    <annotation>      Arithmetic IF

    <interface id>    008B3C84-93A5-11C9-85B0-08002B147A61,1.0
    <member_name>     /.../amoeba/inventory_group
    <priority>        0
    <annotation>      Inventory IF
```

Since some clients use the automatic binding method, set the RPC-specific environment variable **RPC_DEFAULT_ENTRY**, to **/.:/johns_profile** prior to testing.

```
▷ setenv RPC_DEFAULT_ENTRY /.:/johns_profile
```

Clients that use name service import and lookup routines can begin their search at the value specified in the **RPC_DEFAULT_ENTRY** environment variable, by using **NULL** for the entry name argument. You can also change clients to use **/.:/johns_profile** as an entry name.

Accessing the Database Hierarchy with Default Elements

So far we have described how to use a profile to organize a hierarchy of servers from entries you know. In a typical distributed environment, however, you want access not only to your servers, but to servers for many kinds of resources, across many levels of your organization. For example, suppose your program makes a remote procedure call to an interface that manages a database of people in your organization. You should not have to obtain entry names and include them in your profile every time you want another interface already in use by your organization. Profiles not only allow you to create a top-down hierarchy of your servers, they also give you bottom-up access to the name service database hierarchy in a way that frees you from knowing about the details of the hierarchy.

Figure 6-7 shows how your profile can access more of the database hierarchy. Every profile can contain one **default element** which is used as the last resort during a search of that profile. If none of a profile's elements match the interface identifier being sought, the search uses the default element to continue. The default element refers to another profile that is usually the next level up in your name service database hierarchy. The search starts over again with the new profile. If the new profile does not contain an appropriate element, that profile's default element is used, and the search continues until a server is found or the search is exausted. Thus your personal profile can inherit upper levels of the name service database hierarchy by using a default profile.

The default element has a NULL interface identifier, and since there can be only one default element per profile, the priority of a profile element is not relevant.

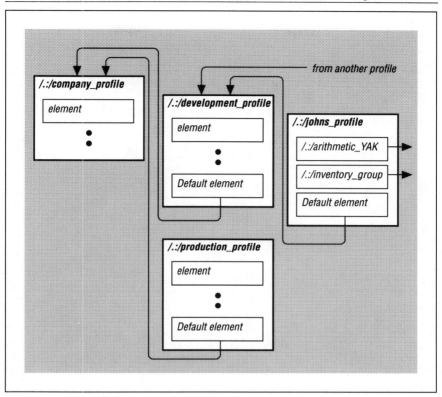

Figure 6-7: Default Elements in a Name Service Database

7

Using Context Handles

Some applications require that a server maintain information between remote procedure calls. This is called **maintaining context** (or maintaining state). Global data is one way a local application can maintain information between procedure calls. In a distributed application, however, the client and server are in different address spaces so the only data common to each are passed as parameters. Even if a set of remote procedures use server global data, there is nothing to prevent more than one client from making calls that modify the data. A **context handle** is the mechanism that maintains information on a particular server for a particular client. An **active context handle** refers to valid (non-null) context, and includes binding information because a specific server maintains information for a particular client.

The Remote_file Application

The remote_file application is a simple file transfer example that copies text from the client to the server.* A client uses a context handle to refer to server context. The server context is the file handle used by remote procedures to open, write, and close the file. In this application, the filename on the server may be the same or different from the filename on the client, but the server does not overwrite an existing file on the server system. If you do not select any filenames, this application uses standard input (**stdin**) of the client and standard output (**stdout**) of the server to transfer a message from the client to the server. The complete remote_file application is shown in Appendix E.

---

*We use remote file access here as a simple demonstration of how to use a context handle. See Chapter 8 for a more efficient way to transfer files.

7.1 Declaring Context in an Interface Definition

A file handle in a local application is a good analogy to a context handle in a distributed application. The information a file handle refers to is maintained by the C library and the operating system, not your application. You call some library routines to open or close the file, and other routines to read from or write to the file.

A context handle is maintained by the stubs and RPC runtime library, not by your application code. Remote procedures that manipulate the context must include a procedure that returns an active context handle, and one that frees the context when you are finished with it. Other remote procedures can access or manipulate the active context.

Example 7-1 shows how to define context handles in the remote_file interface definition.

Example 7-1: Defining Context Handles

```
/* FILE NAME: remote_file.idl */
[
uuid(016B2B80-F9B4-11C9-B31A-08002B111685),
version(1.0)
]
interface remote_file         /* file manipulation on a remote system */
{
    typedef [context_handle] void *filehandle;  /*❶*/
    typedef                   byte buffer[];

filehandle remote_open(         /* open for write ❷*/
    [in] handle_t binding_h,    /* explicit primitive binding handle      */
    [in, string] char name[],   /* if name is null, use stdout in server */
    [in, string] char mode[]    /* values can be "r", "w", or "a"         */
);

long remote_send(
    [in] filehandle fh,                        /*❸*/
    [in, max_is(max)] buffer buf,
    [in] long max
);

void remote_close(
    [in,out] filehandle *fh                    /*❹*/
);
}
```

❶ To define a context handle data type, apply the **context_handle** attribute to a **void *** type (or a type that resolves to **void ***) in a type definition. If the client-server communication breaks down or the client fails, a context handle data type allows the server to automatically clean up the user-defined context with a call to a **context rundown procedure**. If a context handle is applied in a type definition, then the server application developer must write a context rundown procedure.

❷ At least one remote procedure initializes the context handle, and returns it to the client for later use. A procedure returning a context handle result always returns a new active context handle. Also, if a parameter is an out-only context handle, the procedure creates a new active context handle.

❸ A procedure with a context handle parameter that is input only must use an active context handle.

❹ When the client application is finished with the server context, the context must be freed.

If the context handle is null upon return from a procedure, the remote procedure on the server has freed the context and the client stub has freed the context handle. A remote procedure that frees a context handle requires the parameter to have the **in** directional attribute so the server can free the context, and the **out** directional attribute so the client stub can also free the client's copy of the context handle.

7.2 Using a Context Handle in a Client

The client uses a context handle to refer to the server context through the remote procedure calls. In the client, the context handle refers to an **opaque structure**. This means that the data is hidden and cannot be manipulated by the client application code. The context handle can be tested for null but not assigned any values by the client application. The server code accomplishes all context modification, but the status of the context is communicated to the client through the context handle. The client stub manipulates the context handle in the client, on behalf of the server. Example 7-2 shows a typical sequence of remote procedure calls when using context handles.

Example 7-2: Using a Context Handle in a Client

```
/* FILE NAME: r_client.c */
#include <stdio.h>
#include <string.h>
#include "remote_file.h"
#define MAX 200          /* maximum line length for a file */

main(argc, argv)
int argc;
char *argv[];
{
```

Example 7-2: Using a Context Handle in a Client (continued)

```
FILE        *local_fh;        /* file handle for client file input */
char        host[100];    /* name or network address of remote host */
idl_char    remote_name[100];           /* name of remote file */
rpc_binding_handle_t binding_h;             /* binding handle */
filehandle  remote_fh;                    /* context handle */
buffer      *buf_ptr;            /* buffer pointer for data sent */
int         size;                   /* size of data buffer */
void exit();
char *malloc();

    get_args(argc, argv, &local_fh, host, (char *)remote_name);
#ifndef LOCAL
    if(do_string_binding(host, &binding_h) < 0) {               /*❶*/
        fprintf(stderr, "Cannot get binding\n");
        exit(1);
    }
#endif
    remote_fh = remote_open(binding_h, remote_name, (idl_char *)"w"); /*❷*/
    if(remote_fh == NULL) {
        fprintf(stderr, "Cannot open remote file\n");
        exit(1);
    }
    /* The buffer data type is a conformant array of bytes; */
    /* memory must be allocated for a conformant array.     */
    buf_ptr = (buffer *)malloc((MAX+1) * sizeof(buffer));

    while( fgets((char *)buf_ptr, MAX, local_fh) != NULL) {
        size = (int)strlen((char *)buf_ptr); /* data sent won't include */
        if( remote_send(remote_fh, (*buf_ptr), size) < 1) {        /*❸*/
            fprintf(stderr, "Cannot write to remote file\n");
            exit(1);
        }
    }
    remote_close(&remote_fh);                                      /*❹*/
}
```

❶ Before a context handle becomes valid, a client must establish a binding with the server that will maintain the context. For the explicit or implicit binding methods, your application requires this step. For the automatic binding method, binding occurs in the client stub during the first remote procedure call. Then, to find the server after the context handle is established, subsequent calls use it instead of a binding handle. The `do_string_binding` procedure is an application-specific procedure that creates a binding handle from a host input and a generated protocol sequence (see Section 3.2.3).

The symbol `LOCAL` is used in applications in this book, to distinguish compiling this client to test in a local environment, from compiling to run in a distributed environment.

❷ To establish an active context handle, a procedure must either return the context handle as the procedure result or have only the **out** directional attribute on a context handle parameter. The context handle cannot be used by any other procedure until it is active. For the `remote_open` procedure, an explicit binding handle is the first parameter.

❸ Procedures using only an active context handle can be used however the application requires. Note that for a procedure to use the context handle, a context handle parameter must have at least the **in** attribute. The `remote_send` procedure sends a buffer of text data to the server, where the remote procedure writes the data to the file referred to by the context handle.

❹ When you have finished with the context, free the context handle to release resources.

7.2.1 Binding Handles and Context Handles

A procedure can use a binding handle and one or more context handles. However, make sure all handles in the parameter list refer to the same server because a remote procedure call cannot directly refer to more than one server at a time.

Table 7-1 shows how to determine whether a binding handle or a context handle directs the remote procedure call to the server.

Table 7-1 Binding Handles and Context Handles in a Call

Procedure Format	Other Parameters	Handle that Directs Call
`proc( . . . )`	No binding or context handles	The interface-wide automatic or implicit binding handle directs the call.
`proc( [in] bh . . . )`	May include context handles	The explicit binding handle, bh, directs the call.
`proc( . . . [in] ch . . . )`	May include other context handles but no binding handles	The first context handle that is an input only parameter directs the call. If it is null, the call will fail.

Table 7-1 Binding Handles and Context Handles in a Call (continued)

Procedure Format	Other Parameters	Handle that Directs Call
proc(. . . [in,out]ch. . .)	May include other input /output or output only context handles but no binding handles or input only context handles	The first non-null context handle that is an input/output parameter directs the call. If all are null, the call will fail.

7.3 Managing Context in a Server

When more than one remote procedure call from a particular client needs context on a server, the server stub and server application maintain the context. This section describes how to implement the procedures that manipulate context in a server.

A **server context handle** refers to context in the server code. It communicates the status of the context back to the client. From the perspective of the server developer, a server context handle is an untyped pointer that can be tested for null, assigned null, or assigned any value within the server address space.

Once the server context handle is active (non-null), the server maintains the context for the particular client until one of the following occurs:

* The client performs a remote procedure call that frees the context.

* The client terminates while context is being maintained.

* Communication breaks between the client and server.

If the client terminates or the client-server communication breaks while the server maintains context, the server's RPC runtime library may invoke a context rundown procedure to clean up user data. Section 7.3.2 shows how to write a context rundown procedure.

7.3.1 Writing Procedures That Use a Context Handle

The procedures that manipulate server context can be organized into categories, depending on the input and output requirements of the context handle. Example 7-3 shows how to implement a procedure that obtains an active context handle, one that uses the active context handle, and one that frees the context handle.

Example 7-3: Procedures that Use Context Handles

```
/* FILE NAME: r_procedures.c */
#include <stdio.h>
#include <string.h>
#include <unistd.h>
#include "remote_file.h"

filehandle remote_open(binding_h, name, mode)   /*❶*/
rpc_binding_handle_t binding_h;
idl_char            name[];
idl_char            mode[];
{
   FILE *FILEh;

   if(strlen((char *)name) == 0)                        /* no filename given */
      if(strcmp((char *)mode, "r") == 0)
         FILEh = NULL;                          /* cannot read nonexistent file */
      else FILEh = stdout;                      /* use server stdout */

   else if(access((char *)name, F_OK) == 0)              /* file exists */
      if(strcmp((char *)mode, "w") == 0)
         FILEh = NULL;                  /* do not overwrite existing file */
      else FILEh = fopen((char *)name, (char *)mode); /*open read/append */

   else                                         /* file does not exist */
      if(strcmp((char *)mode, "r") == 0)
         FILEh = NULL;                  /* cannot read nonexistent file */
      else FILEh = fopen((char *)name, (char *)mode);/*open write/append */

   return( (filehandle)FILEh );    /* cast FILE handle to context handle */
}

idl_long_int remote_send(fh, buf, max)          /*❷*/
filehandle fh;
buffer buf;
idl_long_int max;
{
   /* write data to the file (context), which is cast as a FILE pointer */
   return( fwrite(buf, sizeof(buffer), max, (FILE *)fh) );
}

void remote_close(fh)                           /*❸*/
filehandle *fh;  /* the client stub needs the changed value upon return */
{
   if( (FILE *)(*fh) != stdout )
      fclose( (FILE *)(*fh) );
   (*fh) = NULL;          /* assign NULL to the context handle to free it */
   return;
}
```

❶ Initialize data as required by later calls, and assign the application context to the server context handle. In this example, a file handle is obtained and assigned to the context handle when the procedure returns. Outside of the server process this file handle is meaningless, but when the client makes subsequent calls, the server uses this file handle to write data or close the file.

❷ Use the server context handle parameter defined with the **in** directional attribute. This procedure must have an active context handle as input. For this example, the buffer (**buf**) of **max** number of items is written to the file. Cast the server context handle to the context's data type (**FILE ***).

❸ Free the context by using a procedure whose context handle parameter is defined with the **in** and **out** directional attributes. This procedure must have an active context handle as input. To free the context, assign null to the server context handle and use the C library procedure **free** or a corresponding method to clean up your application. In this example, before freeing the file handle, the context is tested to be sure it does not refer to **stdout**. The server context handle is cast to the context's data type.

When this procedure returns to the client, the client stub automatically frees the context handle on the client side, if the server context handle is set to NULL.

If memory must be allocated for the context, use the C library procedure **malloc**, or another method. Do *not* use the stub support procedure **rpc_ss_allocate** because you do not want the allocated memory to be automatically freed by the server stub after the procedure completes.

7.3.2 Writing a Context Rundown Procedure

A context rundown procedure allows orderly cleanup of the server context. The server RPC runtime library automatically calls it when a context is maintained for a client, and either of the following occurs:

- The client terminates without requesting that the server free the context.

- Communication breaks between the client and server.

In our example, the interface definition defines the following type as a context handle:

```
typedef [context_handle] void *filehandle;
```

Example 7-4 shows the context rundown procedure to implement in the server code. The procedure name is created by appending **_rundown** to the type name (**filehandle**). The procedure does not return a value and the only parameter is the context handle. In this example, when the context rundown procedure executes, it closes the file that represents the context.

Example 7-4: A Context Rundown Procedure

```
/* FILE NAME: context_rundown.c */
#include <stdio.h>
#include "remote_file.h"

void filehandle_rundown(remote_fh)
filehandle remote_fh;                /* the context handle is passed in  */
{
    fprintf(stderr, "Server executing context rundown\n");
    if( (FILE *)remote_fh != stdout )
        fclose( (FILE *)remote_fh );  /* file is closed if client is gone */
    remote_fh = NULL;                /* must set context handle to NULL  */
    return;
}
```

The context handle must be defined as a type in the interface definition in order for the server runtime to automatically call the context rundown procedure. And if you define the context handle as a type, then you must implement a context rundown procedure in the server.

8

Using Pipes for Large Quantities of Data

A **pipe** in a DCE application efficiently passes very large or incrementally produced quantities of data in a remote procedure call. The following kinds of data are candidates for pipes:

- large quantities of data

- data of unknown size that cannot be in memory all at once

- data incrementally produced or consumed and not in memory all at once

The idea of a pipe is to put the RPC mechanism in charge of data transfer because it can use the underlying transport protocol more efficiently than the high-level application can. A pipe is defined in the IDL interface definition, and encompasses a collection of data structures, procedures, and stub routines. In the remote procedure declaration, a pipe can appear as a parameter with the same **in** and **out** attributes as other parameters. As an input parameter, the pipe transfers data from client to server, while as an output parameter it transfers data from server to client. Unlike the familiar pipes of UNIX shell commands, you can use an RPC pipe to transfer data in both directions.

Transfer through a pipe starts after the client issues a remote procedure call and while the server executes the remote procedure. The server and client now enter loops in which the stubs transfer chunks of data. The server calls special stub routines that load or unload a buffer of pipe data, and the client calls application programmer's procedures that allocate buffers and load or unload them. Because the server controls the loops, we use the term **pull** for an input pipe (transferring data from client to server), and **push** for an output pipe (transferring data from server to client).

The Transfer_data Application

The transfer_data application (see Appendix F) shows how pipes are used to transfer binary data to and from the server. As described in Section 3.3, a customized binding handle controls binding.

8.1 Defining Pipes in an Interface Definition

Example 8-1 shows how pipes are defined in an interface definition.

Example 8-1: Defining Pipes

```
/* FILE NAME: transfer_data.idl */
[
uuid(A6876974-F555-11CA-BAE1-08002B245A28),
version(1.0)
]
interface transfer_data    /* data transfer to and from a remote system */
{
  const long NAME_LENGTH = 200;

    typedef [handle] struct {              /* a customized handle type */
       char host[NAME_LENGTH+1];
       char filename[NAME_LENGTH+1];
    } file_spec;

    typedef pipe float pipe_type;               /* a pipe data type❶*/

void send_floats(       /* send pipe of floats to a file on the server */
    [in] file_spec  cust_binding_h,    /* customized binding for server */
    [in] pipe_type data                 /* input pipe of float data❷*/
);

void receive_floats(    /* get pipe of floats from a file on the server */
    [in] file_spec  cust_binding_h,    /* customized binding for server */
    [out] pipe_type *data               /* output pipe of float data❸*/
);
}
```

❶ You define a pipe in a type definition using the keyword **pipe**. The base type for a pipe defines the size of one element in the transfer buffer. In this example, the base type is a **float**.

❷ In this procedure, we use an input pipe to transfer data of type **float** from the client to a file on the server system.

❸ In this procedure, we use an output pipe to transfer data of type **float** to the client from a file on the server system.

When you pass the interface definition of Example 8-1 through the IDL compiler, it creates a C structure in the output header file for the pipe data type. The structure outline is shown in Example 8-2 and contains pointers to procedures and a pipe state. We describe the parameters required for each procedure later in this chapter.

Example 8-2: A Pipe Structure Generated by the IDL Compiler

```
       .
       .
       .
typedef struct pipe_type {
  void (* pull)(
       .
       .
       .
  );
  void (* push)(
       .
       .
       .
  );
  void (* alloc)(
       .
       .
       .
  );
  rpc_ss_pipe_state_t state;
} pipe_type;
       .
       .
       .
```

Figure 8-1 shows where an application defines and uses the procedures, stub routines, and pipe state.

Your client has to manage the data. For an input pipe, write a **pull** procedure that provides a chunk of data (for instance, by reading it from a file). For an output pipe, write a **push** procedure that processes a chunk of data (for instance, by writing it to a file). In both cases, write an **alloc** procedure that allocates or points to a buffer of memory for each chunk. Finally, to coordinate these procedures over multiple calls, define an application-specific state structure. Your client application never calls the procedures directly; instead, the client stub calls them during each pass in its internal loop.

During data transfer, the following information is required:

- The size of the chunk transferred each time.

- Where the data transfer starts (for instance, the beginning of a file or the first element of an array).

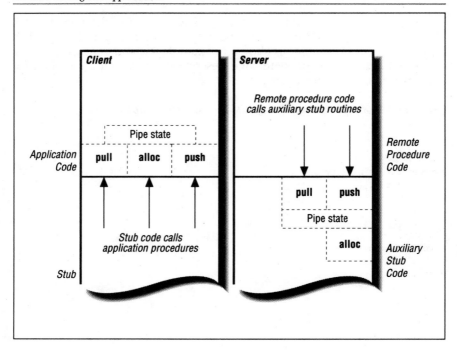

Figure 8-1: Structure of Pipe Application Code

- Where the data transfer ends (for instance, check for the end of the file, or count the number of elements being transferred and stop at the end of the array). A chunk of zero length indicates the end of pipe data.

For the server, the IDL compiler generates the pipe state and **alloc, pull,** and **push** stub routines, and places them in a server auxiliary stub file. Your server calls the **pull** stub routine for an input pipe and the **push** stub routine for an output pipe in loops from the remote procedure. On the server side, the **alloc** stub routine and the pipe state are used exclusively by the stub.

This chapter describes the rules that you must follow to make pipes work. The examples show an input pipe first, and then an output pipe that performs the reverse operation.

The Pipe State

A pipe state is application-specific and local to each side. That is, the client and the server each have a separate state that is used just to communicate between application code and stub code. For most applications, the state is a structure.

The client developer defines and manipulates the pipe state for the client. The main task of the state for all applications is to keep track of where to find or place the data. For example, if you are transferring chunks of data from a large array in memory, you set a structure member of the state to start at zero for the first element. During each **pull** or **push** loop cycle, you update the member so that it points to the starting element for the next transfer. The example in this chapter transfers data from one file to another, so all that is needed for the state is the file handle. It keeps track internally, of the current data location in the file.

Many clients have additional uses for the state structure, and can define extra members to meet these needs. For example, suppose you are using a pipe for both input and output in a remote procedure call. Your application may need to perform specific activities after input data is transferred to the server, but before output data is transferred back to the client. In order for the **pull** and **push** procedures to coordinate and perform these activities, the state can include whatever data is necessary. For example, let's assume pipe data from a file on a client is transferred to a server for processing, and then the pipe data is transferred back to the same file on the client. If the file is opened and the data in it transferred to the server with an input pipe, the file must be reset to write data back to the file with an output pipe. If the last time the **pull** procedure is called it closes the file, the **push** procedure needs the filename in the state structure to reopen the file.

In the server, the IDL compiler generates the pipe state structure. It is used only in the server stub. The server developer does not manipulate the pipe state.

Example 8-3 shows the pipe state structure used by the client of the transfer_data application.

Example 8-3: A Pipe State Structure

```
/* FILE NAME: pipe_state.h */
/* Definition of application-specific state structure of client pipe data.*/
typedef struct pipe_state {
    int  filehandle;         /* handle of client data file ❶*/
    char *filename;          /* name of client data file   ❷*/
} pipe_state;
```

❶ This application requires the handle of the opened data file so our **pull** procedure can find the data and so our **push** procedure knows where to put the data.

❷ The name of the client data file is part of this pipe state structure, so the file can be opened in the **pull** and **push** procedures. The application requires this information for a pipe that is both input and output, so the file can be reset from read to write.

8.2 Using an Input Pipe

In this section we first describe how to write a client for an input pipe parameter. Then we describe how to write a remote procedure to manage an input pipe for a server.

8.2.1 Using an Input Pipe in a Client

For an input pipe, you write the following:

- an **alloc** procedure, that the client stub calls to allocate a buffer of client memory for pipe data

- a **pull** procedure, that the client stub calls to load the allocated buffer

- a **pipe state** structure that coordinates **alloc** and **pull**

Figure 8-2 shows how the client processes pipe data that is transferred to the server.

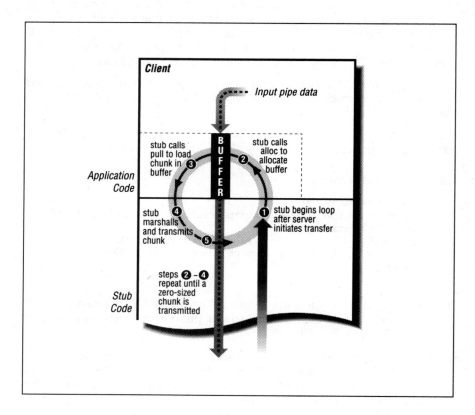

Figure 8-2: Pipe Data Transfer from a Client

When the server initiates data transfer, the client stub begins to process data in a loop. On each pass, the stub calls the **alloc** procedure to create a buffer, then it calls the **pull** procedure to fill the buffer, and finally it marshalls and transmits data from the buffer to the server. The loop repeats until the stub transmits a zero-sized chunk of data. Example 8-4 shows an example of a remote procedure call with an input pipe parameter.

Example 8-4: Using an Input Pipe in a Client

```
/* FILE NAME: client_send.c */
/* Client for customized handle and input pipe test */
#include <stdio.h>
#include "transfer_data.h"
#include "pipe_state.h"   /* definition of state structure for pipe data❶*/

main(argc, argv)
int argc;
char *argv[];
{
    file_spec  cust_binding_h;              /* customized binding handle */
    pipe_state state;
    pipe_type  data;                 /* a pipe structure is allocated❷*/
    char       local_source[100];
               /* procedures in other modules */
    void       client_alloc(), in_pull();
    void       send_floats();
               /* get user input */
    if(argc < 4) {
      printf("USAGE: %s  local_source  host  file\n", argv[0]);
      exit(0);
    }
    /* initialize customized binding handle structure */
    strcpy(local_source, argv[1]);
    strcpy(cust_binding_h.host, argv[2]);
    strcpy(cust_binding_h.filename, argv[3]);

    /* initialize pipe structure */
    state.filehandle = -1;
    state.filename = local_source;
    data.state = (rpc_ss_pipe_state_t)&state;    /* initialize pipe state❸*/
    data.alloc = client_alloc;   /* initialize alloc procedure for a pipe❹*/
    data.pull = in_pull;     /* Initialize pull procedure for input pipe❺*/

    send_floats(cust_binding_h, data);/* remote procedure with input pipe❻*/
}
```

❶ Example 8-3 shows the `pipe_state` structure. This structure allows your **pull** and **alloc** procedures to coordinate activities during the data transfer loop.

❷ Allocate a pipe structure.

❸ To initialize the pipe state, assign your application-specific state structure to the **state** member of the pipe structure. Since you define the state to be anything appropriate for your application, cast your application state structure when it is assigned to the **state** member.

❹ To initialize the **alloc** procedure, assign your application procedure, `client_alloc`, to the **alloc** member of the pipe structure. Then, when the client stub needs a buffer for pipe data, it calls `client_alloc`. This procedure is shown in Example 8-5.

❺ To initialize the **pull** procedure, assign your application procedure, `in_pull`, to the **pull** member of the pipe structure. Then, when the client stub needs input pipe data, it calls `in_pull`. This procedure is shown in Example 8-6.

❻ Call the remote procedure that has the input pipe parameter. The `send_floats` procedure takes an input pipe of floating-point file data and copies it to the target file on the server.

Example 8-5 shows the **alloc** procedure for the input pipe of Example 8-4. This example simply returns a pointer to the same array each time the client stub calls this procedure. Sophisticated applications may need to allocate a different amount of memory each time the stub calls this procedure.

Example 8-5: A Client Alloc Procedure for a Pipe

```
/* FILE NAME: client_alloc.c */
#include <stdio.h>
#include "transfer_data.h"
#include "pipe_state.h"

#define BUFFER_SIZE 2000
idl_short_float client_buffer[BUFFER_SIZE];

void client_alloc(state, bsize, buf, bcount)    /* allocation for a pipe❶*/
pipe_state         *state;          /* coordinates pipe procedure calls❷*/
idl_ulong_int      bsize;           /* desired size of buffer in bytes❸*/
idl_short_float    **buf;                             /* allocated buffer❹*/
idl_ulong_int      *bcount;         /* allocated buffer size in bytes  ❺*/
{
    *buf = client_buffer;
    *bcount = BUFFER_SIZE;
    return;
}
```

❶ The header file generated by the IDL compiler specifies arguments that you must include in your **alloc** procedure.

❷ The pipe state is available to coordinate calls that the stub makes to the pipe procedures. In this example, the state is not used.

❸ The stub passes in the number of bytes it would prefer to use for the transfer buffer. This value is set by the IDL compiler and is read-only in your **alloc** procedure. In this example, this value is not used.

❹ The procedure obtains a pointer to the allocated buffer.

❺ The procedure obtains the actual size of the buffer in bytes.

After the client stub calls your **alloc** procedure, the stub calls your **pull** procedure to load a chunk of data into the buffer. This procedure must perform the following tasks:

- Find the chunk of data, usually by referring to the state structure.

- Read the chunk of data into the buffer, usually from a data structure, file, or device.

- Set the number of bytes to be transferred. To indicate the end of data, set this argument to zero.

- Do application-specific cleanup when all data is transferred. Cleanup can include tasks in preparation for the transfer of output data back through the pipe.

Example 8-6 shows the **pull** procedure and the arguments you must include for the input pipe of Example 8-4. In this example, the procedure opens the source file on the client and reads a chunk of data.

Example 8-6: A Client Pull Procedure for an Input Pipe

```
/* FILE NAME: in_pull.c */
#include <stdio.h>
#include <sys/file.h>
#include "transfer_data.h"
#include "pipe_state.h" /* definition of a state structure for pipe data */

void in_pull(state, buf, esize, ecount)/* input pipe uses pull procedure❶*/
pipe_state      *state;           /* coordinates pipe procedure calls❷*/
idl_short_float *buf;             /* buffer of data pulled          ❸*/
idl_ulong_int   esize;            /* maximum element count in buffer ❹*/
idl_ulong_int   *ecount;          /* actual element count in buffer  ❺*/
{
    /* for this application, open local source file if not open already */
    if(state->filehandle == -1) {
       state->filehandle = open(state->filename, O_RDONLY);
       if(state->filehandle == -1) {
           fprintf(stderr, "Cannot open file %s for read\n", state->filename);
           exit(0);
       }
    }
    /* process buffer for your application */
    *ecount = read(state->filehandle, buf, (sizeof(float)*esize)) /
                sizeof(float);
```

Example 8-6: A Client Pull Procedure for an Input Pipe (continued)

```
        /* To signal the end of data, pull procedure must set count to 0.   ❻*/
        if(*ecount == 0) {      /* end of data reached, do application cleanup❼*/
            close(state->filehandle);
        }
        return;
    }
```

❶ The required parameters are declared in the pipe structure of the header file, generated by IDL.

❷ You refer to the pipe state to find the start of a chunk of data, and any other state information you need. In this example, the state contains a filename and handle for the open file.

❸ The stub passes in a pointer to the buffer allocated by the previous call to the **alloc** procedure.

❹ The stub passes in the size of the buffer in terms of data elements. You should try to read this amount of data into the buffer. In this example, a pipe data element is a float.

❺ The procedure returns the actual number of pipe data elements in the buffer. The stub needs this value in order to marshall and transmit the correct amount of data.

❻ Send one empty data buffer by setting the element count to 0. This is the signal to the stub that it has reached the end of data. In this example, the last read from a file returns 0 elements in **ecount**, so the pull procedure simply passes it back to the client stub.

❼ Do application-specific cleanup. If an input parameter is also an output parameter, some preparation may be necessary before the stub calls the **push** procedure. In this example, the data file is closed.

Some applications use a pipe when data already has the proper form in memory, such as an array of pipe type elements. You can use your **alloc** procedure to assign the data to the buffer and make your **pull** procedure a null procedure.

8.2.2   Managing an Input Pipe in the Server

Figure 8-3 shows how the remote procedure processes input pipe data. You initiate data transfer by calling the server stub's **pull** routine in a loop. This routine tells the client stub to begin transmitting chunks of pipe data. It also unmarshalls the data into the server's buffer for use by the remote procedure. The loop repeats until the remote procedure receives a zero-sized chunk of data.

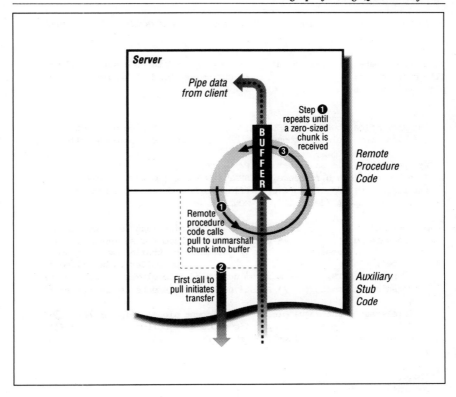

Figure 8-3: Input Pipe Data Transfer to a Server

Example 8-7 shows the steps to process an input pipe in a remote procedure implementation. Your remote procedure must call the **pull** stub routine in a loop until all data elements are received. Parameters passed to the stub routine include the pipe state (controlled by the stub) and the maximum number of data elements requested. Parameters returned include the buffer for the data and the actual count of elements pulled. The stub puts into the buffer no more elements than the maximum requested. It could put in less; for instance, in this application, when the last chunk of data from the client's input file is sent, it could be shorter than the rest. When a zero-sized chunk is received, the process loop can quit. Exiting the loop before this leads to an exception condition. Once the pipe is empty, the **pull** stub routine must not be called for this parameter again.

Example 8-7: Processing an Input Pipe in a Remote Procedure

```
/* FILE NAME: send_floats.c */
#include <stdio.h>
#include <sys/file.h>
#include "transfer_data.h"
#define MAX_ELEMENTS  1000
```

Example 8-7: Processing an Input Pipe in a Remote Procedure (continued)

```
void send_floats(c_b_h, in_data)    /* copy input data to a server file */
file_spec  c_b_h;                   /* customized binding handle        */
pipe_type in_data;
{
    int              file_h;
    idl_short_float buf[MAX_ELEMENTS];              /* pipe data buffer */
    idl_ulong_int    element_count;       /* number of elements pulled */

    /* open local file on server for write */
    file_h = open(c_b_h.filename, O_CREAT | O_TRUNC | O_WRONLY, 0777);
    if(file_h < 0)  /* If can't open file, need to discard the pipe data */
        file_h = open("/dev/null", O_WRONLY);

    while(true) {                     /* entire pipe must be processed ❶*/
        (in_data.pull)(          /* pull routine is used for an input pipe ❷*/
            in_data.state,          /* state is controlled by the stub */
            buf,                          /* the buffer to be filled */
            MAX_ELEMENTS,      /* maximum number of data elements in buffer */
            &element_count      /* actual number of elements in the buffer */
        );
        if(element_count == 0) break;   /* 0 count signals pipe is empty ❸*/
        /****          application specific process of buffer     **** ❹*/
        write(file_h, buf, (sizeof(idl_short_float) * element_count));
    }

    close(file_h);
    return;
}
```

❶ Keep looping until all data is received.

❷ Call the **pull** stub routine to obtain pipe data from the client.

❸ A chunk of data with 0 elements indicates that the pipe is empty.

❹ Process the data buffer appropriately for your implementation. In this example, the chunk of data is written to a file on the server.

8.3 Using an Output Pipe

Using an output pipe is similar to using an input pipe. However, an output pipe requires a **push** procedure instead of a **pull** procedure. In this section we first describe how to write a client for an output pipe parameter. Then we describe how to write a remote procedure to manage an output pipe for a server.

8.3.1   Using an Output Pipe in a Client

For an output pipe, you write the following:

- an **alloc** procedure, that the client stub calls to allocate a buffer of client memory for the pipe data

- a **push** procedure, that the client stub calls to unload the allocated buffer

- a **pipe state** structure that coordinates **alloc** and **push**

Figure 8-4 shows how the client processes pipe data that is transferred from the server.

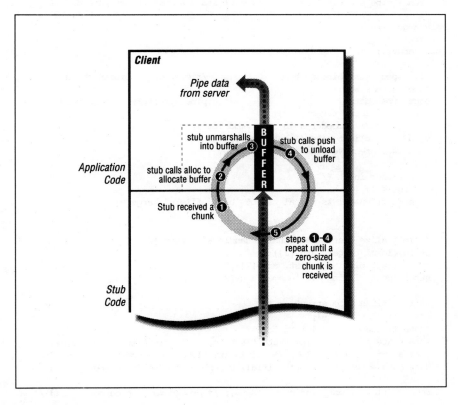

Figure 8-4: Pipe Data Transfer to a Client

The client stub enters a loop in which it receives a chunk of data, calls the **alloc** procedure to create a buffer, unmarshalls data into the buffer, and calls the **push** procedure to use the data. The size of the chunk sent by the server can be different than the size allocated by your **alloc** procedure. If the chunk sent is larger than your allocated buffer, the stub repeats this sequence for the remainder of the chunk sent. The loop repeats until the stub receives a zero-sized chunk of data. Example 8-8 shows a remote procedure call with an output pipe parameter. In this example, the **state** structure and the **alloc** procedure are the same as those used for the input pipe in Example 8-4.

Example 8-8: Using an Output Pipe in a Client

```
/* FILE NAME: client_receive.c */
/* Client for customized handle and output pipe test */
#include <stdio.h>
#include "transfer_data.h"
#include "pipe_state.h"  /* definition of state structure for pipe data❶*/

main(argc, argv)
int argc;
char *argv[];
{
    file_spec   cust_binding_h;             /* customized binding handle */
    pipe_state  state;
    pipe_type   data;                       /* a pipe structure is allocated❷*/
    char        local_target[100];
                /* procedures in other modules */
    void        client_alloc(),out_push();
    void        receive_floats();

    /* get user input */
    if(argc < 4) {
       printf("USAGE: %s  local_target  host  file\n", argv[0]);
       exit(0);
    }
    /* initialize customized binding handle structure */
    strcpy(local_target, argv[1]);
    strcpy(cust_binding_h.host, argv[2]);
    strcpy(cust_binding_h.filename, argv[3]);

    /* initialize pipe structure */
    state.filehandle = -1;
    state.filename = local_target;
    data.state = (rpc_ss_pipe_state_t)&state;  /* initialize pipe state❸*/
    data.alloc = client_alloc; /* initialize alloc procedure for a pipe ❹*/
    data.push = out_push;    /* initialize push procedure for output pipe❺*/

    receive_floats(cust_binding_h, &data); /* procedure with output pipe❻*/
}
```

❶ Example 8-3 defined the `pipe_state` structure. This structure allows your **push** and **alloc** procedures to coordinate activities during the data transfer loop. In this example, the state is a structure of client data file information including the filename and the handle of the open file.

❷ Allocate a pipe structure.

❸ To initialize the pipe state, assign the client-specific state structure to the **state** member of the pipe structure.

❹ To initialize the **alloc** procedure, assign your application procedure, client_alloc, to the **alloc** member of the pipe structure. Then, when the client stub needs a buffer for pipe data, it calls client_alloc. The procedure is the same one used for the input pipe. (See Example 8-5.)

❺ To initialize the **push** procedure, assign your application procedure, out_push, to the **push** member of the pipe structure. Then, when the client stub has output pipe data, it calls out_push. This procedure is shown in Example 8-9.

❻ Call the remote procedure that has the output pipe parameter. The receive_floats procedure copies a server file of floating-point data to the target file on the client.

After the client stub calls your **alloc** procedure to allocate the buffer for a chunk of output pipe data, the stub unmarshalls data into the buffer. The stub then calls your **push** procedure to unload the chunk of data from the buffer to your application. This procedure must perform the following tasks:

- Check the number of data elements transferred. If the number is zero, data transfer is finished.

- Take the chunk of data from the buffer, and process it or store it as required by the application.

Example 8-9 shows the **push** procedure and the arguments you must include for the output pipe of Example 8-8. For each chunk of data the server sends, the client stub calls this procedure, to retrieve the data in a manner appropriate to your application.

Example 8-9: A Client Push Procedure for an Output Pipe

```
/* FILE NAME: out_push.c */
#include <stdio.h>
#include <sys/file.h>
#include "transfer_data.h"
#include "pipe_state.h" /* definition of a state structure for pipe data */
```

Example 8-9: A Client Push Procedure for an Output Pipe (continued)

```
void out_push(state, buf, ecount)  /* output pipe needs push procedure ❶*/
pipe_state      *state;            /* coordinates pipe procedure calls ❷*/
idl_short_float *buf;              /* buffer of data pushed            ❸*/
idl_ulong_int   ecount;            /* number of elements for buffer    ❹*/
{
    /* for this application, open local target file if not open already  */
    if(state->filehandle == -1) {
        if(ecount <= 0)     /* if first buffer is empty, don't do anything */
            return;
        state->filehandle = open(state->filename,
                                 O_CREAT | O_TRUNC | O_WRONLY, 0777);
        if(state->filehandle == -1) {
            fprintf(stderr, "Cannot open file %s for write\n", state->filename);
            exit(0);
        }
    }
    /* To detect end of data, push routine must test the count for 0.    ❺*/
    if(ecount == 0)                     /* do application specific cleanup */
        close(state->filehandle);
    else                                /* process buffer for application  */
        write(state->filehandle, buf, (sizeof(float) * ecount));
    return;
}
```

❶ The required parameters are declared in the pipe structure of the header file, generated by IDL.

❷ The pipe state coordinates calls that the stub makes to your pipe procedures. In this example, the state is used to determine whether the input file is open and to hold the file handle.

❸ The client stub passes in a pointer to the buffer containing a chunk of data.

❹ The client stub passes in the number of data elements in the buffer.

❺ The procedure must test the element count for 0. This indicates that the end of data has been reached. In this example, if the element count is 0, the procedure closes the file; otherwise the data in the buffer is written to the file.

8.3.2 Managing an Output Pipe in the Server

Figure 8-5 shows how the remote procedure processes output pipe data. You initiate data transfer by calling the server stub's **push** routine in a loop. This stub routine marshalls and transmits chunks of pipe data. The loop repeats until a zero-sized chunk of data is sent.

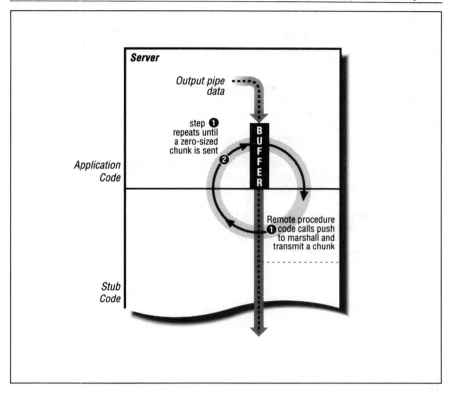

Figure 8-5: Output Pipe Data Transfer from a Server

Example 8-10 shows the steps needed to process an output pipe in a remote procedure. Your remote procedure must call the **push** stub routine in a loop until all data items are sent. Parameters passed to the stub routine include the pipe state (controlled by the stub), the buffer of data, and the number of data elements to send.

Example 8-10: Processing an Output Pipe in a Remote Procedure

```
/* FILE NAME: receive_floats.c */
#include <stdio.h>
#include <sys/file.h>
#include "transfer_data.h"
#define MAX_ELEMENTS  1000

void receive_floats(c_b_h, out_data) /* copy server file data to a client */
file_spec c_b_h;            /* customized binding handle */
pipe_type *out_data;
{
    int           file_h;
    idl_short_float buf[MAX_ELEMENTS];          /* pipe data buffer          */
```

Example 8-10: Processing an Output Pipe in a Remote Procedure (continued)

```
idl_ulong_int    element_count;           /* number of elements pushed */
int              nbytes;

/* open local file on server for read */
file_h = open(c_b_h.filename, O_RDONLY);
nbytes = sizeof(idl_short_float) * MAX_ELEMENTS;

if(file_h > 0) {
   while(true)  {
        /*****          application specific process of buffer      *****❶*/
        element_count = read(file_h, buf, nbytes) / sizeof(idl_short_float);
        if(element_count == 0) break;

        out_data->push(      /* push routine is used for an output pipe ❷*/
            out_data->state,       /* the state is controlled by the stub */
            buf,                   /* the buffer of data to send          */
            element_count          /* the number of data elements to send */
        );
   }
   close(file_h);
}

out_data->push(out_data->state, buf, 0);    /* 0 indicates end of pipe❸*/
return;
}
```

❶ Process the data buffer for the given implementation. In this example, we read a chunk of data from a file.

❷ Call the **push** stub routine to transfer data to the client. The pipe state is an input parameter, and is controlled by the stub. Other input parameters include the buffer of data to send and the number of elements to push.

❸ The last call to the push stub routine for this pipe must have an element count of 0 to indicate the end of the data.

8.4 Managing Multiple Pipes

IDL assumes that the client and server have a stream-like connection between them when they use pipes. This means data for a remote procedure transmits in a specific order, without "handshaking" in between transmission of parameters. This allows the underlying network protocol to transmit data in the most efficient way it can. For example, data for all non-pipe parameters are transmitted first, followed by data for each input pipe parameter. What this means, however, is that when a remote procedure has more than one pipe, each must be completely processed and in a specific order. Suppose the following procedure is declared in an interface definition:

```
void proc([in,out] pipe_type *a, [out] pipe_type *b, [in] pipe_type c);
```

For this example assume **pipe_type** is any valid pipe previously defined in the interface definition. Example 8-11 demonstrates the order in which the pipes must be processed in the remote procedure implementation. Examples 8-7 and 8-10 show the details of processing the individual input and output portion of a pipe.

Example 8-11: Processing Multiple Pipes in a Remote Procedure

```
void proc(a, b, c)
pipe_type *a;        /* in, out pipe */
pipe_type *b;        /* out pipe     */
pipe_type c;         /* in pipe      */
{
    .
    .
    .
    while(true) {/* process first input pipe with its pull stub routine ❶*/
        (a->pull) ( . . . )
        .
        .
    while(true) {/* process next input pipe with its pull stub routine  ❷*/
        (c.pull) ( . . . )
        .
        .
    while(true) {/* process first output pipe with its push stub routine❸*/
        .
        .
        .
        (a->push)( . . . )
        .
        .
    while(true) {/* process next output pipe with its push stub routine ❹*/
        .
        .
        .
        (b->push)( . . . )
        .
        .
    return;      /* return only when all pipes are completely processed ❺*/
}
```

❶ Obtain all data from the first input pipe of the parameter list. The output portion is not processed until all input pipes are processed.

❷ Obtain all data from the rest of the input pipes of the parameter list, one parameter at a time.

❸ Send data for the first output pipe only after all input pipes are complete. All output pipes are processed in the order shown in the parameter list.

❹ Send all data from the rest of the output pipes of the parameter list, one parameter at a time.

❺ The procedure returns only when all pipes have been completely processed.

IDL and ACF Attributes Quick Reference

All IDL attributes are shown in Tables A-1 through A-8, and all ACF attributes are shown in Table A-9, but not all are demonstrated in this book.

Table A-1 IDL Interface Header Attributes

Attribute	Description
uuid(*uuid_string*)	A universal unique identifier is generated by the **uuidgen** utility and assigned to the interface to distinguish it from other interfaces. This attribute is required unless the local attribute is used.
version(*major.minor*)	A particular version of a remote interface is identified when more than one version exists.
pointer_default(*kind*)	The default treatment for pointers is specified. Kinds of pointers include reference (**ref**) and full (**ptr**).
endpoint(*string*)	An endpoint is a number representing the transport-layer address of a server process. Well-known endpoints may be specified on which servers will listen for remote procedure calls. Usually established by the authority responsible for a particular transport protocol.
local	The IDL compiler can be used as a C language header file generator. When this attribute is used, all other interface header attributes are ignored and no stub files are generated by the IDL compiler.

Table A-2 IDL Array Attributes

Attribute	Description
string	An array is specified to have the properties of a string.
Conformant Array Attributes	
size_is(*size*)	A variable is defined in the interface definition and used at runtime to establish the array size.
max_is(*max*)	A variable is defined in the interface definition and used at runtime to establish the maximum index value.
Varying Array Attributes	
first_is(*first*)	A variable is defined in the interface definition and used at runtime to establish the lowest index value of transmitted data. The value is not necessarily the lowest bound of the array.
last_is(*last*)	A variable is defined in the interface definition and used at runtime to establish the highest index value of transmitted data. The value is not necessarily the highest bound of the array.
length_is(*length*)	A variable is defined in the interface definition and used at runtime to establish the number of elements transmitted for a portion of the array.

Table A-3 IDL Pointer Type Attributes

Attribute	Description
ptr	A pointer is specified as a full pointer with the ptr attribute, which gives all the capabilities usually associated with pointers.
ref	A pointer is specified as a reference pointer with the ref attribute. This attribute gives basic indirection without the implementation overhead associated with full pointers.
string	A pointer is specified as pointing to a string.

Table A-4 IDL Data Type Attributes

Attribute	Description
pointer type attributes	A data type with a visible pointer operator may be specified with a pointer type attribute. See Table A-3.
context_handle	A state is maintained on a particular server between remote procedure calls from a specific client by maintaining a context handle as a data type. The context handle identifies the state.
handle	A defined data type is specified as a customized handle so that the client-server binding information is associated with it.
transmit_as(*type***)**	A data type that is manipulated by clients and servers may be specified so that it is converted to a different data type for transmission over the network.

Table A-5 IDL Structure Member Attributes

Attribute	Description
array attributes	A structure member can have array attributes if it has array dimensions or a visible pointer operator. (A structure member that has a visible pointer operator and the **size_is** or **max_is** attribute defines a pointer to a conformant array, not an array structure member.) See Table A-2.
pointer type attributes	A structure member can have a pointer type attribute if it has a visible pointer operator. See Table A-3.
ignore	A structure member that is a pointer is specified as not to be transmitted in a remote procedure call. This can save the overhead of copying and transmitting data to which the pointer refers.

Table A-6 IDL Union Case Attributes

Attribute	Description
pointer type attributes	A union case can have a pointer type attribute if it has a visible pointer operator. See Table A-3.

Table A-7 IDL Procedure Parameter Attributes

Attribute	Description
in	The parameter is input when the remote procedure is called.
out	The parameter is output when the remote procedure returns.
array attributes	A parameter with array dimensions can have array attributes. An alternative way to define a conformant array is a procedure parameter with a visible pointer operator and the **size_is** or **max_is** attribute. See Table A-2.
pointer type attributes	A parameter with a visible pointer operator can have a pointer type attribute. See Table A-3.
context_handle	A parameter that is a void * type can have the context handle attribute.

Table A-8 IDL Procedure Attributes

Attribute	Description
Procedure Result Attributes	
string	A procedure result is specified to have the properties of a string with the **string** attribute.
ptr	A procedure that returns a pointer result always returns a full pointer. It may be specified with the **ptr** attribute but this is not necessary. Full pointers give all the capabilities normally associated with pointers.
context_handle	A procedure returns a context handle result in order to indicate a state on a particular server, which is then referred to in successive remote procedure calls from a specific client.
Procedure Execution Attributes	
idempotent	An idempotent procedure, when invoked multiple times, does not cause any state to change in the called procedure.
broadcast	A procedure can be broadcast to all hosts on the network. The client receives output from the first reply to return successfully.
maybe	A procedure is specified with the **maybe** attribute if it does not need to execute every time it is invoked, or if it does not require a response.

Most of the ACF attributes affect only the client side of an application but **in_line**, **out_of_line**, and **represent_as** also affect the server side. The **heap** and **enable_allocate** attributes affect only the server side.

Table A-9 ACF Attributes

Attribute	Description
	Binding Methods
auto_handle	The automatic binding method is selected.
implicit_handle(*type name***)**	The implicit binding method is selected.
explicit_handle	The explicit binding method is selected.
	Exceptions as Parameters
comm_status	Names a parameter or the procedure result to which a status code is written if a communication error is reported by the client runtime to the client stub. If an error is reported and this attribute is not used, the client stub raises an exception.
fault_status	Names a parameter or the procedure result to which a status code is written if: an error is reported by the server runtime to the server stub; an exception occurs in the server stub; or an exception occurs in the remote procedure. If an error is reported and this attribute is not used, the client stub raises an exception.
	Excluding Unused Procedures
code	All or selected procedures from the interface have the associated client stub code generated by the IDL compiler.
nocode	All or selected procedures from the interface do not have the associated client stub code generated by the IDL compiler.
	Controlling Marshalling
in_line	The code for marshalling and unmarshalling data is in the flow of stub code rather than in generated routines.
out_of_line	The code for marshalling and unmarshalling data is in routines in auxiliary files generated by the IDL compiler.

Table A-9 ACF Attributes (continued)

Attribute	Description
	Other ACF Attributes
represent_as(*type***)**	Data types in an interface definition are represented as local data types from your application code.
enable_allocate	The memory allocation stub support routine **rpc_ss_allocate** is enabled for use in a server. This routine is automatically enabled for remote procedures that use full pointers.
heap	Parameters are specified for allocation in server heap memory. If this attribute is not specified, the parameter may be allocated on the server stub's stack.

B

DCE RPC Runtime Routines Quick Reference

The following tables organize the RPC runtime routines so you can determine which ones you need. Table B-1 shows all the routines client applications can use, and Table B-2 shows all the routines server applications can use. All DCE RPC runtime routines are shown in these tables but not all are used in examples in this book.

The following abreviations are used in RPC runtime routine names:

auth	authentication, authorization
com	communication
dce	distributed computing environment
dflt	default
elt	element
ep	endpoint
exp	expiration
fn	function
id	identifier
if	interface
inq	inquire
mbr	member
mgmt	management
ns	name service
protect	protection
protseq	protocol sequence
princ	principle
rpc	remote procedure call
stats	statistics

Table B-1 Client RPC Runtime Routines

Manage Binding Handles	Find Servers from a Name Service
rpc_binding_copy	rpc_ns_binding_import_begin
rpc_binding_free	rpc_ns_binding_import_next
rpc_binding_reset	rpc_ns_binding_import_done
rpc_ep_resolve_binding	rpc_ns_binding_inq_entry_name
rpc_binding_inq_object	rpc_ns_binding_lookup_begin
rpc_binding_set_object	rpc_ns_binding_lookup_next
rpc_binding_inq_auth_info	rpc_ns_binding_select
rpc_binding_set_auth_info	rpc_ns_binding_lookup_done
rpc_binding_vector_free	**Manage Name Service Entries**
rpc_string_binding_compose	rpc_ns_mgmt_entry_create
rpc_binding_from_string_binding	rpc_ns_entry_object_inq_begin
rpc_binding_to_string_binding	rpc_ns_entry_object_inq_next
rpc_string_binding_parse	rpc_ns_entry_object_inq_done
General Utility	rpc_ns_entry_expand_name
dce_error_inq_text	rpc_ns_mgmt_entry_inq_if_ids
rpc_string_free	rpc_ns_mgmt_binding_unexport
Inquire of Protocol Sequences	rpc_ns_mgmt_entry_delete
rpc_network_is_protseq_valid	**Manage Name Service Groups**
rpc_network_inq_protseqs	rpc_ns_group_mbr_add
rpc_protseq_vector_free	rpc_ns_group_mbr_inq_begin
Manage Interface Information	rpc_ns_group_mbr_inq_next
rpc_if_inq_id	rpc_ns_group_mbr_inq_done
rpc_if_register_auth_info	rpc_ns_group_mbr_remove
rpc_if_id_vector_free	rpc_ns_group_delete
Manage the Client	**Manage Name Service Profiles**
rpc_mgmt_inq_com_timeout	rpc_ns_profile_elt_add
rpc_mgmt_set_com_timeout	rpc_ns_profile_elt_inq_begin
rpc_mgmt_inq_dflt_protect_level	rpc_ns_profile_elt_inq_next
rpc_mgmt_set_cancel_timeout	rpc_ns_profile_elt_inq_done
Manage Local or Remote Applications	rpc_ns_profile_elt_remove
rpc_mgmt_is_server_listening	rpc_ns_profile_delete
rpc_mgmt_stop_server_listening	**Manage Name Service Expirations**
rpc_mgmt_inq_if_ids	rpc_ns_mgmt_inq_exp_age
rpc_mgmt_inq_server_princ_name	rpc_ns_mgmt_set_exp_age
rpc_mgmt_inq_stats	rpc_ns_mgmt_handle_set_exp_age
rpc_mgmt_stats_vector_free	**Manage UUIDs**
Manage an Endpoint Map	uuid_create_nil
	uuid_create
rpc_mgmt_ep_elt_inq_begin	uuid_from_string
rpc_mgmt_ep_elt_inq_next	uuid_to_string
rpc_mgmt_ep_unregister	uuid_is_nil
rpc_mgmt_ep_elt_inq_done	uuid_equal
	uuid_compare
	uuid_hash

Table B-2 Server RPC Runtime Routines

Manage Interfaces	Export Servers to a Name Service
rpc_server_register_if rpc_server_inq_if rpc_server_unregister_if rpc_if_inq_id rpc_if_id_vector_free	rpc_ns_binding_export rpc_ns_binding_unexport rpc_ns_binding_inq_entry_name
Create Binding Information	**Manage Name Service Expirations**
rpc_server_use_protseq rpc_server_use_all_protseqs rpc_server_use_protseq_ep rpc_server_use_protseq_if rpc_server_use_all_protseqs_if rpc_network_is_protseq_valid rpc_network_inq_protseqs rpc_protseq_vector_free	rpc_ns_mgmt_inq_exp_age rpc_ns_mgmt_set_exp_age rpc_ns_mgmt_handle_set_exp_age
	Manage Name Service Entries
Manage Binding Handles	rpc_ns_mgmt_entry_create rpc_ns_entry_object_inq_begin rpc_ns_entry_object_inq_next rpc_ns_entry_object_inq_done rpc_ns_entry_expand_name rpc_ns_mgmt_entry_inq_if_ids rpc_ns_mgmt_binding_unexport rpc_ns_mgmt_entry_delete
rpc_server_inq_bindings rpc_binding_to_string_binding rpc_string_binding_parse rpc_string_binding_compose rpc_binding_copy rpc_binding_free rpc_binding_inq_object rpc_binding_server_from_client rpc_binding_vector_free	
	Manage Name Service Groups
Listen for RPCs	rpc_ns_group_mbr_add rpc_ns_group_mbr_inq_begin rpc_ns_group_mbr_inq_next rpc_ns_group_mbr_inq_done rpc_ns_group_mbr_remove rpc_ns_group_delete
rpc_server_listen	
General Utility	**Manage Name Service Profiles**
dce_error_inq_text rpc_string_free	rpc_ns_profile_elt_add rpc_ns_profile_elt_inq_begin rpc_ns_profile_elt_inq_next rpc_ns_profile_elt_inq_done rpc_ns_profile_elt_remove rpc_ns_profile_delete
Manage Endpoints	
rpc_ep_register rpc_ep_register_no_replace rpc_ep_resolve_binding rpc_ep_unregister	**Manage Local or Remote Applications**
	rpc_mgmt_is_server_listening rpc_mgmt_stop_server_listening rpc_mgmt_inq_if_ids rpc_mgmt_inq_server_princ_name rpc_mgmt_inq_stats rpc_mgmt_stats_vector_free
Manage Object Types	
rpc_object_set_type rpc_object_set_inq_fn rpc_object_inq_type	
	Manage Authentication
Manage an Endpoint Map	rpc_server_register_auth_info rpc_binding_inq_auth_client
rpc_mgmt_ep_elt_inq_begin rpc_mgmt_ep_elt_inq_next rpc_mgmt_ep_unregister rpc_mgmt_ep_elt_inq_done	**Manage UUIDs**
	uuid_create_nil uuid_create uuid_from_string uuid_to_string uuid_is_nil uuid_equal uuid_compare uuid_hash
Manage the Server	
rpc_mgmt_set_authorization_level rpc_mgmt_inq_dflt_protect_level rpc_mgmt_set_server_stack_size	

C

The Arithmetic Application

The arithmetic application makes a remote procedure call to a procedure named **sum_arrays**, which adds together the values for the same array index in two long integer arrays, and returns the sums in another long integer array.

The application demonstrates the basics of a distributed application with a remote procedure call and includes these features:

- Defining a simple array in an interface definition.

- Using the automatic binding method.

- Exporting a server to the name service.

- Checking the error status of RPC runtime calls.

How to Run the Application

To run the nondistributed local test of the application, type the following:

```
C> make local
C> local_client
```

To run the server of the distributed application, set the application-specific environment variable ARITHMETIC_SERVER_ENTRY to the server entry name **/.:/arithmetic_*serverhost***, where *serverhost* is the name of your server system. Type the following:

```
S> make server
S> setenv ARITHMETIC_SERVER_ENTRY /.:/arithmetic_serverhost
S> server
```

To run the client of the distributed application, set the RPC environment variable RPC_DEFAULT_ENTRY to the server entry name **/.:/arithme-tic_serverhost**. The **serverhost** is the server host name, not the client host name. Type the following:

```
▷ make client
▷ setenv RPC_DEFAULT_ENTRY /.:/arithmetic_serverhost
▷ client
```

Application Files

Makefile contains descriptions of how the application is compiled. Use the compilation **make all** to create all the executable files for the application. See Example C-1.

client.sh is a shell script to set the environment and execute the client. See Example C-2.

server.sh is a shell script to set the environment and execute the server. See Example C-3.

arithmetic.idl contains the description of the constants, data types, and procedures for the interface. See Example C-4.

client.c initializes two arrays, calls the remote procedure **sum_arrays**, and displays the results of the returned array. See Example C-5.

procedure.c is the remote procedure implementation. See Example C-6.

server.c initializes the server with a series of RPC runtime calls. See Example C-7.

check_status.h defines the CHECK_STATUS macro which interprets error status codes that may return from RPC runtime calls. See Example C-8.

Example C-1: The Makefile for the Arithmetic Application

```
# FILE NAME: Makefile
# Makefile for the arithmetic application
#
# definitions for this make file
#
APPL=arithmetic
IDLCMD=idl -v
DCELIBS=-ldce -lcma          #OSF/1: DCE Libraries
LIBS=$(DCELIBS) -li -ldnet   #MIPS ULTRIX: DCE, internationalization & DECnet
CFLAGS=
CC=cc
```

Example C-1: The Makefile for the Arithmetic Application (continued)

```
#
# COMPLETE BUILD of the application
#
all:    local interface client server


#
# LOCAL BUILD of the client application to test locally
#
local:interface client.c procedure.c
        $(CC)   -DLOCAL -o local_client client.c procedure.c
# remove object files so they do not interfere with a real build
        rm client.o procedure.o


#
# INTERFACE BUILD
#
interface:   $(APPL).h $(APPL)_cstub.o $(APPL)_sstub.o
$(APPL).h $(APPL)_cstub.o $(APPL)_sstub.o: $(APPL).idl
        $(IDLCMD) $(APPL).idl


#
# CLIENT BUILD
#
client:     $(APPL).h client.o $(APPL)_cstub.o
        $(CC) $(CFLAGS) -o client client.o $(APPL)_cstub.o $(LIBS)


#
# SERVER BUILD
#
server:     $(APPL).h server.o procedure.o $(APPL)_sstub.o
        $(CC) $(CFLAGS) -o server server.o procedure.o $(APPL)_sstub.o $(LIBS)
```

Example C-2: The Client Shell Script for the Arithmetic Application

```
# FILE NAME: client.sh
setenv RPC_DEFAULT_ENTRY /.:/arithmetic_serverhost
client
```

Example C-3: The Server Shell Script for the Arithmetic Application

```
# FILE NAME: server.sh
setenv ARITHMETIC_SERVER_ENTRY /.:/arithmetic_serverhost
server
```

Example C-4: The IDL File of the Arithmetic Application

```
/* FILE NAME: arithmetic.idl */
/* This Interface Definition Language file represents a basic arithmetic    */
/* procedure that a remote procedure call application can use.              */
[
uuid(C985A380-255B-11C9-A50B-08002B0ECEF1)            /* Universal Unique ID */
]
interface arithmetic                          /* interface name is arithmetic  */
{
   const unsigned short ARRAY_SIZE = 10;/* an unsigned integer constant    */
   typedef long long_array[ARRAY_SIZE]; /* an array type of long integers  */

   void sum_arrays ( /* The sum_arrays procedure does not return a value    */
      [in] long_array a,                     /* 1st parameter is passed in  */
      [in] long_array b,                     /* 2nd parameter is passed in  */
      [out] long_array c                     /* 3rd parameter is passed out */
   );
}
```

Example C-5: The Client File of the Arithmetic Application

```
/* FILE NAME: client.c */
/* This is the client module of the arithmetic example. */
#include <stdio.h>
#include "arithmetic.h"    /* header file created by IDL compiler   */

long_array a ={100,200,345,23,67,65,0,0,0,0};
long_array b ={4,0,2,3,1,7,5,9,6,8};

main ()
{
   long_array    result;
   int i;

   sum_arrays(a, b, result);          /* A Remote Procedure Call   */
   puts("sums:");
   for(i = 0; i < ARRAY_SIZE; i++)
      printf("%ld\n", result[i]);
}
```

Example C-6: Remote Procedure of the Arithmetic Application

```
/* FILE NAME: procedure.c */
/* An implementation of the procedure defined in the arithmetic interface. */
#include <stdio.h>
#include "arithmetic.h"              /* header file produced by IDL compiler   */

void sum_arrays(a, b, c)     /* implementation of the sum_arrays procedure   */
    long_array a;
    long_array b;
    long_array c;
    {
        int i;

        for(i = 0; i < ARRAY_SIZE; i++)
            c[i] = a[i] + b[i];    /* array elements are each added together   */
    }
```

Example C-7: Server Initialization of the Arithmetic Application

```
/* FILE NAME: server.c */
#include <stdio.h>
#include "arithmetic.h"              /* header created by the idl compiler */
#include "check_status.h"            /* header with the CHECK_STATUS macro */

main ()
{
    unsigned32           status;                    /* error status (nbase.h) */
    rpc_binding_vector_t *binding_vector; /*set of binding handles(rpcbase.h)*/
    unsigned_char_t      *entry_name; /*entry name for name service (lbase.h)*/
    char *getenv();

    rpc_server_register_if(     /* register interface with the RPC runtime   */
        arithmetic_v0_0_s_ifspec,   /* interface specification (arithmetic.h) */
        NULL,
        NULL,
        &status                                     /* error status */
    );
    CHECK_STATUS(status, "Can't register interface\n", ABORT);

    rpc_server_use_all_protseqs(                 /* create binding information   */
        rpc_c_protseq_max_reqs_default,   /* queue size for calls (rpcbase.h) */
        &status
    );
    CHECK_STATUS(status, "Can't create binding information\n", ABORT);

    rpc_server_inq_bindings(    /* obtain this server's binding information   */
        &binding_vector,
        &status
    );
    CHECK_STATUS(status, "Can't get binding information\n", ABORT);
```

Example C-7: Server Initialization of the Arithmetic Application (continued)

```
        entry_name = (unsigned_char_t *)getenv("ARITHMETIC_SERVER_ENTRY");
        rpc_ns_binding_export(          /* export entry to name service database   */
            rpc_c_ns_syntax_default,    /* syntax of the entry name   (rpcbase.h) */
            entry_name,                 /* entry name for name service            */
            arithmetic_v0_0_s_ifspec,   /* interface specification (arithmetic.h)*/
            binding_vector,             /* the set of server binding handles      */
            NULL,
            &status
        );
        CHECK_STATUS(status, "Can't export to name service database\n", ABORT);


        rpc_ep_register(            /* register endpoints in local endpoint map   */
            arithmetic_v0_0_s_ifspec,   /* interface specification (arithmetic.h) */
            binding_vector,             /* the set of server binding handles      */
            NULL,
            NULL,
            &status
        );
        CHECK_STATUS(status, "Can't add address to the endpoint map\n", ABORT);


        rpc_binding_vector_free(        /* free set of server binding handles     */
            &binding_vector,
            &status
        );
        CHECK_STATUS(status, "Can't free binding handles and vector\n", ABORT);


        puts("Listening for remote procedure calls...");
        rpc_server_listen(                              /* listen for remote calls    */
            rpc_c_listen_max_calls_default, /*concurrent calls to server (rpcbase.h)*/
            &status
        );
        CHECK_STATUS(status, "rpc listen failed\n", ABORT);
}
```

Example C-8: The Check Error Status Macro

```
/* FILE NAME: check_status.h */
#include <stdio.h>
#include <dce/dce_error.h> /* required to call dce_error_inq_text routine   */
#include <dce/pthread.h>   /* needed if application uses threads            */
#include <dce/rpcexc.h>    /* needed if application uses exception handlers */

#define RESUME 0
#define ABORT  1
```

Example C-8: The Check Error Status Macro (continued)

```
#define CHECK_STATUS(input_status, comment, action) \
{ \
   if(input_status != rpc_s_ok) { \
      dce_error_inq_text(input_status, error_string, &error_stat); \
      fprintf(stderr, "%s %s\n", comment, error_string); \
      if(action == ABORT) \
         exit(1); \
   } \
}

static int            error_stat;
static unsigned char  error_string[dce_c_error_string_len];

void exit();
```

D

The Inventory Application

The inventory application allows a user to inquire about, and order from, a simple inventory. Data structures are defined for the following items:

— Part number (to identify a part)

— Part name

— Part description

— Part price

— Quantity of part

— Part list

— Account number (to identify a user)

Procedures are also defined in the interface definition to do the following:

— Confirm if a part is available.

— Obtain a part name.

— Obtain a part description.

— Obtain a part price.

— Obtain the quantity of parts available.

— Obtain a list of subpart numbers.

— Order a part.

The application demonstrates many features of DCE application development including:

• Using strings, pointers, structures, a union, and a conformant array.

- Allocating new memory in a remote procedure for data returned to the client using stub support routines. The **get_part_description** and **whatare_subparts** remote procedures demonstrate server allocation of a string and a conformant structure.

- Managing protocol sequences, interpreting binding information, selecting binding information, and using exception handler macros.

- Variations on a client using ACFs and the automatic, implicit, and explicit binding methods.

- Finding a server by importing from a name service database.

How to Run the Application

To run the local test of the client, type the following:

```
C> make local
C> local_i_client.exe
```

To run the server of the distributed application, type the following:

```
S> make server
S> i_server.exe
```

Before you run the client that uses the automatic binding method for the first time, set the RPC environment variable, RPC_DEFAULT_ENTRY, to the name service group name for the inventory application. Type the following:

```
C> make client
C> setenv RPC_DEFAULT_ENTRY /.:/inventory_group
C> i_client.exe
```

To run a nondistributed local test of the implicit client, type the following in the **implicit** subdirectory:

```
C> make local
C> local_implicit_client.exe
```

To run the implicit client of the distributed application, type the following in the **implicit** subdirectory:

```
C> make client
C> implicit_client.exe
```

To run the explicit client of the distributed application, type the following in the **explicit** subdirectory:

```
C> make client
C> explicit_client.exe
```

Application Files

Makefile contains descriptions of how the application is compiled. Some files depend on the header file **check_status.h** from the arithmetic application for the CHECK_STATUS macro. See Example D-1.

i_client.sh is a shell script to set the environment and execute the client that uses automatic binding management. See Example D-2.

inventory.idl contains the description of the constants, data types, and procedures for the interface. See Example D-3.

i_procedures.c is the implementation of all the remote procedures defined in this interface. See Example D-4.

implement_inventory.c is the implementation of the inventory database. For simplicity, only three inventory items are included. The part numbers for these are printed when the inventory is opened. See Example D-5.

i_server.c initializes the server with a series of runtime calls prior to servicing remote procedure calls. In addition to the required calls, this server also selects a specific protocol sequence, uses exception handling macros, and does some basic cleanup when the server quits. See Example D-6.

i_client.c displays the instructions for the user and processes user input in a loop until exit is selected. Each remote procedure is exercised depending on the input from the user. See Example D-7.

implicit/implicit_client.c imports a binding handle from the name service database. See Example D-8.

explicit/explicit_client.c imports a binding handle from the name service database. All procedures have a binding handle as the first parameter. See Example D-9.

implicit/Makefile contains descriptions of how the implicit client is compiled. Some files depend on the header file **check_status.h** from the arithmetic application for the CHECK_STATUS macro.

The server for the implicit client is the same as the one for the automatic client. See Example D-10 for the Makefile.

implicit/inventory.acf customizes how you use an interface. In this application it is used to select the implicit binding method. See Example D-11.

implicit/do_import_binding.c contains the **do_import_binding** procedure, that shows how to import a binding handle from the name service database. See Example D-12.

implicit/do_interpret_binding.c contains the **do_interpret_binding** procedure, that shows how to obtain the binding information to which a binding handle refers. See Example D-13.

explicit/Makefile contains descriptions of how the explicit client is compiled. Some files depend on the header file **check_status.h** from the arithmetic application for the CHECK_STATUS macro. The compilation depends on some files from the implicit client development.

The server for the explicit client is the same as the one for the automatic and implicit clients. See Example D-14. for the Makefile.

explicit/inventory.acf customizes how you use an interface. In this application it is used to select the explicit binding method for all remote procedures in the interface. See Example D-15.

Example D-1: The Makefile for the Inventory Application

```
# FILE NAME: Makefile
# Makefile for the inventory application
#
# definitions for this make file
#
APPL=inventory
IDLCMD=idl -v
CHECK=../arithmetic      # directory containing check_status.h
LIBDCE=-ldce -lcma       #OSF\1: DCE libraries
LIBS=$(LIBDCE) -li -ldnet #MIPS ULTRIX: DCE, internationalization, DECnet

CFLAGS=
CC= cc


#
# COMPLETE BUILD of the application.
#
all:   local interface client server


#
# LOCAL BUILD of the application to test locally.
#
local: interface i_client.c i_procedures.c implement_inventory.c
        $(CC) $(CFLAGS) -DLOCAL -o local_i_client.exe i_client.c \
             i_procedures.c implement_inventory.c
#remove the object files so they do not interfere with a real build
        rm i_client.o i_procedures.o implement_inventory.o


#
# INTERFACE BUILD
#
interface:  $(APPL).h $(APPL)_cstub.o $(APPL)_sstub.o
$(APPL).h $(APPL)_cstub.o $(APPL)_sstub.o: $(APPL).idl
        $(IDLCMD) $(APPL).idl
```

Example D-1: The Makefile for the Inventory Application (continued)

```
#
# CLIENT BUILD
#
client:     i_client
i_client:   i_client.o $(APPL)_cstub.o
        $(CC) $(CFLAGS) -o i_client.exe i_client.o $(APPL)_cstub.o $(LIBS)


#
# SERVER BUILD
#
server:     i_server
i_server:   $(APPL).h i_server.o i_procedures.o implement_inventory.o \
    $(APPL)_sstub.o
        $(CC) $(CFLAGS) -I$(CHECK) -o i_server.exe i_server.o i_procedures.o \
            implement_inventory.o \
            $(APPL)_sstub.o $(LIBS)
i_server.o: i_server.c
        $(CC) $(CFLAGS) -I$(CHECK) -c i_server.c
```

Example D-2: The Client Shell Script for the Inventory Application

```
# FILE NAME: i_client.sh
setenv RPC_DEFAULT_ENTRY /.:/inventory_group
i_client.exe
```

Example D-3: The IDL File of the Inventory Application

```
/* FILE NAME: inventory.idl */
[                                       /* brackets enclose attributes  */
uuid(008B3C84-93A5-11C9-85B0-08002B147A61), /* universal unique identifier */
version(1.0),                           /* version of this interface   */
pointer_default(ptr)                    /* pointer default             */
] interface  inventory                  /* interface name              */
{
    const long MAX_STRING = 30;             /* constant for string size   */

    typedef long      part_num;             /* inventory part number      */

    typedef [string] char part_name[MAX_STRING+1];    /* name of part    */

    typedef [string, ptr] char *paragraph;      /* description of part    */

    typedef enum {
        ITEM, GRAM, KILOGRAM
    } part_units;                               /* units of measurement   */
```

Example D-3: The IDL File of the Inventory Application (continued)

```
typedef struct part_price {                              /* price of part   */
   part_units units;
   double      per_unit;
} part_price;

typedef union switch(part_units units) total {      /* quantity of part   */
   case ITEM:     long int number;
   case GRAM:
   case KILOGRAM: double   weight;
} part_quantity;

typedef struct part_list{                            /* list of part numbers   */
   long                    size;                     /* number of parts in array */
   [size_is(size)] part_num numbers[*];              /* conformant array of parts */
} part_list;

typedef struct part_record {                         /* data for each part */
   part_num       number;
   part_name      name;
   paragraph      description;
   part_price     price;
   part_quantity quantity;
   part_list      subparts;
} part_record;

typedef long account_num;                            /* user account number */

/*********************** Procedure Declarations ***********************/
boolean is_part_available(                /* return true if in inventory    */
   [in] part_num number                   /* input part number */
);

void whatis_part_name(                    /* get part name from inventory    */
   [in]  part_num  number,                /* input part number */
   [out] part_name name                   /* output part name   */
);

paragraph get_part_description(           /* return a pointer to a string    */
   [in]  part_num  number
);

void whatis_part_price(                   /* get part price from inventory    */
   [in]  part_num   number,
   [out] part_price *price
);
```

Example D-3: The IDL File of the Inventory Application (continued)

```
    void whatis_part_quantity(          /* get part quantity from inventory */
        [in]  part_num       number,
        [out] part_quantity *quantity
    );

    void whatare_subparts(              /* get list of subpart numbers    */
        [in]  part_num  number,
        [out] part_list **subparts      /* structure containing the array */
    );

    /* Order part from inventory with part number, quantity desired, and  */
    /* account number.  If inventory does not have enough, output lesser  */
    /* quantity ordered.  Return values: 1=ordered OK,                    */
    /* -1=invalid part, -2=invalid quantity, -3=invalid account.          */

    long order_part(    /* order part from inventory, return OK or error code */
        [in]      part_num       number,
        [in,out]  part_quantity *quantity,              /* quantity ordered   */
        [in]      account_num    account
    );
} /* end of interface definition */
```

Example D-4: Remote Procedures of the Inventory Application

```
/* FILE NAME: i_procedures.c */
/** Implementation of the remote procedures for the inventory application. **/
#include <stdio.h>
#include "inventory.h"
#ifdef LOCAL
    /* stub support procedures are redefined for a local test of application */
#define rpc_ss_allocate malloc
    /* In a distributed RPC application, rpc_ss_free is called automatically */
    /* by the server stub. In a local test, data is not automatically freed. */
#define rpc_ss_free free
#endif

idl_boolean is_part_available(number)
part_num number;
{
    part_record *part;                  /* a pointer to a part record */
    int found;

    found = read_part_record(number, &part);
    if(found)
        return(idl_true);
    else
        return(idl_false);
}
```

Example D-4: Remote Procedures of the Inventory Application (continued)

```
void whatis_part_name(number, name)
part_num  number;
part_name name;
{
   part_record *part;                       /* a pointer to a part record */
   char * strncpy();

   read_part_record(number, &part);
   strncpy((char *)name, (char *)part->name, MAX_STRING);
   return;
}


paragraph get_part_description(number)
part_num  number;
{
   part_record *part;                       /* a pointer to a part record */
   paragraph description;
   int size;
   char *strcpy();

   if( read_part_record(number, &part) ) {
      /* Allocated data that is returned to the client must be allocated */
      /* with the rpc_ss_allocate stub support routine.                  */
      size = strlen((char *)part->description) + 1;
      description = (paragraph)rpc_ss_allocate((unsigned)size);
      strcpy((char *)description, (char *)part->description);
   }
   else
      description = NULL;
   return(description);
}


void whatis_part_price(number, price)
part_num    number;
part_price  *price;
{
   part_record *part;                       /* a pointer to a part record */

   read_part_record(number, &part);
   price->units = part->price.units;
   price->per_unit = part->price.per_unit;
   return;
}
```

Example D-4: Remote Procedures of the Inventory Application (continued)

```
void whatis_part_quantity(number, quantity)
part_num        number;
part_quantity *quantity;
{
    part_record *part;                     /* a pointer to a part record */

    read_part_record(number, &part);
    quantity->units = part->quantity.units;
    switch(quantity->units) {
        case ITEM: quantity->total.number = part->quantity.total.number;
                break;
        case KILOGRAM:
        case GRAM: quantity->total.weight = part->quantity.total.weight;
                break;
    }
    return;
}


void whatare_subparts(number, subpart_ptr)
part_num   number;
part_list **subpart_ptr;
{
    part_record *part;                      /* pointer to a part record */
    int i;
    int size;

    read_part_record(number, &part);

    /* Allocated data that is output to the client must be allocated with  */
    /* the rpc_ss_allocate stub support routine.  Allocate for a part_list */
    /* struct plus the array of subpart numbers.  Remember the part_list   */
    /* struct already has an array with one element, hence the -1.         */
    size = sizeof(part_list) + (sizeof(part_num) * (part->subparts.size-1));
    *subpart_ptr = (part_list *)rpc_ss_allocate((unsigned)size);

    /* fill in the values */
    (*subpart_ptr)->size = part->subparts.size;
    for(i = 0; i < (*subpart_ptr)->size; i++)
        (*subpart_ptr)->numbers[i] = part->subparts.numbers[i];
    return;
}


idl_long_int order_part(number, quantity, account)
part_num        number;
part_quantity *quantity;
account_num    account;
{
    part_record *part;              /* pointer to a part record */
```

Example D-4: Remote Procedures of the Inventory Application (continued)

```
long error = 1;   /* assume no error to start */
/* Test for valid input */
if( !read_part_record(number, &part) ) /* invalid part number input */
    error = -1;
else if(quantity->units == ITEM)        /* invalid quantity input    */
    error = (quantity->total.number <= 0) ? -2 : error;
else if(quantity->units == GRAM || quantity->units == KILOGRAM)
    error = (quantity->total.weight <= 0.0) ? -2 : error;
/* else if()   invalid account, not implemented */
/*     error = -3;                               */
if(error < 0)
    return(error);

/* convert input quantity & units if units are not correct for part */
if(quantity->units != part->quantity.units) {
    if(part->quantity.units == ITEM)      /* convert weight to items   */
        quantity->total.number = (idl_long_int)quantity->total.weight;
    else if(quantity->units == ITEM)      /* convert items to weight   */
        quantity->total.weight = (idl_long_float)quantity->total.number;
    else if(quantity->units == GRAM && part->quantity.units == KILOGRAM)
        quantity->total.weight /= 1000.0; /* convert grams to kilograms */
    else if(quantity->units == KILOGRAM && part->quantity.units == GRAM)
        quantity->total.weight *= 1000.0; /* convert kilograms to grams */
    quantity->units = part->quantity.units;
}

/* check if enough in inventory for this order */
switch(part->quantity.units) {
case ITEM:
    if(part->quantity.total.number > quantity->total.number)
        /* reduce quantity in inventory by amount ordered */
        part->quantity.total.number -= quantity->total.number;
    else {
        /* order all available and reduce quantity in inventory to 0 */
        quantity->total.number = part->quantity.total.number;
        part->quantity.total.number = 0;
    }
    break;
case KILOGRAM:
case GRAM:
    if(part->quantity.total.weight > quantity->total.weight)
        /* reduce quantity in inventory by amount ordered */
        part->quantity.total.weight -= quantity->total.weight;
    else {
        /* order all available and reduce quantity in inventory to 0.0 */
        quantity->total.weight = part->quantity.total.weight;
        part->quantity.total.weight = 0.0;
    }
    break;
}
```

Example D-4: Remote Procedures of the Inventory Application (continued)

```
        write_part_record(part);    /* update inventory */

        return(1); /* order ok */
}
```

Example D-5: The Inventory Implementation

```
/* FILE NAME: implement_inventory.c */
/* A sample implementation of an inventory.                          */
/* For simplicity, a few inventory items are maintained in the inventory.  */
/* The valid numbers are printed when the open_inventory() procedure is    */
/* called so the user knows what numbers to test.                    */
#include <stdio.h>
#include "inventory.h"
#define MAX_PARTS     10      /* maximum number of parts in this inventory */
#define MAX_SUBPARTS 5        /* maximum number of subparts for a part     */

static part_record *rec[MAX_PARTS]; /* array of pointers for this inventory */
static inventory_is_open = 0;       /* flag is reset to non-zero when open  */

/* Data for empty record or unknown part number */
static part_record no_part = {0,"UNKNOWN"};
static part_num    no_subparts[MAX_SUBPARTS];


void open_inventory()  /***** setup inventory ****************************/
{
    int i,j;
    unsigned size;
    char *malloc(), *strcpy(), *strncpy();

    /* Allocate memory for the inventory array.  Each part gets the size of */
    /* a part_record plus enough memory for a subpart list.  Since the      */
    /* subpart list is already defined in the part_record as an array of 1, */
    /* the new array memory only needs to be MAX_SUBPARTS-1 in size.        */
    for(i = 0; i < MAX_PARTS; i++) {
        size = sizeof(part_record) + (sizeof(part_num) * (MAX_SUBPARTS-1));
        rec[i] = (part_record *)malloc(size);
    }
    /* assign some data to the inventory array (part of an exercise machine) */
    rec[0]->number          = 102;
    strncpy((char *)rec[0]->name, "electronics display module", MAX_STRING);
    rec[0]->description = (paragraph)malloc(1000);
    strcpy((char *)rec[0]->description,
        "The electronics display module is a liquid crystal display containing\n\
a timer, counter, metronome, and calorie counter.");
    rec[0]->price.units        = ITEM;
    rec[0]->price.per_unit     = 7.00;
    rec[0]->quantity.units     = rec[0]->price.units;
    rec[0]->quantity.total.number = 432;
```

Example D-5: The Inventory Implementation (continued)

```
rec[0]->subparts.size        = 4;  /* cannot be greater than MAX_SUBPARTS */
for(i = 0; i < rec[0]->subparts.size; i++) /* values used are not relevant */
    rec[0]->subparts.numbers[i] = rec[0]->number + 1 + i;

rec[1]->number               = 203;
strncpy((char *)rec[1]->name, "base assembly", MAX_STRING);
rec[1]->description = (paragraph)malloc(1000);
strcpy((char *)rec[1]->description,
    "The base assembly rests on the floor to stabilize the machine.\n\
The arm and bench assemblies are attached to it.");
rec[1]->price.units          = ITEM;
rec[1]->price.per_unit       = 85.00;
rec[1]->quantity.units       = rec[1]->price.units;
rec[1]->quantity.total.number = 1078;
rec[1]->subparts.size        = 5;  /* cannot be greater than MAX_SUBPARTS */
for(i = 0; i < rec[1]->subparts.size; i++) /* values used are not relevant */
    rec[1]->subparts.numbers[i] = rec[1]->number + 17 + i;

rec[2]->number               = 444;
strncpy((char *)rec[2]->name, "ballast", MAX_STRING);
rec[2]->description = (paragraph)malloc(1000);
strcpy((char *)rec[2]->description,
    "The ballast is used to counter balance the force exerted by the user.");
rec[2]->price.units          = KILOGRAM;
rec[2]->price.per_unit       = 1.59;
rec[2]->quantity.units       = rec[2]->price.units;
rec[2]->quantity.total.weight = 13456.2;
rec[2]->subparts.size        = 0;  /* cannot be greater than MAX_SUBPARTS */
for(i = 0; i < MAX_SUBPARTS; i++)  /* zero out subpart array */
    rec[2]->subparts.numbers[i] = no_subparts[i];

/* fill in rest of inventory as "empty" data */
for(i = 3; i < MAX_PARTS; i++) {
    rec[i] = &no_part;
    for(j = 0; j < MAX_SUBPARTS; j++)
        rec[i]->subparts.numbers[j] = no_subparts[j];
}
puts("Part numbers in inventory:");
for(i = 0; i < MAX_PARTS; i++)
    if(rec[i]->number > 0)
        printf("%ld0, rec[i]->number);
inventory_is_open = 1;
return;
}
```

Example D-5: The Inventory Implementation (continued)

```c
void close_inventory()  /**** close inventory *****************************/
{
    /* Undo whatever is done in open_inventory.  Free memory and so forth.  */
    /* (not implemented) */
    return;
}


int read_part_record(number, part_ptr) /** get record for this part number **/
part_num number;
part_record **part_ptr;
{
    int i;

    if(inventory_is_open == 0)
        open_inventory();
    *part_ptr = &no_part;                   /* initialize assuming no part */
    for(i = 0; i < MAX_PARTS; i++)          /* search the inventory        */
        if(rec[i]->number == number) {      /* found the part              */
            *part_ptr = rec[i];
            break;
        }
    if( (*part_ptr)->number > 0)
        return(1);
    else                                    /* not a valid part            */
        return(0);
}


int write_part_record(part)  /*** update inventory for this part number *****/
part_record *part;
{
    int i;

    if(inventory_is_open == 0)
        open_inventory();
    for(i = 0; i < MAX_PARTS; i++)
        if(rec[i]->number == part->number) {
            rec[i] = part;   /* overwrite inventory with new data */
            return(1);
        }
    return(0);
}

/*<COMMENT> dump the part data to the screen.
static dump_part_record(index)
int index;
{
    printf("number input:%ld  part number:%ld0, number, rec[index]->number);
    printf("part name:%s0, rec[index]->name);
    printf("description:%s0, rec[index]->description);
```

Example D-5: The Inventory Implementation (continued)

```
        printf("price:%f per %s0, rec[index]->price.per_unit,\
            (rec[index]->price.units == ITEM) ? "item" : "gram");
        printf("quantity:");
        switch(rec[index]->quantity.units) {
        case ITEM: printf("%ld items0, rec[index]->quantity.total.number); break;
        case GRAM: printf("%f grams0, rec[index]->quantity.total.weight); break;
        case KILOGRAM: printf("%f kilos0, rec[index]->quantity.total.weight); break;
        }
        printf("subparts: ");
        for(i = 0; i < rec[index]->subparts.size; i++)
            printf("%ld  ", rec[index]->subparts.numbers[i]);
        printf("0);
}<ENDCOMMENT>*/
```

Example D-6: Server Initialization of the Inventory Application

```
/* FILE NAME: i_server.c */
#include <stdio.h>
#include <ctype.h>
#include "inventory.h"          /* header created by the IDL compiler   */
#include "check_status.h"       /* contains the CHECK_STATUS macro       */
#define STRINGLEN 50

main (argc, argv)
int argc;
char *argv[];
{
    unsigned32          status;         /* error status (nbase.h)        */
                                        /* RPC vectors                   */
    rpc_binding_vector_t *binding_vector; /* binding handle list (rpcbase.h) */
    rpc_protseq_vector_t *protseq_vector; /*protocol sequence list(rpcbase.h)*/

    char entry_name[STRINGLEN];         /* name service entry name       */
    char group_name[STRINGLEN];         /* name service group name       */
    char annotation[STRINGLEN];         /* annotation for endpoint map   */
    char hostname[STRINGLEN];
    char *strcpy(), *strcat();
    /*************************** REGISTER INTERFACE ***************************/
    rpc_server_register_if(                                          /*  */
        inventory_v1_0_s_ifspec,    /* interface specification (inventory.h) */
        NULL,
        NULL,
        &status
    );
    CHECK_STATUS(status, "Can't register interface:", ABORT);        /*  */
```

Example D-6: Server Initialization of the Inventory Application (continued)

```
/****************** CREATING SERVER BINDING INFORMATION ******************/
if(argc > 1) {
    rpc_server_use_protseq(                 /* use a protocol sequence      */
        (unsigned_char_t *)argv[1],         /* the input protocol sequence  */
        rpc_c_protseq_max_calls_default,    /* (rpcbase.h)                  */
        &status
    );
    CHECK_STATUS(status, "Can't use this protocol sequence:", ABORT);
}
else {
    puts("You can invoke the server with a protocol sequence argument.");
    rpc_server_use_all_protseqs(            /* use all protocol sequences   */
        rpc_c_protseq_max_calls_default,    /* (rpcbase.h)                  */
        &status
    );
    CHECK_STATUS(status, "Can't register protocol sequences:", ABORT);
}

rpc_server_inq_bindings(      /* get all binding information for server   */
    &binding_vector,
    &status
);
CHECK_STATUS(status, "Can't get binding information:", ABORT);

/************************* ADVERTISE SERVER *************************/

strcpy(entry_name, "/.:/inventory_");
gethostname(hostname, STRINGLEN);
strcat(entry_name, hostname);
rpc_ns_binding_export(              /* export to a name service database    */
    rpc_c_ns_syntax_default,        /* syntax of entry name (rpcbase.h)     */
    (unsigned_char_t *)entry_name,  /* name of entry in name service        */
    inventory_v1_0_s_ifspec,        /* interface specification (inventory.h) */
    binding_vector,                 /* binding information                  */
    NULL,                           /* no object UUIDs exported             */
    &status
);
CHECK_STATUS(status, "Can't export to name service database:", RESUME);

strcpy(group_name, "/.:/inventory_group");
rpc_ns_group_mbr_add(              /* add as member of name service group  */
    rpc_c_ns_syntax_default,        /* syntax of group name (rpcbase.h)     */
    (unsigned_char_t *)group_name,  /* name of group in name service        */
    rpc_c_ns_syntax_default,        /* syntax of member name (rpcbase.h)    */
    (unsigned_char_t *)entry_name,  /* name of member in name service       */
    &status
);
CHECK_STATUS(status, "Can't add member to name service group:", RESUME);
```

Example D-6: Server Initialization of the Inventory Application (continued)

```
/************************* MANAGE ENDPOINTS **************************/
strcpy(annotation, "Inventory interface");
rpc_ep_register(                     /* add endpoints to local endpoint map   */
    inventory_v1_0_s_ifspec,    /* interface specification (inventory.h) */
    binding_vector,              /* vector of server binding handles      */
    NULL,                        /* no object UUIDs to register           */
    (unsigned_char_t *)annotation,  /* annotation supplied (not required) */
    &status
);
CHECK_STATUS(status, "Can't add endpoints to local endpoint map:", RESUME);

rpc_binding_vector_free(                /* free server binding handles   */
    &binding_vector,
    &status
);
CHECK_STATUS(status, "Can't free server binding handles:", RESUME);

open_inventory();                       /* application specific procedure */

/****************** LISTEN FOR REMOTE PROCEDURE CALLS *****************/
TRY                              /* thread exception handling macro   */
    rpc_server_listen(                                          /*  */
        1,                       /* process one remote procedure call at a time */
        &status
    );
    CHECK_STATUS(status, "rpc listen failed:", RESUME);

FINALLY                                  /* error recovery and cleanup */
    close_inventory();                   /* application specific procedure */
    rpc_server_inq_bindings(             /* get binding information    */
        &binding_vector,
        &status
    );
    CHECK_STATUS(status, "Can't get binding information:", RESUME);

    rpc_ep_unregister(       /* remove endpoints from local endpoint map    */
        inventory_v1_0_s_ifspec,  /* interface specification (inventory.h) */
        binding_vector,           /* vector of server binding handles */
        NULL,                     /* no object UUIDs */
        &status
    );
    CHECK_STATUS(status, "Can't remove endpoints from endpoint map:", RESUME);

    rpc_binding_vector_free(                /* free server binding handles   */
        &binding_vector,
        &status
    );
    CHECK_STATUS(status, "Can't free server binding handles:", RESUME);
```

Example D-6: Server Initialization of the Inventory Application (continued)

```
        puts("\nServer quit!");
    ENDTRY
}   /* END SERVER INITIALIZATION */
```

Example D-7: The Automatic Client File of the Inventory Application

```
/* FILE NAME: i_client.c */
/******************** Client of the inventory application ********************/
#include <stdio.h>
#include <stdlib.h>
#include "inventory.h"            /* header file created by the IDL compiler */

char instructions[] = "Type character followed by appropriate argument(s).\n\
    Is part available?          a  [part_number]\n\
    What is part name?          n  [part_number]\n\
    Get part description.       d  [part_number]\n\
    What is part price?         p  [part_number]\n\
    What is part quantity?      q  [part_number]\n\
    What are subparts of this part?  s  [part_number]\n\
    Order part.                 o  part_number  quantity\n\
    REDISPLAY                   r\n\
    EXIT                        e\n";

main()
{
    part_record part;            /* structure for all data about a part  */
    part_list  *subparts;        /* pointer to parts list data structure */
    account_num account = 1234;  /* a user account number                */

    int i, num_args, done = 0;
    long result;
    char input[100], selection[20], quantity[20];
    char *strcpy();

    puts(instructions);
    part.number = 0;
    strcpy(quantity, "");
    while(!done) {               /* user makes selections and each is processed */
        printf("Selection: "); fflush(stdout); gets(input);
        num_args = sscanf(input, "%s%ld%s", selection, &(part.number), quantity);

        switch (tolower(selection[0])) {
        case 'a': if (is_part_available(part.number))
                    puts("available: Yes");
                else
                    puts("available: No");
                break;
        case 'n': whatis_part_name(part.number, part.name);
                printf("name:%s\n", part.name);
                break;
```

Example D-7: The Automatic Client File of the Inventory Application (continued)

```
case 'd': part.description = get_part_description(part.number);
          printf("description:\n%s\n", part.description);
          if(part.description != NULL)
              free(part.description);      /* free memory allocated */
          break;
case 'p': whatis_part_price(part.number, &(part.price));
          printf("price:%10.2f\n", part.price.per_unit);
          break;
case 'q': whatis_part_quantity(part.number, &(part.quantity));
          if(part.quantity.units == ITEM)
              printf("total items:%ld\n", part.quantity.total.number);
          else if(part.quantity.units == GRAM)
              printf("total grams:%10.2f\n", part.quantity.total.weight);
          else if(part.quantity.units == KILOGRAM)
              printf("total kilos:%10.2f\n", part.quantity.total.weight);
          break;
case 's': whatare_subparts(part.number, &subparts);
          for(i = 0; i < subparts->size; i++)
              printf("%ld  ", subparts->numbers[i]);
          printf("\ntotal number of subparts:%ld\n", subparts->size);
          free(subparts);          /* free memory for conformant struct */
          break;
case 'o': if(num_args < 3) {
              puts("Not enough arguments");
              break;
          }
          /* Assume KILOGRAM units and assign quantity input */
          part.quantity.units = KILOGRAM;
          part.quantity.total.weight = atof(quantity);
          result = order_part(part.number, &(part.quantity), account);
          if(result > 0) {
            if(part.quantity.units == ITEM)
              printf("order:%ld items\n", part.quantity.total.number);
            else if(part.quantity.units == GRAM)
              printf("order:%10.2f grams\n", part.quantity.total.weight);
            else if(part.quantity.units == KILOGRAM)
              printf("order:%10.2f kilos\n", part.quantity.total.weight);
          }
          else { /* error cases */
            if(result == -1) puts("Invalid part number");
            else if(result == -2) puts("Invalid quantity");
            else if(result == -3) puts("Invalid account number");
          }
          break;
```

Example D-7: The Automatic Client File of the Inventory Application (continued)

```
        case 'r':    /* redisplay selection or bad input displays instructions */
        default: puts(instructions);  break;
        case 'e': done = 1;  break;
        } /*end case */
    } /* end while */
} /* end main() */
```

Example D-8: The Implicit Client of the Inventory Application

```
/* FILE NAME: implicit_client.c */
/******* Client of the inventory application with implicit method ***********/
#include <stdio.h>
#include <stdlib.h>
#include "inventory.h"            /* header file created by the IDL compiler */

char instructions[] = "Type character followed by appropriate argument(s).\n\
    Is part available?              a  [part_number]\n\
    What is part name?              n  [part_number]\n\
    Get part description.           d  [part_number]\n\
    What is part price?             p  [part_number]\n\
    What is part quantity?          q  [part_number]\n\
    What are subparts of this part? s  [part_number]\n\
    Order part.                     o  part_number  quantity\n\
    REDISPLAY                       r\n\
    EXIT                            e\n";

main()
{
    part_record part;            /* structure for all data about a part  */
    part_list   *subparts;       /* pointer to parts list data structure */
    account_num account = 1234;  /* a user account number                */

    int i, num_args, done = 0;
    long result;
    char input[100], selection[20], quantity[20];
    char *strcpy();

    puts(instructions);
    part.number = 0;
    strcpy(quantity, "");

#ifndef LOCAL                            /* find server in name service database */
    do_import_binding("/.:/inventory_group", &global_binding_h);
#endif

    while(!done) {                /* user makes selections and each is processed */
        printf("Selection: ");  fflush(stdout);  gets(input);
        num_args = sscanf(input, "%s%ld%s", selection, &(part.number), quantity);
```

Example D-8: The Implicit Client of the Inventory Application (continued)

```
switch (tolower(selection[0])) {
case 'a': if (is_part_available(part.number))
              puts("available: Yes");
          else
              puts("available: No");
          break;
case 'n': whatis_part_name(part.number, part.name);
          printf("name:%s\n", part.name);
          break;
case 'd': part.description = get_part_description(part.number);
          printf("description:\n%s\n", part.description);
          if(part.description != NULL)
              free(part.description);       /* free memory allocated */
          break;
case 'p': whatis_part_price(part.number, &(part.price));
          printf("price:%10.2f\n", part.price.per_unit);
          break;
case 'q': whatis_part_quantity(part.number, &(part.quantity));
          if(part.quantity.units == ITEM)
              printf("total items:%ld\n", part.quantity.total.number);
          else if(part.quantity.units == GRAM)
              printf("total grams:%10.2f\n", part.quantity.total.weight);
          else if(part.quantity.units == KILOGRAM)
              printf("total kilos:%10.2f\n", part.quantity.total.weight);
          break;
case 's': whatare_subparts(part.number, &subparts);
          for(i = 0; i < subparts->size; i++)
              printf("%ld  ", subparts->numbers[i]);
          printf("\ntotal number of subparts:%ld\n", subparts->size);
          free(subparts);         /* free memory for conformant struct */
          break;
case 'o': if(num_args < 3) {
              puts("Not enough arguments");
              break;
          }
          /* Assume KILOGRAM units and assign quantity input */
          part.quantity.units = KILOGRAM;
          part.quantity.total.weight = atof(quantity);
          result = order_part(part.number, &(part.quantity), account);
          if(result > 0) {
            if(part.quantity.units == ITEM)
              printf("order:%ld items\n", part.quantity.total.number);
            else if(part.quantity.units == GRAM)
              printf("order:%10.2f grams\n", part.quantity.total.weight);
            else if(part.quantity.units == KILOGRAM)
              printf("order:%10.2f kilos\n", part.quantity.total.weight);
          }
```

Example D-8: The Implicit Client of the Inventory Application (continued)

```
                else { /* error cases */
                    if(result == -1) puts("Invalid part number");
                    else if(result == -2) puts("Invalid quantity");
                    else if(result == -3) puts("Invalid account number");
                }
                break;
        case 'r':   /* redisplay selection or bad input displays instructions */
        default: puts(instructions);  break;
        case 'e': done = 1;  break;
        } /*end case */
    } /* end while */
} /* end main() */
```

Example D-9: The Explicit Client of the Inventory Application

```
/* FILE NAME: explicit_client.c */
/****** Client of the inventory application with explicit method ***********/
#include <stdio.h>
#include <stdlib.h>
#include "inventory.h"          /* header file created by the IDL compiler */

char instructions[] = "Type character followed by appropriate argument(s).\n\
    Is part available?             a  [part_number]\n\
    What is part name?             n  [part_number]\n\
    Get part description.          d  [part_number]\n\
    What is part price?            p  [part_number]\n\
    What is part quantity?         q  [part_number]\n\
    What are subparts of this part? s [part_number]\n\
    Order part.                    o  part_number  quantity\n\
    REDISPLAY                      r\n\
    EXIT                           e\n";

main()
{
    part_record part;           /* structure for all data about a part  */
    part_list   *subparts;      /* pointer to parts list data structure */
    account_num account = 1234; /* a user account number                */

    handle_t    binding_h;      /* declare a binding handle */

    int i, num_args, done = 0;
    long result;
    char input[100], selection[20], quantity[20];
    char *strcpy();

    puts(instructions);
    part.number = 0;
    strcpy(quantity, "");
```

Example D-9: The Explicit Client of the Inventory Application (continued)

```
#ifndef LOCAL                        /* find server in name service database */
    do_import_binding("/.:/inventory_group", &binding_h);
#endif

    while(!done) {                    /* user makes selections and each is processed */
        printf("Selection: ");  fflush(stdout);  gets(input);
        num_args = sscanf(input, "%s%ld%s", selection, &(part.number), quantity);

        switch (tolower(selection[0])) {
        case 'a': if (is_part_available(binding_h, part.number))
                      puts("available: Yes");
                  else
                      puts("available: No");
                  break;
        case 'n': whatis_part_name(binding_h, part.number, part.name);
                  printf("name:%s\n", part.name);
                  break;
        case 'd': part.description =
                      get_part_description(binding_h, part.number);
                  printf("description:\n%s\n", part.description);
                  if(part.description != NULL)
                      free(part.description);      /* free memory allocated */
                  break;
        case 'p': whatis_part_price(binding_h, part.number, &(part.price));
                  printf("price:%10.2f\n", part.price.per_unit);
                  break;
        case 'q': whatis_part_quantity(binding_h, part.number, &(part.quantity));
                  if(part.quantity.units == ITEM)
                      printf("total items:%ld\n", part.quantity.total.number);
                  else if(part.quantity.units == GRAM)
                      printf("total grams:%10.2f\n", part.quantity.total.weight);
                  else if(part.quantity.units == KILOGRAM)
                      printf("total kilos:%10.2f\n", part.quantity.total.weight);
                  break;
        case 's': whatare_subparts(binding_h, part.number, &subparts);
                  for(i = 0; i < subparts->size; i++)
                      printf("%ld ", subparts->numbers[i]);
                  printf("\ntotal number of subparts:%ld\n", subparts->size);
                  free(subparts);         /* free memory for conformant struct */
                  break;
        case 'o': if(num_args < 3) {
                      puts("Not enough arguments");
                      break;
                  }
                  /* Assume KILOGRAM units and assign quantity input */
                  part.quantity.units = KILOGRAM;
                  part.quantity.total.weight = atof(quantity);
                  result =
                      order_part(binding_h, part.number, &(part.quantity), account);
```

Example D-9: The Explicit Client of the Inventory Application (continued)

```
                if(result > 0) {
                  if(part.quantity.units == ITEM)
                    printf("order:%ld items\n", part.quantity.total.number);
                  else if(part.quantity.units == GRAM)
                    printf("order:%10.2f grams\n", part.quantity.total.weight);
                  else if(part.quantity.units == KILOGRAM)
                    printf("order:%10.2f kilos\n", part.quantity.total.weight);
                }
                else { /* error cases */
                    if(result == -1) puts("Invalid part number");
                    else if(result == -2) puts("Invalid quantity");
                    else if(result == -3) puts("Invalid account number");
                }
                break;
      case 'r':   /* redisplay selection or bad input displays instructions */
      default: puts(instructions);  break;
      case 'e': done = 1;  break;
      } /*end case */
   } /* end while */
} /* end main() */
```

Example D-10: The Makefile for the Implicit Client

```
# FILE NAME: Makefile
# Makefile for the inventory client that uses an ACF and implicit binding
#
# definitions for this make file
#
APPL=inventory
IDLCMD=idl -v
LIBDCE=-ldce -lcma        #OSF/1: DCE libraries
LIBS=$(LIBDCE) -li -ldnet #MIPS ULTRIX: DCE, internationalization & DECnet
CHECK=../../arithmetic    # directory containing check_status.h
CFLAGS=
CC= cc


#
# COMPLETE BUILD of this application.
#
all:  local interface client server


#
# LOCAL BUILD of the implicit client to test locally.
#
local:interface implicit_client.c ../i_procedures.c ../implement_inventory.c
        $(CC) $(CFLAGS) -I../ -I$(CHECK) -DLOCAL -o local_implicit_client.exe \
                implicit_client.c ../i_procedures.c ../implement_inventory.c
#remove object files so they do not interfere with the distributed build
        rm implicit_client.o i_procedures.o implement_inventory.o
```

Example D-10: The Makefile for the Implicit Client (continued)

```
#
# INTERFACE BUILD that uses an ACF for implicit binding.
# Notice this builds only the client stub and the header files.
#
interface:  $(APPL).acf $(APPL).h $(APPL)_cstub.o
$(APPL).h $(APPL)_cstub.o:    ../$(APPL).idl $(APPL).acf
        $(IDLCMD) -I../ -server none ../$(APPL).idl


#
# CLIENT BUILD
#
client:     implicit_client
implicit_client:   interface implicit_client.o \
   do_import_binding.o do_interpret_binding.o
        $(CC) $(CFLAGS) -I../ -o implicit_client.exe implicit_client.o \
             do_import_binding.o do_interpret_binding.o \
                $(APPL)_cstub.o $(LIBS)

do_import_binding.o:    do_import_binding.c
        $(CC) $(CFLAGS) -I../ -I$(CHECK) -c do_import_binding.c

do_interpret_binding.o: do_interpret_binding.c
        $(CC) $(CFLAGS) -I../ -I$(CHECK) -c do_interpret_binding.c


#
# SERVER BUILD
#
server:
        @echo make server in directory ../


#
# files needed from other directories
#
i_procedures.o:   ../i_procedures.c
        $(CC) $(CFLAGS) -I../ -c ../i_procedures.c

implement_inventory.o:   ../implement_inventory.c
        $(CC) $(CFLAGS) -I../ -c ../implement_inventory.c
```

Example D-11: An ACF File for Implicit Binding

```
/* FILE NAME: inventory.acf (implicit version)*/
/* This Attribute Configuration File is used in conjunction with the    */
/* associated IDL file (inventory.idl) when the IDL compiler is invoked. */
[
implicit_handle(handle_t global_binding_h)  /* implicit binding method   */
]
interface  inventory    /* The interface name must match the idl file.   */
{
}
```

Example D-12: The do_import_binding Procedure

```
/* FILE NAME: do_import_binding.c */
/* Get binding from name service database. */
#include <stdio.h>
#include "inventory.h"
#include "check_status.h"

void do_import_binding(entry_name, binding_h)
char                  entry_name[];       /* entry name to begin search   */
rpc_binding_handle_t  *binding_h;         /* a binding handle (rpcbase.h)  */
{
    unsigned32        status;             /* error status (nbase.h)        */
    rpc_ns_handle_t   import_context;     /* required to import (rpcbase.h) */
    char              protseq[20];        /* protocol sequence             */

    rpc_ns_binding_import_begin(  /* set context to import binding handles */
        rpc_c_ns_syntax_default,        /* use default syntax              */
        (unsigned_char_t *)entry_name, /* begin search with this name      */
        inventory_v1_0_c_ifspec,        /* interface specification (inventory.h) */
        NULL,                           /* no optional object UUID required */
        &import_context,                /* import context obtained         */
        &status
    );
    CHECK_STATUS(status, "Can't begin import:", RESUME);

    while(1) {
        rpc_ns_binding_import_next(               /* import a binding handle */
            import_context,       /* context from rpc_ns_binding_import_begin */
            binding_h,            /* a binding handle is obtained            */
            &status
        );
        if(status != rpc_s_ok) {
            CHECK_STATUS(status, "Can't import a binding handle:", RESUME);
            break;
        }
```

Example D-12: The do_import_binding Procedure (continued)

```
    /** application-specific selection criteria (by protocol sequence) *  */
    do_interpret_binding(*binding_h ,protseq);
    if(strcmp(protseq, "ncacn_ip_tcp") == 0)  /*select connection protocol*/
        break;
    else {
       rpc_binding_free(         /* free binding information not selected   */
          binding_h,
          &status
       );
       CHECK_STATUS(status, "Can't free binding information:", RESUME);
    }
} /*end while */

rpc_ns_binding_import_done(               /* done with import context   */
   &import_context,         /* obtained from rpc_ns_binding_import_begin */
   &status
);
return;
}
```

Example D-13: The do_interpret_binding Procedure

```
/* FILE NAME: do_interpret_binding.c */
/* Interpret binding information and return the protocol sequence. */
#include <stdio.h>
#include <dce/rpc.h>
#include "check_status.h"

void do_interpret_binding(binding, protocol_seq)
rpc_binding_handle_t binding;    /* binding handle to interpret (rpcbase.h) */
char                 *protocol_seq;  /* protocol sequence to obtain        */
{
   unsigned32     status;          /* error status                        */
   unsigned_char_t *string_binding; /* string of binding info. (lbase.h)  */
   unsigned_char_t *protseq;        /* binding component of interest       */

   rpc_binding_to_string_binding(/* convert binding information to string  */
      binding,                       /* the binding handle to convert */
      &string_binding,               /* the string of binding data   */
      &status
   );
   CHECK_STATUS(status, "Can't get string binding:", RESUME);
```

Example D-13: The do_interpret_binding Procedure (continued)

```
    rpc_string_binding_parse(           /* get components of string binding   */
        string_binding,        /* the string of binding data              */
        NULL,                  /* an object UUID string is not obtained    */
        &protseq,              /* a protocol sequence string IS obtained   */
        NULL,                  /* a network address string is not obtained */
        NULL,                  /* an endpoint string is not obtained       */
        NULL,                  /* a network options string is not obtained */
        &status
    );
    CHECK_STATUS(status, "Can't parse string binding:", RESUME);

    strcpy(protocol_seq, (char *)protseq);

    /* free all strings allocated by other runtime routines               */
    rpc_string_free(&string_binding,  &status);
    rpc_string_free(&protseq,         &status);
    return;
}
```

Example D-14: The Makefile for the Explicit Client

```
# FILE NAME: Makefile
# Makefile for the inventory client that uses an ACF and explicit binding
#
# definitions for this make file
#
APPL=inventory
IDLCMD=idl -v
LIBDCE=-ldce -lcma      #OSF/1: DCE libraries
LIBS=$(LIBDCE) -li -ldnet #MIPS ULTRIX: DCE, internationalization, DECnet
CHECK=../../arithmetic  # directory containing check_status.h
CFLAGS=
CC= cc


#
# COMPLETE BUILD of this application.
#
all:  interface client server


#
# LOCAL BUILD
# No local build is developed for the explicit client because the remote
# procedure implementations for the server have been developed without
# explicit binding.  In order to test this client locally, the remote
# procedure implementations need to have a binding handle as the first
# parameter.
#
```

Example D-14: The Makefile for the Explicit Client (continued)

```
#
# INTERFACE BUILD that uses an ACF for explicit binding.
# Notice this builds only the client stub and the header files.
#
interface:   $(APPL).acf $(APPL).h $(APPL)_cstub.o
$(APPL).h $(APPL)_cstub.o:    ../$(APPL).idl $(APPL).acf
         $(IDLCMD) -I../ -server none ../$(APPL).idl


#
# CLIENT BUILD
#
client:     explicit_client
explicit_client:   interface explicit_client.o \
   do_import_binding.o do_interpret_binding.o
         $(CC) $(CFLAGS) -I../ -o explicit_client.exe explicit_client.o \
            do_import_binding.o do_interpret_binding.o \
               $(APPL)_cstub.o $(LIBS)


#
# SERVER BUILD
#
server:
         @echo make server in directory ../


#
# files needed from other directories
#
i_procedures.o:    ../i_procedures.c
         $(CC) $(CFLAGS) -I../ -c ../i_procedures.c

implement_inventory.o:   ../implement_inventory.c
         $(CC) $(CFLAGS) -I../ -c ../implement_inventory.c


do_import_binding.o:    ../implicit/do_import_binding.c
         $(CC) $(CFLAGS) -I$(CHECK) -c ../implicit/do_import_binding.c

do_interpret_binding.o:   ../implicit/do_interpret_binding.c
         $(CC) $(CFLAGS) -I$(CHECK) -c ../implicit/do_interpret_binding.c
```

Example D-15: An ACF File for Explicit Binding

```
/* FILE NAME: inventory.acf (explicit version) */
/* This Attribute Configuration File is used in conjunction with the     */
/* associated IDL file (inventory.idl) when the IDL compiler is invoked. */
[
explicit_handle                             /* explicit binding method */
]
interface  inventory     /* The interface name must match the idl file. */
{
}
```

E

The Remote_file Application

The remote_file client copies ASCII data from the client to the server. The source can be a data file or the standard input of the client. The target on the server system is either a file or the server standard output. The remote_file application demonstrates some advanced features of DCE application development including:

- Using a context handle with a context rundown procedure

- Using the explicit binding method with a primitive binding handle

- Finding a server using strings of binding information

How to Run the Application

To run the local test of the application, use an ASCII text file as input and a new data file as output. The host is not relevant for the local test. Type the following:

```
C> make local
C> local_r_client.exe input   host   output
```

To run the server of the distributed application, type the following:

```
S> make server
S> r_server.exe
```

To run the client of the distributed application to transfer ASCII data, use an ASCII text file as input and a new data file on the server host as output. Type the following:

```
C> make client
C> r_client.exe input   host   output
```

Application Files

Makefile contains descriptions of how the application is compiled. See Example E-1.

remote_file.idl contains descriptions of the data types and procedures for the interface. See Example E-2.

r_client.c interprets the user input by calling the application-specific procedure **get_args**. A binding handle representing the information about a client-server relationship is obtained from strings of binding information. The remote procedure **remote_open** is called to open the server target file. A buffer is allocated for a conformant array. The application loops, reading source data and sending the data to the target with a remote procedure call to **remote_send**. Finally, the remote procedure **remote_close** is called to close the target file. See Example E-3.

get_args.c interprets the user input to obtain the name of a local client ASCII file of source data, the server host to use, and the server target file. See Example E-4.

do_string_binding.c contains the **do_string_binding** procedure that shows how to find a server from strings of binding information. A host name or network address is input, and then combined with a generated protocol sequence to create a valid binding handle, which is returned as a parameter. See Example E-5.

context_rundown.c is the implementation of a context rundown procedure. The server stub calls this procedure automatically if communication breaks between a client and the server which is maintaining context for the client. For this application, the context is a file handle of a server data file. This context rundown procedure closes the file. See Example E-6.

r_procedures.c is the implementation of the remote procedures defined in the remote_file interface. See Example E-7.

r_server.c initializes the server with a series of runtime calls prior to servicing remote procedure calls. In this application, all available protocol sequences are registered. The server is not advertised in a name service database. The server's dynamic endpoints are added to the server's local endpoint map. A client finds this server by constructing a string binding containing a protocol sequence and the host name or network address. See Example E-8.

Example E-1: The Makefile for the Remote_file Application

```
# FILE NAME: Makefile
# Makefile for the remote_file application
#
# definitions for this make file
#
APPL=remote_file
IDLCMD=idl -v
CHECK=../arithmetic        # Directory containing check_status.h
LIBDCE=-ldce -lcma         #OSF1:  DCE libraries
LIBS=$(LIBDCE) -li -ldnet #MIPS ULTRIX: DCE, internationalization, DECnet
CFLAGS=
CC= cc


#
# COMPLETE BUILD of the distributed application.
#
all:  local interface client server


#
# LOCAL BUILD of the client application to test locally.
#
local: interface r_client.c get_args.c r_procedures.c
        $(CC) $(CFLAGS) -DLOCAL -o local_r_client.exe \
               r_client.c get_args.c r_procedures.c
# remove object files so they do not interfere with a real build
        rm r_client.o get_args.o r_procedures.o


#
# INTERFACE BUILD
#
interface:  $(APPL).h $(APPL)_cstub.o $(APPL)_sstub.o
$(APPL).h $(APPL)_cstub.o $(APPL)_sstub.o: $(APPL).idl
        $(IDLCMD) $(APPL).idl


#
# CLIENT BUILD
#
client:     r_client
r_client:   $(APPL).h r_client.o get_args.o do_string_binding.o \
   $(APPL)_cstub.o
        $(CC) $(CFLAGS) -o r_client.exe r_client.o \
               get_args.o do_string_binding.o $(APPL)_cstub.o $(LIBS)

do_string_binding.o:    do_string_binding.c
        $(CC) $(CFLAGS) -I$(CHECK) -c do_string_binding.c
```

Example E-1: The Makefile for the Remote_file Application (continued)

```
#
# SERVER BUILD
#
server:     r_server
r_server:   $(APPL).h r_server.o r_procedures.o context_rundown.o \
    $(APPL)_sstub.o
            $(CC) $(CFLAGS) -I$(CHECK) -o r_server.exe r_server.o \
                r_procedures.o context_rundown.o $(APPL)_sstub.o $(LIBS)

r_server.o:  r_server.c
            $(CC) $(CFLAGS) -I$(CHECK) -c r_server.c
```

Example E-2: The IDL File of the Remote_file Application

```
/* FILE NAME: remote_file.idl */
[
uuid(016B2B80-F9B4-11C9-B31A-08002B111685),
version(1.0)
]
interface remote_file            /* file manipulation on a remote system */
{
    typedef [context_handle] void *filehandle;  /* */
    typedef                  byte buffer[];

filehandle remote_open(          /* open for write   */
    [in] handle_t binding_h,     /* explicit primitive binding handle   */
    [in, string] char name[],    /* if name is null, use stdout in server */
    [in, string] char mode[]     /* values can be "r", "w", or "a"      */
);

long remote_send(
    [in] filehandle fh,                      /* */
    [in, max_is(max)] buffer buf,
    [in] long max
);

void remote_close(
    [in,out] filehandle *fh                  /* */
);
}
```

Example E-3: A Client File of the Remote_file Application

```c
/* FILE NAME: r_client.c */
#include <stdio.h>
#include <string.h>
#include "remote_file.h"
#define MAX 200          /* maximum line length for a file */

main(argc, argv)
int argc;
char *argv[];
{
    FILE        *local_fh;          /* file handle for client file input */
    char        host[100];          /* name or network address of remote host */
    idl_char    remote_name[100];           /* name of remote file */
    rpc_binding_handle_t binding_h;             /* binding handle */
    filehandle  remote_fh;              /* context handle */
    buffer      *buf_ptr;           /* buffer pointer for data sent */
    int         size;               /* size of data buffer */
    void exit();
    char *malloc();

    get_args(argc, argv, &local_fh, host, (char *)remote_name);
#ifndef LOCAL
    if(do_string_binding(host, &binding_h) < 0) {               /* */
        fprintf(stderr, "Cannot get binding\n");
        exit(1);
    }
#endif
    remote_fh = remote_open(binding_h, remote_name, (idl_char *)"w");    /* */
    if(remote_fh == NULL) {
        fprintf(stderr, "Cannot open remote file\n");
        exit(1);
    }

    /* The buffer data type is a conformant array of bytes; */
    /* memory must be allocated for a conformant array.      */
    buf_ptr = (buffer *)malloc((MAX+1) * sizeof(buffer));

    while( fgets((char *)buf_ptr, MAX, local_fh) != NULL) {
        size = (int)strlen((char *)buf_ptr); /* data sent will not include \0 */
        if( remote_send(remote_fh, (*buf_ptr), size) < 1) {             /* */
            fprintf(stderr, "Cannot write to remote file\n");
            exit(1);
        }
    }
    remote_close(&remote_fh);                                       /* */
}
```

Example E-4: The get_args Procedure

```
/* FILE NAME: get_args.c */
#include <stdio.h>

get_args(argc, argv, local_fh, host, remote_name)
int  argc;
char *argv[];
FILE **local_fh;
char host[];
char remote_name[];
{
   char local_name[100];
   char *strcpy();
   void exit();

   switch(argc) {
   case 1:
   case 2: printf("Usage: %s [local_file] host [remote_file]0, argv[0]);
           puts("Use \"\" for local stdin.");
           exit(0);
           break;
   case 3: strcpy(local_name, argv[1]);  /* use the same file name */
           strcpy(remote_name, local_name);
           strcpy(host, argv[2]);
           break;
   default: strcpy(local_name, argv[1]);
            strcpy(host, argv[2]);
            strcpy(remote_name, argv[3]);
            break;
   }
   if(strlen(local_name) == 0) {
      (*local_fh) = stdin;
      puts("Using stdin.  Type input:");
   }
   else
      if( ( (*local_fh) = fopen(local_name, "r")) == NULL ) {
         puts("Cannot open local file");
         exit(1);
      }
   return;
}
```

Example E-5: The do_string_binding Procedure

```
/* FILE NAME: do_string_binding.c */
/* Find a server binding handle from strings of binding information    */
/* including protocol sequence, host address, and server process endpoint. */
#include <stdio.h>
#include <dce/rpc.h>
#include "check_status.h"              /* contains the CHECK_STATUS macro */

int do_string_binding(host, binding_h) /*return=0 if binding valid, else -1 */
char            host[];       /* server host name or network address input  */
rpc_binding_handle_t *binding_h;   /* binding handle is output (rpcbase.h) */
{
    rpc_protseq_vector_t *protseq_vector;  /* protocol sequence list       */
    unsigned_char_t      *string_binding;  /* string of binding information */
    unsigned32           status;           /* error status                 */
    int                  i, result;

    rpc_network_inq_protseqs( /* obtain a list of valid protocol sequences  */
        &protseq_vector,               /* list of protocol sequences obtained */
        &status
    );
    CHECK_STATUS(status, "Can't get protocol sequences:", ABORT);

    /* loop through protocol sequences until a binding handle is obtained */
    for(i=0; i < protseq_vector->count; i++) {

        rpc_string_binding_compose(  /* make string binding from components  */
            NULL,                       /* no object UUIDs are required       */
            protseq_vector->protseq[i], /* protocol sequence                  */
            (unsigned_char_t *)host,    /* host name or network address       */
            NULL,                       /* no endpoint is required            */
            NULL,                       /* no network options are required    */
            &string_binding,            /* the constructed string binding     */
            &status
        );
        CHECK_STATUS(status, "Can't compose a string binding:", RESUME);

        rpc_binding_from_string_binding(/* convert string to binding handle  */
            string_binding,             /* input string binding               */
            binding_h,                  /* binding handle is obtained here    */
            &status
        );
        if(status != rpc_s_ok) {
            result = -1;
            CHECK_STATUS(status, "Can't get binding handle from string:", RESUME);
        }
        else
            result = 0;

        rpc_string_free(                              /* free string binding created   */
            &string_binding,
            &status
        );
```

Example E-5: The do_string_binding Procedure (continued)

```
        CHECK_STATUS(status, "Can't free string binding:", RESUME);
        if(result == 0) break;                      /* got a valid binding */
    }

    rpc_protseq_vector_free(          /* free the list of protocol sequences    */
        &protseq_vector,
        &status
    );
    CHECK_STATUS(status, "Can't free protocol sequence vector:", RESUME);
    return(result);
}
```

Example E-6: The Context Rundown of the Remote_file Application

```
/* FILE NAME: context_rundown.c */
#include <stdio.h>
#include "remote_file.h"

void filehandle_rundown(remote_fh)
filehandle remote_fh;                     /* the context handle is passed in  */
{
    fprintf(stderr, "Server executing context rundown0);
    if( (FILE *)remote_fh != stdout )
        fclose( (FILE *)remote_fh );  /* file is closed if client is gone */
    remote_fh = NULL;                 /* must set context handle to NULL  */
    return;
}
```

Example E-7: Remote Procedures of the Remote_file Application

```
/* FILE NAME: r_procedures.c */
#include <stdio.h>
#include <string.h>
#include <unistd.h>
#include "remote_file.h"

filehandle remote_open(binding_h, name, mode)  /*  */
rpc_binding_handle_t binding_h;
idl_char                name[];
idl_char                mode[];
{
    FILE *FILEh;

    if(strlen((char *)name) == 0)                      /* no file name given */
        if(strcmp((char *)mode, "r") == 0)
            FILEh = NULL;                        /* cannot read nonexistent file */
        else FILEh = stdout;                          /* use server stdout */
```

Example E-7: Remote Procedures of the Remote_file Application (continued)

```
    else if(access((char *)name, F_OK) == 0)                    /* file exists */
        if(strcmp((char *)mode, "w") == 0)
            FILEh = NULL;                          /* do not overwrite existing file */
        else FILEh = fopen((char *)name, (char *)mode);    /* open read/append */

    else                                                      /* file does not exist */
        if(strcmp((char *)mode, "r") == 0)
            FILEh = NULL;                          /* cannot read nonexistent file */
        else FILEh = fopen((char *)name, (char *)mode);   /* open write/append */

    return( (filehandle)FILEh );          /* cast FILE handle to context handle */
}


idl_long_int remote_send(fh, buf, max)          /*  */
filehandle fh;
buffer buf;
idl_long_int max;
{
    /* write data to the file (context), which is cast as a FILE pointer */
    return( fwrite(buf, sizeof(buffer), max, (FILE *)fh) );
}


void remote_close(fh)                            /*  */
filehandle *fh;   /* the client stub needs the changed value upon return */
{
    if( (FILE *)(*fh) != stdout )
        fclose( (FILE *)(*fh) );
    (*fh) = NULL;          /* assign NULL to the context handle to free it */
    return;
}
```


Example E-8: Server Initialization of the Remote_file Application

```
/* FILE NAME: r_server.c */
#include <stdio.h>
#include "remote_file.h"            /* header created by the idl compiler */
#include "check_status.h"           /* contains the CHECK_STATUS macro     */
main ()
{
    unsigned32              status;            /* error status (nbase.h)        */
    rpc_binding_vector_t    *binding_vector; /* binding handle list (rpcbase.h)*/
```

Example E-8: Server Initialization of the Remote_file Application (continued)

```
    rpc_server_register_if(        /* register interface with the RPC runtime */
        remote_file_v1_0_s_ifspec, /* handle for interface specification      */
        NULL,
        NULL,
        &status                    /* error status */
    );
    CHECK_STATUS(status, "Can't register interface\n", ABORT);

    rpc_server_use_all_protseqs(             /* establish protocol sequences */
        rpc_c_protseq_max_reqs_default,      /* queue length for remote calls */
        &status
    );
    CHECK_STATUS(status, "Can't establish protocol sequences\n", ABORT);

    rpc_server_inq_bindings(     /* get set of this server's binding handles */
        &binding_vector,
        &status
    );
    CHECK_STATUS(status, "Can't get binding handles\n", ABORT);

    rpc_ep_register(                       /* add endpoint to local endpoint map  */
        remote_file_v1_0_s_ifspec,         /* handle for interface specification  */
        binding_vector,                    /* vector of server binding handles    */
        NULL,                              /* no object UUIDs to register         */
        (unsigned_char_t *)"remote_file server", /* annotation (not required) */
        &status
    );
    CHECK_STATUS(status, "Can't add endpoints to local endpoint map:", ABORT);

    puts("Listening for remote procedure calls...");
    TRY
        rpc_server_listen(                       /* listen for remote calls */
            rpc_c_listen_max_calls_default,      /* number of threads       */
            &status
        );
        CHECK_STATUS(status, "rpc listen failed:", RESUME);
    FINALLY
        puts("Removing endpoints from local endpoint map.");
        rpc_ep_unregister(         /* remove endpoints from local endpoint map */
            remote_file_v1_0_s_ifspec,   /* handle for interface specificaiton */
            binding_vector,              /* vector of server binding handles   */
            NULL,                        /* no object UUIDs to unregister       */
            &status
        );
        CHECK_STATUS(status,"Can't remove endpoints from endpoint map:", RESUME);
```

Example E-8: Server Initialization of the Remote_file Application (continued)

```
    rpc_binding_vector_free(              /* free set of binding handles */
        &binding_vector,
        &status
    );
    CHECK_STATUS(status, "Can't free binding handles and vector\n", ABORT);
ENDTRY
}
```

F

The Transfer_data Application

There are two clients for the transfer_data application. One sends a binary file of floating-point data from a client to a server. The other receives a binary file of floating-point data from a server. The transfer_data application demonstrates the following advanced features of DCE application development:

- Using input and output pipes

- Using the explicit binding method

- Using a customized binding handle and the associated bind and unbind procedures

How to Run the Application

To create a binary file of float data for the application, type the following:

```
C> make utility
C> float_util.exe write datafile
```

To run the local tests of the application, use the binary file of float data as a source file and a new data file as the target file. The host is not relevant for the local test. Type the following:

```
C> make local
C> local_client_send.exe source  host  target
C> local_client_receive.exe target  host  source
```

To run the server for the clients of the distributed application type the following:

```
S> make server
S> t_server.exe
```

To run the clients of the distributed application, type the following:

```
C> make client
C> client_send.exe source   host   target
C> client_receive.exe target   host   source
```

Application Files

Makefile contains descriptions of how the application is compiled. See Example F-1.

float_util.c contains code that generates and writes a binary file of float data or reads a binary file of float data. See Example F-2.

transfer_data.idl contains the description of the constants, data types, and procedures for the interface. See Example F-3.

client_send.c demonstrates the use of a pipe that is an input parameter. The customized binding handle is initialized; the pipe structure is initialized for an input pipe; and the remote procedure **send_floats** is called to transfer pipe data to the server. See Example F-4.

client_receive.c demonstrates the use of a pipe that is an output parameter. The customized binding handle is initialized; the pipe structure is initialized for an output pipe; and the remote procedure **receive_floats** is called to transfer pipe data from the server to the client. See Example F-5.

binding.c contains the bind and unbind procedures that the client stub calls to obtain and free a binding handle. After the customized binding information is initialized in the client application, the binding is handled entirely by the client stub with these routines. See Example F-6.

send_floats.c contains the implementation of the **send_floats** remote procedure. See Example F-7.

receive_floats.c contains the implementation of the **receive_floats** remote procedure. See Example F-8.

t_server.c initializes the server with a series of runtime calls prior to servicing remote procedure calls. In this application, all protocol sequences available are registered. The server is not advertised in a name service database. The server's dynamic endpoints are added to the server's local endpoint map. A client finds this server by constructing a string binding containing a protocol sequence and the host name or network address. See Example F-9.

pipe_state.h contains a structure with client file handle and file name members. See Example F-10.

client_alloc.c contains the **client_alloc** procedure that the client stub calls to allocate a buffer for pipe data. See Example F-11.

in_pull.c contains the **in_pull** procedure that the client stub calls to process input pipe data. See Example F-12.

out_push.c contains the **out_push** procedure that the client stub calls to process output pipe data. See Example F-13.

Example F-1: The Makefile for the Transfer_data Application

```
# FILE NAME: Makefile
# Makefile for the customized handle and pipes application
#
# definitions for this make file
#
APPL=transfer_data
IDLCMD=idl -v
CHECK=../arithmetic       # Directory containing check_status.h
LIBDCE=-ldce -lcma        #OSF/1: DCE libraries
LIBS=$(LIBDCE) -li -ldnet  #MIPS ULTRIX: DCE, internationalization, DECnet
CFLAGS=
CC= cc


#
# COMPLETE BUILD of the application
#
all:  utility local interface client server


#
# BUILD OF UTILITY to create and read files of float data
#
utility:    float_util
float_util: float_util.c
        $(CC) $(CFLAGS) -o float_util.exe float_util.c


#
# LOCAL BUILD of the clients to test locally.
#
local:interface  local_client_send  local_client_receive

local_client_send: client_send.c client_alloc.c in_pull.c \
                 send_floats.c
            $(CC) $(CFLAGS) -DLOCAL -I. -o local_client_send.exe \
                 client_send.c client_alloc.c in_pull.c send_floats.c
# remove object files so they do not interfere with a real build
            rm client_send.o send_floats.o client_alloc.o in_pull.o
```

Example F-1: The Makefile for the Transfer_data Application (continued)

```
local_client_receive:    client_receive.c client_alloc.c out_push.c \
                   receive_floats.c
        $(CC) $(CFLAGS) -DLOCAL -I. -o local_client_receive.exe \
                client_receive.c client_alloc.c out_push.c receive_floats.c
# remove object files so they do not interfere with a real build
          rm  client_receive.o receive_floats.o client_alloc.o out_push.o


#
# INTERFACE BUILD
#
interface:  $(APPL).h $(APPL)_cstub.o $(APPL)_sstub.o $(APPL)_saux.o
$(APPL).h $(APPL)_cstub.o $(APPL)_sstub.o $(APPL)_saux.o:    $(APPL).idl
        $(IDLCMD) $(APPL).idl


#
# CLIENT BUILDS
#
client:     client_send   client_receive
client_send: client_send.o client_alloc.o in_pull.o \
            binding.o do_string_binding.o $(APPL)_cstub.o
        $(CC) $(CFLAGS) -I$(CHECK) -o client_send.exe \
            client_send.o client_alloc.o in_pull.o \
            binding.o do_string_binding.o $(APPL)_cstub.o $(LIBS)

client_receive:    client_receive.o client_alloc.o out_push.o \
            binding.o do_string_binding.o $(APPL)_cstub.o
        $(CC) $(CFLAGS) -I$(CHECK) -o client_receive.exe \
            client_receive.o client_alloc.o out_push.o \
            binding.o do_string_binding.o $(APPL)_cstub.o $(LIBS)

#
# module needed by both clients
#
binding.o:  binding.c
        $(CC) $(CFLAGS) -I$(CHECK) -c binding.c

# module needed from remote_file application
do_string_binding.o:    ../remote_file/do_string_binding.c
        $(CC) $(CFLAGS) -I$(CHECK) -c ../remote_file/do_string_binding.c
```

Example F-1: The Makefile for the Transfer_data Application (continued)

```
#
# SERVER BUILD.  Notice the server stub auxiliary file is required.
#
server:       t_server
t_server:     $(APPL).h t_server.o send_floats.o receive_floats.o \
   $(APPL)_sstub.o $(APPL)_saux.o
          $(CC) $(CFLAGS) -I$(CHECK) -o t_server.exe t_server.o \
               send_floats.o receive_floats.o \
               $(APPL)_sstub.o $(APPL)_saux.o $(LIBS)


t_server.o: t_server.c
          $(CC) $(CFLAGS) -I$(CHECK) -c t_server.c
```

Example F-2: The Float File Generating Utility

```
/* FILE NAME: float_util.c */
/* utility to generate or read a file of float data to test pipes */
#include <stdio.h>
#include <string.h>
#include <sys/file.h>
void exit();
char *malloc();

main(argc, argv)
int argc;
char *argv[];
{
    char choice[20], filename[100];

    if(argc == 1)  {
       printf("Usage: %s [write | read] [filename]\n", argv[0]);
       puts("Enter w to create a file, r to read:");
       gets(choice);
    }
    else
       strcpy(choice, argv[1]);
    if(argc > 2)
       strcpy(filename, argv[2]);
    else
       strcpy(filename, "");

    if(choice[0] == 'w')
       write_floats(filename);
    else
       read_floats(filename);
}
```

Example F-2: The Float File Generating Utility (continued)

```
write_floats(file)
char file[];
{
    char filename[100];
    int filehand;
    long num, i;
    float *buf, x;

    strcpy(filename, file);
    if(strlen(filename) == 0) {
        puts("enter name of data file to create");
        gets(filename);
    }
    filehand = open(filename, O_CREAT | O_TRUNC | O_WRONLY, 0777);
    if(filehand == 0) {
        fprintf(stderr, "Cannot open file %s for write\n", filename);
        exit(0);
    }
    puts("enter number of data items desired");
    fscanf(stdin, "%ld", &num);
    buf = (float *)malloc(sizeof(float) * num);
    for(i=0, x=1.1; i < num; i++, x+=0.4567) {   /* insert arbitrary numbers */
        buf[i] =  x;
        printf("%f\n", buf[i]);
    }
    write(filehand, (char *)buf, (int)(sizeof(float) * num) );
    close(filehand);
}


read_floats(file)
char file[];
{
    char filename[100];
    int filehand;
    long num, i, total, bytesread, numread;
    float *buf;

    strcpy(filename, file);
    if(strlen(filename) == 0) {
        puts("enter name of data file to read");
        gets(filename);
    }
    filehand = open(filename, O_RDONLY);
    if(filehand == 0) {
        fprintf(stderr, "Cannot open file %s for read", filename);
        exit(0);
    }
    num = 5; total = 0;
    buf = (float *)malloc(sizeof(float) * num);
```

Example F-2: The Float File Generating Utility (continued)

```
while((bytesread =
            read(filehand, (char *)buf, (int)(sizeof(float) * num) )) > 0) {
    numread = bytesread/sizeof(float);
    for(i=0; i < numread; i++)
        printf("%f   ", buf[i]);
    puts("");
    total+=numread;
}
printf("Total read: %ld\n", total);
close(filehand);
}
```

Example F-3: The IDL File of the Transfer_data Application

```
/* FILE NAME: transfer_data.idl */
[
uuid(A6876974-F555-11CA-BAE1-08002B245A28),
version(1.0)
]
interface transfer_data    /* data transfer to and from a remote system */
{
    const long NAME_LENGTH = 200;

    typedef [handle] struct {              /* a customized handle type */
        char host[NAME_LENGTH+1];
        char filename[NAME_LENGTH+1];
    } file_spec;

    typedef pipe float pipe_type;       /* a pipe data type           */

void send_floats(        /* send pipe of floats to a file on the server */
    [in] file_spec  cust_binding_h,    /* customized binding for server */
    [in] pipe_type data                /* input pipe of float data      */
);

void receive_floats(    /* get pipe of floats from a file on the server */
    [in] file_spec  cust_binding_h,    /* customized binding for server */
    [out] pipe_type *data              /* output pipe of float data     */
);
}
```

Example F-4: A Client that Uses an Input Pipe

```
/* FILE NAME: client_send.c */
/* Client for customized handle and input pipe test */
#include <stdio.h>
#include "transfer_data.h"
#include "pipe_state.h"     /* definition of state structure for pipe data    */

main(argc, argv)
int argc;
char *argv[];
{
    file_spec  cust_binding_h;          /* customized binding handle   */
    pipe_state state;
    pipe_type  data;                    /* a pipe structure is allocated    */
    char       local_source[100];
               /* procedures in other modules */
    void       client_alloc(), in_pull();
    void       send_floats();

    /* get user input */
    if(argc < 4) {
        printf("USAGE: %s  local_source  host  file\n", argv[0]);
        exit(0);
    }
    /* initialize customized binding handle structure */
    strcpy(local_source, argv[1]);
    strcpy(cust_binding_h.host, argv[2]);
    strcpy(cust_binding_h.filename, argv[3]);

    /* initialize pipe structure */
    state.filehandle = -1;
    state.filename = local_source;
    data.state = (rpc_ss_pipe_state_t)&state;       /* initialize pipe state    */
    data.alloc = client_alloc;   /* initialize alloc procedure for a pipe    */
    data.pull = in_pull;         /* Initialize pull procedure for input pipe    */

    send_floats(cust_binding_h, data); /* remote procedure with input pipe    */
}
```

Example F-5: A Client that Uses an Output Pipe

```
/* FILE NAME: client_receive.c */
/* Client for customized handle and output pipe test */
#include <stdio.h>
#include "transfer_data.h"
#include "pipe_state.h"      /* definition of state structure for pipe data    */

main(argc, argv)
int argc;
char *argv[];
{
    file_spec  cust_binding_h;                /* customized binding handle   */
    pipe_state state;
    pipe_type  data;                          /* a pipe structure is allocated    */
    char       local_target[100];
               /* procedures in other modules */
    void       client_alloc(),out_push();
    void       receive_floats();

    /* get user input */
    if(argc < 4) {
        printf("USAGE: %s  local_target  host  file\n", argv[0]);
        exit(0);
    }
    /* initialize customized binding handle structure */
    strcpy(local_target, argv[1]);
    strcpy(cust_binding_h.host, argv[2]);
    strcpy(cust_binding_h.filename, argv[3]);

    /* initialize pipe structure */
    state.filehandle = -1;
    state.filename = local_target;
    data.state = (rpc_ss_pipe_state_t)&state;      /* initialize pipe state    */
    data.alloc = client_alloc;    /* initialize alloc procedure for a pipe    */
    data.push = out_push;        /* Initialize push procedure for output pipe    */

    receive_floats(cust_binding_h, &data);    /* procedure with output pipe    */

}
```

Example F-6: Bind and Unbind Procedures

```
/* FILE NAME: binding.c */
#include "transfer_data.h"    /* header created by the IDL compiler */
#include "check_status.h"     /* contains the CHECK_STATUS macro     */


handle_t file_spec_bind(spec) /* "bind" procedure for customized handle   */
file_spec spec;
{
    rpc_binding_handle_t binding_h;

    if(do_string_binding(spec.host, &binding_h) < 0) {
        fprintf(stderr, "Cannot get binding\n");
        exit(1);
    }
    return(binding_h);
}

void file_spec_unbind(spec, binding_h) /* "unbind" for customized handle   */
file_spec spec;
handle_t binding_h;
{
    unsigned32 status;  /* error status */

    rpc_binding_free(&binding_h, &status);
    CHECK_STATUS(status, "Can't free binding handle:", RESUME);
    return;
}
```

Example F-7: The send_floats Procedure

```
/* FILE NAME: send_floats.c */
#include <stdio.h>
#include <sys/file.h>
#include "transfer_data.h"
#define MAX_ELEMENTS  1000

void send_floats(c_b_h, in_data) /* copy input data to a server file */
file_spec   c_b_h;                 /* customized binding handle      */
pipe_type in_data;
{
    int             file_h;
    idl_short_float buf[MAX_ELEMENTS];         /* pipe data buffer          */
    idl_ulong_int   element_count;             /* number of elements pulled */
```

Example F-7: The send_floats Procedure (continued)

```
/* open local file on server for write */
file_h = open(c_b_h.filename, O_CREAT | O_TRUNC | O_WRONLY, 0777);
if(file_h < 0)      /* If can't open file, need to discard the pipe data */
   file_h = open("/dev/null", O_WRONLY);

while(true) {             /* entire pipe must be processed           */
   (in_data.pull)(        /* pull routine is used for an input pipe  */
      in_data.state,      /* state is controlled by the stub         */
      buf,                /* the buffer to be filled                 */
      MAX_ELEMENTS,       /* maximum number of data elements in buffer */
      &element_count      /* actual number of elements in the buffer */
   );
   if(element_count == 0) break;      /* 0 count signals pipe is empty  */
   /****           application specific process of buffer        ****   */
   write(file_h, buf, (sizeof(idl_short_float) * element_count));
}

close(file_h);
return;
}
```

Example F-8: The receive_floats Procedure

```
/* FILE NAME: receive_floats.c */
#include <stdio.h>
#include <sys/file.h>
#include "transfer_data.h"
#define MAX_ELEMENTS  1000

void receive_floats(c_b_h, out_data)   /* copy server file data to a client */
file_spec c_b_h;              /* customized binding handle */
pipe_type *out_data;
{
   int            file_h;
   idl_short_float buf[MAX_ELEMENTS];      /* pipe data buffer          */
   idl_ulong_int   element_count;          /* number of elements pushed */
   int            nbytes;

   /* open local file on server for read */
   file_h = open(c_b_h.filename, O_RDONLY);
   nbytes = sizeof(idl_short_float) * MAX_ELEMENTS;

   if(file_h > 0) {
      while(true) {
         /*****           application specific process of buffer        ***** */
         element_count = read(file_h, buf, nbytes) / sizeof(idl_short_float);
         if(element_count == 0) break;
```

Example F-8: The receive_floats Procedure (continued)

```
            out_data->push(    /* push routine is used for an output pipe    */
                out_data->state, /* the state is controlled by the stub        */
                buf,             /* the buffer of data to send                 */
                element_count    /* the number of data elements to send        */
            );
        }
        close(file_h);
    }

    out_data->push(out_data->state, buf, 0);    /* 0 indicates end of pipe    */
    return;
}
```

Example F-9: Server Initialization of the Transfer_data Application

```
/* FILE NAME: t_server.c */
#include <stdio.h>
#include "transfer_data.h"            /* header created by the idl compiler */
#include "check_status.h"             /* contains the CHECK_STATUS macro    */
main ()
{
    unsigned32             status;            /* error status (nbase.h)         */
    rpc_binding_vector_t   *binding_vector;   /* binding handle list (rpcbase.h)*/

    rpc_server_register_if(        /* register interface with the RPC runtime */
        transfer_data_v1_0_s_ifspec, /* handle to interface specification     */
        NULL,
        NULL,
        &status                    /* error status */
    );
    CHECK_STATUS(status, "Can't register interface\n", ABORT);

    rpc_server_use_all_protseqs(            /* establish protocol sequences */
        rpc_c_protseq_max_reqs_default,     /* queue length for remote calls */
        &status
    );
    CHECK_STATUS(status, "Can't establish protocol sequences\n", ABORT);

    rpc_server_inq_bindings(      /* get set of this server's binding handles */
        &binding_vector,
        &status
    );
    CHECK_STATUS(status, "Can't get binding handles\n", ABORT);
```

Example F-9: Server Initialization of the Transfer_data Application (continued)

```
rpc_ep_register(                              /* add endpoint to local endpoint map */
    transfer_data_v1_0_s_ifspec,      /* handle to interface specification  */
    binding_vector,                        /* vector of server binding handles   */
    NULL,                                  /* no object UUIDs to register        */
    (unsigned_char_t *)"transfer_data server",          /* annotation */
    &status
);
CHECK_STATUS(status, "Can't add endpoints to local endpoint map:", ABORT);

puts("Listening for remote procedure calls...");
TRY
    rpc_server_listen(                         /* listen for remote calls      */
        rpc_c_listen_max_calls_default,   /* number of threads            */
        &status
    );
    CHECK_STATUS(status, "rpc listen failed:", RESUME);
FINALLY
    puts("Removing endpoints from local endpoint map.");
    rpc_ep_unregister(        /* remove endpoints from local endpoint map    */
        transfer_data_v1_0_s_ifspec, /* handle to interface specification  */
        binding_vector,                /* vector of server binding handles   */
        NULL,                          /* no object UUIDs to unregister      */
        &status
    );
    CHECK_STATUS(status,"Can't remove endpoints from endpoint map:",RESUME);

    rpc_binding_vector_free(                    /* free set of binding handles */
        &binding_vector,
        &status
    );
    CHECK_STATUS(status, "Can't free binding handles and vector\n", ABORT);
ENDTRY
}
```

Example F-10: The pipe_state Structure

```
/* FILE NAME: pipe_state.h */
/* Definition of application-specific state structure of client pipe data.*/
typedef struct pipe_state {
    int  filehandle;             /* handle of client data file   */
    char *filename;              /* name of client data file     */
} pipe_state;
```

Example F-11: The client_alloc Procedure

```
/* FILE NAME: client_alloc.c */
#include <stdio.h>
#include "transfer_data.h"
#include "pipe_state.h"

#define BUFFER_SIZE 2000
idl_short_float client_buffer[BUFFER_SIZE];

void client_alloc(state, bsize, buf, bcount)     /* allocation for a pipe   */
pipe_state         *state;        /* coordinates pipe procedure calls   */
idl_ulong_int      bsize;         /* desired size of buffer in bytes    */
idl_short_float    **buf;         /* allocated buffer                   */
idl_ulong_int      *bcount;       /* allocated buffer size in bytes     */
{
    *buf = client_buffer;
    *bcount = BUFFER_SIZE;
    return;
}
```

Example F-12: The in_pull Procedure

```
/* FILE NAME: in_pull.c */
#include <stdio.h>
#include <sys/file.h>
#include "transfer_data.h"
#include "pipe_state.h"     /* definition of a state structure for pipe data */

void in_pull(state, buf, esize, ecount)/* input pipe uses a pull procedure  */
pipe_state       *state;         /* coordinates pipe procedure calls    */
idl_short_float *buf;            /* buffer of data pulled               */
idl_ulong_int   esize;          /* maximum element count in buffer     */
idl_ulong_int   *ecount;        /* actual element count in buffer      */
```

Example F-12: The in_pull Procedure (continued)

```
{
    /* for this application, open local source file if not open already */
    if(state->filehandle == -1) {
        state->filehandle = open(state->filename, O_RDONLY);
        if(state->filehandle == -1) {
            fprintf(stderr, "Cannot open file %s for read\n", state->filename);
            exit(0);
        }
    }
    /* process buffer for your application */
    *ecount = read(state->filehandle, buf, (sizeof(float)*esize)) /
                sizeof(float);

    /* To signal the end of data, pull procedure must set the count to 0.    */
    if(*ecount == 0) {          /* end of data reached, do application cleanup    */
        close(state->filehandle);
    }
    return;
}
```

Example F-13: The out_push Procedure

```
/* FILE NAME: out_push.c */
#include <stdio.h>
#include <sys/file.h>
#include "transfer_data.h"
#include "pipe_state.h"       /* definition of a state structure for pipe data */

void out_push(state, buf, ecount)   /* output pipe needs a push procedure    */
pipe_state      *state;             /* coordinates pipe procedure calls      */
idl_short_float *buf;               /* buffer of data pushed                 */
idl_ulong_int   ecount;             /* number of elements for buffer         */
{
    /* for this application, open local target file if not open already */
    if(state->filehandle == -1) {
        if(ecount <= 0)    /* if first buffer is empty, don't do anything */
            return;
        state->filehandle = open(state->filename,
                                O_CREAT | O_TRUNC | O_WRONLY, 0777);
        if(state->filehandle == -1) {
            fprintf(stderr, "Cannot open file %s for write\n", state->filename);
            exit(0);
        }
    }
    /* To detect the end of data, push routine must test the count for 0.   */
    if(ecount == 0)                         /* do application specific cleanup */
        close(state->filehandle);
    else                                    /* process buffer for application  */
        write(state->filehandle, buf, (sizeof(float) * ecount));
    return;
}
```

Index

V

-**v**, IDL compiler option, 42
varying array, 32
vector, defined, 100
version attribute, 28, 165

W

WAN, protocol sequences for, 61
well-known endpoint, 61

About the Author

John Shirley considers himself a scientist interested in educating himself and others on the use of software tools to analyze and present scientific data. He has developed software and documentation while consulting for companies that include Digital Equipment Corporation, Concurrent Computer Corporation, Inset Systems, NASDAQ, and Tandem Computers. John's work has included the development of C programs to demonstrate not only the use of DCE remote procedure calls, but also multithreaded programming, an application interface for the GEM graphics environment, and storing scientific data. These projects have spanned many operating systems, including OSF/1, UNIX, MS-DOS, and VMS.

John earned a B.A. from Alfred University with a dual major in Mathematics and Geology, an M.S. in Geology from Miami University with a specialty in Structural Geology, and an M.S. in Computer Science from Pace University.

Prior to consulting, John's career included six years in the oil industry as a geophysicist and international explorationist. The work included the analysis of seismic data from New Zealand, Australia, Turkey, Norway, the Dominican Republic, Jamaica, and the United States.

John also worked as a software engineer developing programs for scientific instrument manufacturers.

John lives in Newtown, Connecticut, where he maintains a consulting business specializing in documenting and demonstrating complex software.

UNIX

From the best-selling The Whole Internet *to our Nutshell Handbooks, there's something here for everyone. Whether you're a novice or expert UNIX user, these books will give you just what you're looking for: user-friendly, definitive information on a range of UNIX topics.*

Using UNIX

Connecting to the Internet: An O'Reilly Buyer's Guide **NEW**

By Susan Estrada
1st Edition August 1993
188 pages
ISBN 1-56592-061-9

More and more people are interested in exploring the Internet, and this book is the fastest way for you to learn how to get started. This book provides practical advice on how to determine the level of Internet service right for you, and how to find a local access provider and evaluate the services they offer.

!%@:: A Directory of Electronic Mail Addressing & Networks **NEW**

By Donnalyn Frey & Rick Adams
3rd Edition August 1993
458 pages, ISBN 1-56592-031-7

The only up-to-date directory that charts the networks that make up the Internet, provides contact names and addresses, and describes the services each network provides. It includes all of the major Internet-based networks, as well as various commercial networks such as CompuServe, Delphi, and America Online that are "gatewayed" to the Internet for transfer of electronic mail and other services. If you are someone who wants to connect to the Internet, or someone who already is connected but wants concise, up-to-date information on many of the world's networks, check out this book.

Learning the UNIX Operating System **NEW**

By Grace Todino, John Strang & Jerry Peek
3rd Edition August 1993
108 pages, ISBN 1-56592-060-0

If you are new to UNIX, this concise introduction will tell you just what you need to get started and no more. Why wade through a six-hundred-page book when you can begin working productively in a matter of minutes? This book is the most effective introduction to UNIX in print. This new edition has been updated and expanded to provide increased coverage of window systems and networking. It's a handy book for someone just starting with UNIX, as well as someone who encounters a UNIX system as a visitor via remote login over the Internet.

The Whole Internet User's Guide & Catalog

By Ed Krol
1st Edition September 1992
400 pages, ISBN 1-56592-025-2

A comprehensive—and best-selling—introduction to the Internet, the international network that includes virtually every major computer site in the world. The Internet is a resource of almost unimaginable wealth. In addition to electronic mail and news services, thousands of public archives, databases, and other special services are available: everything from space flight announcements to ski reports. This book is a comprehensive introduction to what's available and how to find it. In addition to electronic mail, file transfer, remote login, and network news, *The Whole Internet* pays special attention to some new tools for helping you find information. Whether you're a researcher, a student, or just someone who likes electronic mail, this book will help you to explore what's possible.

Smileys

By David W. Sanderson, 1st Edition March 1993
93 pages, ISBN 1-56592-041-4

Originally used to convey some kind of emotion in an e-mail message, smileys are some combination of typographic characters that depict sideways a happy or sad face. Now there are hundreds of variations, including smileys that depict presidents, animals, and cartoon characters. Not everyone likes to read mail messages littered with smileys, but almost everyone finds them humorous. The smileys in this book have been collected by David Sanderson, whom the *Wall Street Journal* called the "Noah Webster of Smileys."

UNIX Power Tools

By Jerry Peek, Mike Loukides, Tim O'Reilly, et al.
1st Edition March 1993
1162 pages
(Bantam ISBN)
0-553-35402-7

Ideal for UNIX users who hunger for technical—yet accessible—information, *UNIX Power Tools* consists of tips, tricks, concepts, and freely-available software. Covers add-on utilities and how to take advantage of clever features in the most popular UNIX utilities. CD-ROM included.

Learning the Korn Shell · NEW

By Bill Rosenblatt
1st Edition June 1993
363 pages, ISBN 1-56592-054-6

This new Nutshell Handbook is a thorough introduction to the Korn shell, both as a user interface and as a programming language. Provides a clear explanation of the Korn shell's features, including *ksh* string operations, co-processes, signals and signal handling, and command-line interpretation. Also includes real-life programming examples and a Korn shell debugger *(kshdb)*.

Learning perl · NEW

By Randal L. Schwartz, 1st Edition November 1993 (est.)
220 pages (est.), ISBN 1-56592-042-2

Perl is rapidly becoming the "universal scripting language". Combining capabilities of the UNIX shell, the C programming language, *sed*, *awk*, and various other utilities, it has proved its use for tasks ranging from system administration to text processing and distributed computing. *Learning perl* is a step-by-step, hands-on tutorial designed to get you writing useful perl scripts as quickly as possible. In addition to countless code examples, there are numerous programming exercises, with full answers. For a comprehensive and detailed guide to programming with Perl, read O'Reilly's companion book *Programming perl*.

Programming perl

By Larry Wall & Randal L. Schwartz
1st Edition January 1991, 428 pages, ISBN 0-937175-64-1

Authoritative guide to the hottest new UNIX utility in years, co-authored by its creator. Perl is a language for easily manipulating text, files, and processes.

Learning GNU Emacs

By Deb Cameron & Bill Rosenblatt
1st Edition October 1991
442 pages, ISBN 0-937175-84-6

An introduction to the GNU Emacs editor, one of the most widely used and powerful editors available under UNIX. Provides a solid introduction to basic editing, a look at several important "editing modes" (special Emacs features for editing specific types of documents), and a brief introduction to customization and Emacs LISP programming. The book is aimed at new Emacs users, whether or not they are programmers.

sed & awk

By Dale Dougherty, 1st Edition November 1992
414 pages, ISBN 0-937175-59-5

For people who create and modify text files, *sed* and *awk* are power tools for editing. Most of the things that you can do with these programs can be done interactively with a text editor. However, using *sed* and *awk* can save many hours of repetitive work in achieving the same result.

MH & xmh: E-mail for Users & Programmers

By Jerry Peek, 2nd Edition September 1992
728 pages, ISBN 1-56592-027-9

Customize your e-mail environment to save time and make communicating more enjoyable. *MH & xmh: E-mail for Users & Programmers* explains how to use, customize, and program with the MH electronic mail commands available on virtually any UNIX system. The handbook also covers *xmh*, an X Window System client that runs MH programs. The new second edition has been updated for X Release 5 and MH 6.7.2. We've added a chapter on *mhook*, new sections explaining under-appreciated small commands and features, and more examples showing how to use MH to handle common situations.

Learning the vi Editor

By Linda Lamb, 5th Edition October 1990
192 pages, ISBN 0-937175-67-6

A complete guide to text editing with *vi*, the editor available on nearly every UNIX system. Early chapters cover the basics; later chapters explain more advanced editing tools, such as *ex* commands and global search and replacement.

UNIX in a Nutshell:
For System V & Solaris 2.0

By Daniel Gilly and the staff of O'Reilly & Associates
2nd Edition June 1992, 444 pages, ISBN 1-56592-001-5

You may have seen UNIX quick reference guides, but you've never seen anything like *UNIX in a Nutshell*. Not a scaled-down quick-reference of common commands, *UNIX in a Nutshell* is a complete reference containing all commands and options, along with generous descriptions and examples that put the commands in context. For all but the thorniest UNIX problems this one reference should be all the documentation you need. Covers System V Releases 3 and 4 and Solaris 2.0.

An alternate version of this quick-reference is available for Berkeley UNIX.
Berkeley Edition, December 1986
(latest update October 1990)
272 pages, ISBN 0-937175-20-X

Using UUCP and Usenet

By Grace Todino & Dale Dougherty
1st Edition December 1986 (latest update October 1991)
210 pages, ISBN 0-937175-10-2

Shows users how to communicate with both UNIX and non-UNIX systems using UUCP and *cu* or *tip*, and how to read news and post articles. This handbook assumes that UUCP is already running at your site.

System Administration

Managing UUCP and Usenet

By Tim O'Reilly & Grace Todino
10th Edition January 1992
368 pages, ISBN 0-937175-93-5

For all its widespread use, UUCP is one of the most difficult UNIX utilities to master. This book is for system administrators who want to install and manage UUCP and Usenet software. "Don't even TRY to install UUCP without it!"—Usenet message 456@nitrex.UUCP

sendmail   **NEW**

By Bryan Costales, with Eric Allman & Neil Rickert
1st Edition October 1993 (est.)
600 pages (est.), ISBN 0-937175-056-2

This new Nutshell Handbook is far and away the most comprehensive book ever written on *sendmail*, a program that acts like a traffic cop in routing and delivering mail on UNIX-based networks. Although *sendmail* is the most widespread of all mail programs, it's also one of the last great uncharted territories—and most difficult utilities to learn—in UNIX system administration. The book covers both major versions of *sendmail*: the standard version available on most systems, and IDA *sendmail*, a version from Europe.

termcap & terminfo

By John Strang, Linda Mui & Tim O'Reilly
3rd Edition July 1992
270 pages, ISBN 0-937175-22-6

For UNIX system administrators and programmers. This handbook provides information on writing and debugging terminal descriptions, as well as terminal initialization, for the two UNIX terminal databases.

DNS and BIND

By Cricket Liu & Paul Albitz, 1st Edition October 1992
418 pages, ISBN 1-56592-010-4

DNS and BIND contains all you need to know about the Domain Name System (DNS) and BIND, its UNIX implementation. The Domain Name System (DNS) is the Internet's "phone book"; it's a database that tracks important information (in particular, names and addresses) for every computer on the Internet. If you're a system administrator, this book will show you how to set up and maintain the DNS software on your network.

Essential System Administration

By Æleen Frisch, 1st Edition October 1991
466 pages, ISBN 0-937175-80-3

Provides a compact, manageable introduction to the tasks faced by everyone responsible for a UNIX system. This guide is for those who use a stand-alone UNIX system, those who routinely provide administrative support for a larger shared system, or those who want an understanding of basic administrative functions. Covers all major versions of UNIX.

X Window System Administrator's Guide

By Linda Mui & Eric Pearce
1st Edition October 1992
372 pages, With CD-ROM: ISBN 1-56592-052-X
Without CD-ROM: ISBN 0-937175-83-8

This book is the first and only book devoted to the issues of system administration for X and X-based networks, written not just for UNIX system administrators but for anyone faced with the job of administering X (including those running X on stand-alone workstations). The *X Window System Administrator's Guide* is available either alone or packaged with the XCD. The CD provides X source code and binaries to complement the book's instructions for installing the software. It contains over 600 megabytes of X11 source code and binaries stored in ISO9660 and RockRidge formats. This will allow several types of UNIX workstations to mount the CD-ROM as a filesystem, browse through the source code and install pre-built software.

Practical UNIX Security

By Simson Garfinkel & Gene Spafford
1st Edition June 1991
512 pages, ISBN 0-937175-72-2

Tells system administrators how to make their UNIX system—either System V or BSD—as secure as it possibly can be without going to trusted system technology. The book describes UNIX concepts and how they enforce security, tells how to defend against and handle security breaches, and explains network security (including UUCP, NFS, Kerberos, and firewall machines) in detail.

Managing NFS and NIS

By Hal Stern
1st Edition June 1991
436 pages, ISBN 0-937175-75-7

Managing NFS and NIS is for system administrators who need to set up or manage a network filesystem installation. NFS (Network Filesystem) is probably running at any site that has two or more UNIX systems. NIS (Network Information System) is a distributed database used to manage a network of computers. The only practical book devoted entirely to these subjects, this guide is a must-have for anyone interested in UNIX networking.

TCP/IP Network Administration

By Craig Hunt
1st Edition July 1992
502 pages, ISBN 0-937175-82-X

A complete guide to setting up and running a TCP/IP network for practicing system administrators. Covers how to set up your network, how to configure important network applications including *sendmail*, and discusses troubleshooting and security. Covers BSD and System V TCP/IP implementations.

System Performance Tuning

By Mike Loukides, 1st Edition November 1990
336 pages, ISBN 0-937175-60-9

System Performance Tuning answers the fundamental question, "How can I get my computer to do more work without buying more hardware?" Some performance problems do require you to buy a bigger or faster computer, but many can be solved simply by making better use of the resources you already have.

Computer Security Basics

By Deborah Russell & G.T. Gangemi Sr.
1st Edition July 1991
464 pages, ISBN 0-937175-71-4

Provides a broad introduction to the many areas of computer security and a detailed description of current security standards. This handbook describes complicated concepts like trusted systems, encryption, and mandatory access control in simple terms, and contains a thorough, readable introduction to the "Orange Book."

UNIX Programming

Understanding Japanese Information Processing

By Ken Lunde
1st Edition September 1993 (est.)
450 pages (est.), ISBN 1-56592-043-0

Understanding Japanese Information Processing provides detailed information on all aspects of handling Japanese text on computer systems. It tries to bring all of the relevant information together in a single book. It covers everything from the origins of modern-day Japanese to the latest information on specific emerging computer encoding standards. There are over 15 appendices which provide additional reference material, such as a code conversion table, character set tables, mapping tables, an extensive list of software sources, a glossary, and much more.

lex & yacc

By John Levine, Tony Mason & Doug Brown
2nd Edition October 1992
366 pages, ISBN 1-56592-000-7

Shows programmers how to use two UNIX utilities, *lex* and *yacc*, in program development. The second edition of *lex & yacc* contains completely revised tutorial sections for novice users and reference sections for advanced users. The new edition is twice the size of the original book, has an expanded index, and now covers Bison and Flex.

High Performance Computing **NEW**

By Kevin Dowd, 1st Edition June 1993
398 pages, ISBN 1-56592-032-5

High Performance Computing makes sense of the newest generation of workstations for application programmers and purchasing managers. It covers everything, from the basics of modern workstation architecture, to structuring benchmarks, to squeezing more performance out of critical applications. It also explains what a good compiler can do—and what you have to do yourself. The book closes with a look at the high-performance future: parallel computers and the more "garden variety" shared memory processors that are appearing on people's desktops.

ORACLE Performance Tuning **NEW**

By Peter Corrigan & Mark Gurry
1st Edition September 1993 (est.)
650 pages (est.), ISBN 1-56592-048-1

The ORACLE relational database management system is the most popular database system in use today. With more organizations downsizing and adopting client/server and distributed database approaches, system performance tuning has become vital. This book shows you the many things you can do to dramatically increase the performance of your existing ORACLE system. You may find that this book can save you the cost of a new machine; at the very least, it will save you a lot of headaches.

POSIX Programmer's Guide

By Donald Lewine, 1st Edition April 1991
640 pages, ISBN 0-937175-73-0

Most UNIX systems today are POSIX-compliant because the Federal government requires it for its purchases. However, given the manufacturer's documentation, it can be difficult to distinguish system-specific features from those features defined by POSIX. The *POSIX Programmer's Guide*, intended as an explanation of the POSIX standard and as a reference for the POSIX.1 programming library, helps you write more portable programs.

Understanding DCE

By Ward Rosenberry, David Kenney & Gerry Fisher
1st Edition October 1992
266 pages, ISBN 1-56592-005-8

A technical and conceptual overview of OSF's Distributed Computing Environment (DCE) for programmers and technical managers, marketing and sales people. Unlike many O'Reilly & Associates books, *Understanding DCE* has no hands-on programming elements. Instead, the book focuses on how DCE can be used to accomplish typical programming tasks and provides explanations to help the reader understand all the parts of DCE.

Guide to Writing DCE Applications

By John Shirley
1st Edition July 1992
282 pages, ISBN 1-56592-004-X

A hands-on programming guide to OSF's Distributed Computing Environment (DCE) for first-time DCE application programmers. This book is designed to help new DCE users make the transition from conventional, nondistributed applications programming to distributed DCE programming. Covers the IDL and ACF files, essential RPC calls, binding methods and the name service, server initialization, memory management, and selected advanced topics. Includes practical programming examples.

Power Programming with RPC

By John Bloomer
1st Edition February 1992
522 pages, ISBN 0-937175-77-3

RPC, or remote procedure calling, is the ability to distribute the execution of functions on remote computers. Written from a programmer's perspective, this book shows what you can do with RPC's, like Sun RPC, the de facto standard on UNIX systems. It covers related programming topics for Sun and other UNIX systems and teaches through examples.

Managing Projects with make

By Andrew Oram & Steve Talbott
2nd Edition October 1991
152 pages, ISBN 0-937175-90-0

make is one of UNIX's greatest contributions to software development, and this book is the clearest description of *make* ever written. This revised second edition includes guidelines on meeting the needs of large projects.

Software Portability with imake   **NEW**

By Paul DuBois
1st Edition July 1993
390 pages, 1-56592-055-4

imake is a utility that works with *make* to enable code to be complied and installed on different UNIX machines. This new Nutshell Handbook—the only book available on *imake*—is ideal for X and UNIX programmers who want their software to be portable. It includes a general explanation of *imake*, how to write and debug an *Imakefile*, and how to write configuration files. Several sample sets of configuration files are described and are available free over the Net.

UNIX for FORTRAN Programmers

By Mike Loukides
1st Edition August 1990
264 pages, ISBN 0-937175-51-X

This book provides the serious scientific programmer with an introduction to the UNIX operating system and its tools. The intent of the book is to minimize the UNIX entry barrier and to familiarize readers with the most important tools so they can be productive as quickly as possible. *UNIX for FORTRAN Programmers* shows readers how to do things they're interested in: not just how to use a tool such as *make* or *rcs*, but how to use it in program development and how it fits into the toolset as a whole. "An excellent book describing the features of the UNIX FORTRAN compiler *f77* and related software. This book is extremely well written." — American Mathematical Monthly, February 1991

Practical C Programming

By Steve Oualline
2nd Edition January 1993
396 pages, ISBN 1-56592-035-X

C programming is more than just getting the syntax right. Style and debugging also play a tremendous part in creating programs that run well. *Practical C Programming* teaches you not only the mechanics of programming, but also how to create programs that are easy to read, maintain, and debug. There are lots of introductory C books, but this is the Nutshell Handbook! In the second edition, programs now conform to ANSI C.

Checking C Programs with lint

By Ian F. Darwin
1st Edition October 1988
84 pages, ISBN 0-937175-30-7

The *lint* program is one of the best tools for finding portability problems and certain types of coding errors in C programs. This handbook introduces you to *lint*, guides you through running it on your programs, and helps you interpret *lint's* output.

Using C on the UNIX System

By Dave Curry
1st Edition January 1989
250 pages, ISBN 0-937175-23-4

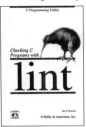

Using C on the UNIX System provides a thorough introduction to the UNIX system call libraries. It is aimed at programmers who already know C but who want to take full advantage of the UNIX programming environment. If you want to learn how to work with the operating system and to write programs that can interact with directories, terminals, and networks at the lowest level you will find this book essential. It is impossible to write UNIX utilities of any sophistication without understanding the material in this book. "A gem of a book. The author's aim is to provide a guide to system programming, and he succeeds admirably. His balance is steady between System V and BSD-based systems, so readers come away knowing both." — SUN Expert, November 1989

Guide to OSF/1

By the staff of O'Reilly & Associates
1st Edition June 1991
304 pages, ISBN 0-937175-78-1

This technically competent introduction to OSF/1 is based on OSF technical seminars. In addition to its description of OSF/1, it includes the differences between OSF/1 and System V Release 4 and a look ahead at DCE.

Understanding and Using COFF

By Gintaras R. Gircys
1st Edition November 1988
196 pages, ISBN 0-937175-31-5

COFF—Common Object File Format—is the formal definition for the structure of machine code files in the UNIX System V environment. All machine-code files are COFF files. This handbook explains COFF data structure and its manipulation.

Career

Love Your Job!   NEW

By Dr. Paul Powers, with Deborah Russell
1st Edition August 1993
210 pages, ISBN 1-56592-036-8

Do you love your job? Too few people do. In fact, surveys show that 80 to 95 percent of Americans are dissatisfied with their jobs. Considering that most of us will work nearly 100,000 hours during our lifetimes (half the waking hours of our entire adult lives!), it's sad that our work doesn't bring us the rewards— both financial and emotional—that we deserve. *Love Your Job!* is an inspirational guide to loving your work. It consists of a series of one-page reflections, anecdotes, and exercises aimed at helping readers think more deeply about what they want out of their jobs. Each can be read individually (anyplace, anytime, whenever you need to lift your spirits), or the book can be read and treated as a whole. *Love Your Job!* informs you, inspires you, and challenges you, not only to look outside at the world of work, but also to look inside yourself at what work means to you.

O'Reilly Online Services

How to Get Information about O'Reilly & Associates

The online O'Reilly Information Resource is a Gopher server that provides you with information on our books, how to download code examples, and how to order from us. There is also a UNIX bibliography you can use to get information on current books by subject area.

Connecting to the O'Reilly Information Resource

Gopher is an interactive tool that organizes the resources found on the Internet as a sequence of menus. If you don't know how Gopher works, see the chapter "Tunneling through the Internet: Gopher" in *The Whole Internet User's Guide and Catalog* by Ed Krol.

An easy way to use Gopher is to download a Gopher client, either the tty Gopher that uses curses or the Xgopher.

Once you have a local Gopher client, you can launch Gopher with:

    gopher gopher.ora.com

To use the Xgopher client, enter:

    xgopher -xrm "xgopher.rootServer:
    gopher.ora.com"

If you have no client, log in on our machine via telnet and run Gopher from there, with:

    telnet gopher.ora.com
    login: gopher (no password)

Another option is to use a World Wide Web browser, and enter the http address:

    gopher://gopher.ora.com

Once the connection is made, you should see a root menu similar to this:

```
Internet Gopher Information Client v1.12
    Root gopher server: gopher.ora.com

->1. News Flash! -- New Products and
       Projects of ORA/.
    2.About O'Reilly & Associates.
    3.Book Descriptions and Information/
    4.Complete Listing of Book Titles.
    5.FTP Archive and E-Mail Information/
    6.Ordering Information/
    7.UNIX Bibliography/

Press ? for Help, q to Quit, u to go up a
menu                         Page: 1/1
```

From the root menu you can begin exploring the information that we have available. If you don't know much about O'Reilly & Associates, choose **About O'Reilly & Associates** from the menu. You'll see an article by Tim O'Reilly that gives an overview of who we are—and a little background on the books we publish.

Getting Information About Our Books

The Gopher server makes available online the same information that we provide in our print catalog, often in more detail.

Choose **Complete Listing of Book Titles** from the root menu to view a list of all our titles. This is a useful summary to have when you want to place an order.

To find out more about a particular book, choose **Book Descriptions and Information**; you will see the screen below:

```
Internet Gopher Information Client v1.12
    Book Descriptions and Information

->1.New Books and Editions/
   2.Computer Security/
   3.Distributed Computing Environment
     (DCE)/
   4.Non-Technical Books/
   5.System Administration/
   6.UNIX & C Programming/
   7.Using UNIX/
   8.X Resource/
   9.X Window System/
   10.CD-Rom Book Companions/
   11.Errata and Updates/
   12.Keyword Search on all Book
      Descriptions <?>
   13.Keyword Search on all Tables of
      Content <?>
```

All of our new books are listed in a single category. The rest of our books are grouped by subject. Select a subject to see a list of book titles in that category. When you select a specific book, you'll find a full description and table of contents.

For example, if you wanted to look at what books we had on administration, you would choose selection 5, **System Administration**, resulting in the following screen:

```
            System Administration

   1.DNS and BIND/
   2.Essential System Administration/
   3.Managing NFS and NIS/
   4.Managing UUCP and Usenet/
   5.sendmail/
   6.System Performance Tuning/
   7.TCP/IP Network Administration/
```

If you then choose Essential System Administration, you will be given the choice of looking at either the book description or the table of contents.

```
        Essential System Administration

-->1.Book Description and Information.
   2.Book Table of Contents.
```

Selecting either of these options will display the contents of a file. Gopher then provides instructions for you to navigate elsewhere or quit the program.

Searching For the Book You Want

Gopher also allows you to locate book descriptions or tables of contents by using a word search. (We have compiled a full-text index WAIS.)

If you choose Book Descriptions and Information from the root menu, the last two selections on that menu allow you to do keyword searches.

Choose Keyword Search on all Book Descriptions and you will be prompted with:

Index word(s) to search for:

Once you enter a keyword, the server returns a list of the book descriptions that match the keyword. For example, if you enter the keyword DCE, you will see:

```
  Keyword Search on all Book Descriptions:
                    DCE

--> 1.Understanding DCE.
    2.Guide to Writing DCE Applications.
    3.Distributed Applications Across DCE
      and Windows NT.
    4.DCE Administration Guide.
    5.Power Programming with RPC.
    6.Guide to OSF/1.
```

Choose one of these selections to view the book description.

Using the keyword search option can be a faster and less tedious way to locate a book than moving through a lot of menus.

You can also use a WAIS client to access the full-text index or book descriptions. The name of the database is

O'Reilly_Book_Descriptions.src

and you can find it in the WAIS directory of servers.

Note: We are always adding functions and listings to the O'Reilly Information Resource. By the time you read this article, the actual screens may very well have changed.

E-mail Accounts

E-mail ordering promises to be quick and easy, even faster than using our 800 number. Because we don't want you to send credit card information over a non-secure network, we ask that you set up an account with us in advance. To do so, either call us at 1-800-998-9938 or use the application provided in Ordering Information on the Gopher root menu. You will then be provided with a confidential account number.

Your account number allows us to retrieve your billing information when you place an order by e-mail, so you only need to send us your account number and what you want to order.

For your security, we use the credit card information and shipping address that we have on file. We also verify that the name of the person sending us the e-mail order matches the name on the account. If any of this information needs to change, we ask that you contact order@ora.com or call our Customer Service department.

Ordering by E-mail

Once you have an account with us, you can send us your orders by e-mail. Remember that you can use our online catalog to find out more about the books you want. Here's what we need when you send us an order:

1. Address your e-mail to: order@ora.com
2. Include in your message:
   - The title of each book you want to order (including ISBN number, if you know it)
   - The quantity of each book
   - Method of delivery: UPS Standard, Fed Ex Priority...
   - Your name and account number
   - Anything special you'd like to tell us about the order

When we receive your e-mail message, our Customer Service representative will verify your order before we ship it, and give you a total cost. If you would like to change your order after confirmation, or if there are ever any problems, please use the phone and give us a call—e-mail has its limitations.

This program is an experiment for us. We appreciate getting your feedback so we can continue improving our service.

How to Order by E-mail

E-mail ordering promises to be quick and easy. Because we don't want you sending credit card information over a non-secure network, we ask that you set up an account with us before ordering by e-mail.
To find out more about setting up an e-mail account, you can either call us at (800) 998-9938 or select `Ordering Information` from the Gopher root menu.

O'Reilly & Associates Inc.
103A Morris Street, Sebastopol, CA 95472

(800) 998-9938 • (707) 829-0515 • FAX (707) 829-0104 • order@ora.com

How to get information about O'Reilly books online
• If you have a local gopher client, then you can launch gopher and connect to our server:
`gopher gopher.ora.com`
• If you want to use the Xgopher client, then enter:
`xgopher -xrm "xgopher.rootServer: gopher.ora.com"`
• If you want to use telnet, then enter:
`telnet gopher.ora.com  login: gopher   [no password]`
• If you use a World Wide Web browser, you can access the gopher server
by typing the following http address:
`gopher://gopher.ora.com`

W E ' D   L I K E   T O   H E A R   F R O M   Y O U

Company Name

Name

Address

City/State

Zip/Country

Telephone

FAX

Internet or *Uunet* e-mail address

Which O'Reilly book did this card come from? _____

Is your job: ❑ SysAdmin? ❑ Programmer?
❑ Other? What?_____

Do you use other computer systems besides UNIX? If so, which one(s)?

Please send me the following:

❑ A free catalog of titles

❑ A list of bookstores in my area that carry O'Reilly books

❑ A list of distributors outside of the U.S. and Canada

❑ Information about bundling O'Reilly books with my product

O'Reilly & Associates Inc.

(800) 998-9938 • (707) 829-0515 • FAX (707) 829-0104 • order@ora.com

How to order books by e-mail:
1. Address your e-mail to: order@ora.com
2. Include in your message:
   - The title of each book you want to order
     (an ISBN number is helpful but not necessary)
   - The quantity of each book
   - Your account number and name
   - Anything special you'd like us to know about your order

Use our online catalog to find out more about our books (see reverse).

_____

O'Reilly Online Account Number